The Lucid View:

Investigations into Occultism, Ufology and Paranoid Awareness

Aeolus Kephas

Other books in this series:

- MIND CONTROL—WORLD CONTROL
- SAUCERS OF THE ILLUMINATI
- INSIDE THE GEMSTONE FILE
- LIQUID CONSPIRACY
- THE SHADOW GOVERNMENT
- MASS CONTROL
- NASA, NAZIS & JFK
- THE ARCH-CONSPIRATOR
- MIND CONTROL, OSWALD & JFK

The Lucid View:

Investigations into Occultism, Ufology and Paranoid Awareness

The Lucid View:
Investigations into Occultism,
Ufology, and Paranoid Awareness

Copyright 2004

Aeolus Kephas

All rights reserved

First Printing July 2004

Cover Art copyright John Coulthart 2004

ISBN 1-931882-30-4

Printed in the United States of America

Published by
Adventures Unlimited Press
One Adventure Place
Kempton, Illinois 60946 USA
www.adventuresunlimitedpress.com
www.adventuresunlimited.co.nl

10 9 8 7 6 5 4 3 2

The
Lucid
View

Openings

The Lucid View

For seekers of knowledge everywhere:
"There are no big secrets: don't believe what you read."
(Talking Heads, *Stop Making Sense*)

With special thanks to the Empress of La La land

Entrails

O: Openings—LUNATIC TUNES............................10

I: Archetypes—MIND FIELDS.....................................15
    Lucifer, Sirius, and the Prime Directive

II: Illuminoids—THE MUNDANE SHELL........................33
    Crowley, Hitler and the Dogs of Reason
    A Brief History of Conspiracy
    Suppressed Technology and Secret Space Colonization

III: Assassins—THEATRE OF HATE............................59
    JFK, the Twin Towers, and the Revelation of the Method
    Charles Manson and Scientology Psi Wars
    Jonestown and the Politics of Genocide

IV: Apostles—CHEMICAL WEDDINGS.................... 89
    Gnostics, Pagans, and Templars

V: Ufos—THE WIZARD OF ID.....................................115

VI: Elves—LOVING THE ALIEN................................135

VII: Extraterrestrials—BABALON FALLING.................153
    Robo Sapiens
    A Brief History of Space Aliens

VIII: Angels and Insects—LUCIFER RISING..................181
    Nazi Ghosts and Final Solutions
    Global Initiation and Emergence of the Other A.E.O.N

Appendix: The Assemblage Point...............................209
Further Reading.. 211

"The essence of reality is not fact but question. There are no facts, only truths."
—*The Key*, by Whitley Strieber

"The Magical method is to act 'as if' a theory is correct until it has done its job, and only then to replace it with another theory. A theory only fails if it cannot take hold in the mind and allow one to act 'as if.' As long as this approach is carried out properly—with a Magician's understanding that the theory is being accepted only because it is 'working,' not because it is 'true'—then there is little danger of delusion."
—Ramsey Dukes, *S.S.O.T.B.M.E: An Essay on Magic*

O: Openings

Lunatic Tunes

Science is the first sin, the germ of all sins, original sin. This alone constitutes morality: "Thou shalt not know."
—Nietzsche, *The Anti-Christ*

The most essential thing about making a case for the impossible is to discredit all rational associations of "cause and effect" entirely: the point is there *is* no point. There are no premises to the argument that paranoid awareness is heightened awareness, save for the premise that the world—and everything in it—is and has always been a vast and unfathomably bizarre mystery, a mystery which we will never understand. Another way of saying this is that life, for all its qualities—or for all its *lack* of them—is simply and wholly what we make of it: a myth-story, ever unfolding. Genesis recurs every day in the matrix of our minds.

The true paranoid is more concerned with the conspiracy of history than the history of conspiracy; he acknowledges that history conspires to make men, and not men to make history, and that man belongs to life, not life to man. He is determined, above all else, *to take no hostages to his meaning.*

From the beginning knowledge has been forbidden to Man, and this concept—that knowledge is something pernicious, harmful, corrupting—is indeed central to the Judeo-Christian ideology which we have inherited, and which forms the backbone of our entire culture and society. It matters not if you accept or even acknowledge this Consensus ideology, you nonetheless belong to it. The Bible itself begins with the fable of Eden, of Adam, Eve and the Serpent, with the forbidding (and punishing) presence of the *Elohim* lurking ever-ominously behind the scenes. And yet, even without departing too radically from the text or diving too deeply between the lines, it can also be reasoned from this myth that knowledge is the very thing that makes us men, that distinguishes us from the other animals (even if it has yet to make us gods).

Perhaps—way back when, at the beginning of Time—the *Elohim* were fully aware of our modern psychological concepts? By forbidding knowledge, these strange gods thereby made sure that we seek after it. The Serpent was really Eve's conscience speaking plainly, goading her on to the inevitable act. This impulse to rebel came about through—or resulted from—the *Elohim's words themselves*, making the Serpent simply the fulfillment of Their secret will. These archetypes in the fable (God and Satan) are as inseparable as cause and effect, as the twin hemispheres of the brain. Indeed, neither has much meaning to the contemporary reader unless seen in psychological terms, as two *apparently* conflicting aspects of the human psyche.

What bearing does any of this have on paranoid awareness? In his insatiable thirst for ever more forbidden lore, the paranoid adheres religiously to the tenet that, so far as knowledge goes, too much is just enough. These metaphors—the warnings and prohibitions—have survived to this day, but the knowledge still eludes us. The peculiar fact is that, even now that knowledge is acknowledged as in many ways *the sine qua non* of being human, and the most valued commodity there is, it is still in its own weird way forbidden to us. Nowadays, we would not dream of submitting meekly to any abstract mandate of a hidden God, yet we are, for all that, coerced and cuckolded into ignorance and slavery.

*

> Legends, of course, tell the truth in a concealed fashion . . . Their success in concealing the truth rests on man's conviction that they are simply stories. . . . So it's been the task of sorcerers for thousands of years to make new legends and to discover the concealed truth of old ones. This is where dreamers come into the picture.
> —Florinda Donner, *Being-In-Dreaming*

Consensus Reality is the ultimate secret society. It is a society so secret that even its members are unaware of its existence. Consensus Reality is a conspiracy to uphold the world; it is the means by which we communicate and agree upon the way things are, and the way they must be. So far as it is a functioning model, such a Consensus is valid. Insofar as it is *not* a functioning model, and is, as in the present case, on the verge of breakdown, then such a Consensus is, by definition, *invalid*. It therefore becomes the right and responsibility of every thinking member of such a Consensus to cancel his membership, and to option a new, higher or broader concept of "reality."

Paranoid awareness is the means to disengaging from Consensus. Paranoid awareness is a leap of the imagination, a leap that we are all preparing (or not, as the case may be) to take. Like everything else however, only more so, paranoid awareness is not what it appears to be to the uninitiated. For example, when I use the word magik, I refer not to spells or incantations, healing balms or lethal broths, night flights or animal transformations. These are no more what define magik than the contents of a laboratory define science. By magik, I refer rather to a shift in perception, a shift from one Consensus to another, a shift of the race assemblage point to a new position. (For a fuller description of the assemblage point, see the Appendix.) This preliminary goal of magik is termed by Castaneda "stopping the world," and at this point, there can be little doubt that the world must be stopped.

Still a ways from such a lucid view, we perceive a darkness on the horizon, drawing inexorably closer; we, for our part, are compelled in our own interests to rise up to meet it. All that follows is a brief and cursory overview of the paranoid perspective, a perspective that insists on every time being the "End Time." This is the only point of view that befits the paranoid, that of the eschatologist—or the romantic—whatever shape, size or form it may assume. For those as yet unenlightened as to the meaning of *eschatology*, Terence McKenna (in *The Archaic Revival*) describes it as follows

> History is the shock wave of eschatology. Something is at the end of time and it is casting an enormous shadow over human history, drawing all human becoming towards it. All the wars, the philosophies, the rapes, the pillaging, the migrations, the cities, the civilizations—all of this is occupying a microsecond of geological, planetary, and galactic time as the monkeys react to the symbiote, which is in the environment and which is feeding information to humanity about the larger picture

The key to paranoid awareness on the edge of the eschaton is that beliefs must be dabbled in without ever really being *believed*: paranoia employs a *pseudo*-belief, conjured like a genie that fades away once it is done, leaving only the residue of smoke. This is a deliberate subterfuge on the part of the paranoid, and depends above all on the idea that reality is elsewhere.

Caught in a Consensus only partially of our own making, we are faced with a system of symbols, metaphors that serve only as "leads" or pointers by which to access a greater, mythic reality. Human beings partake of the lesser myth (with a small "m") of illusory, Consensus reality, and this is the stone from which we must carve our personal myth our "belief system." It is then up to us to use this belief system as a means to prepare for death.

The paranoid knows we can't just make the leap over the Abyss of death. It is too wide for that. Instead, we have to build a bridge, even if we know that this bridge will never actually get us *over* the Abyss. Since death is a complete unknown, and therefore anything is possible, there remains the chance that we may arrive far enough to reach a point from which to *make the leap* into Eternity.

The act of creating "reality" (a personal belief system) is essential to the magician's task. To get rid of "reality" altogether, we must first accept our place in the Consensus, in order to then disband it. What the paranoid is doing is preparing his own consciousness—"strengthening the intellect" as the English poet Keats put it—to assemble a vaster and more mysterious reality—a Consensus of the Gods.

Since I first wrote *The Lucid View* (some ten years ago, back when it was still called *The Mess Age*, and rightly!), I have gone through a whole slew of personal myths and belief systems. Like training wheels, they all went in the end. Now I am relatively free of points to defend. As Charles Fort says, "to investigate anything is to admit prejudice." The only way to investigate these present matters without falling into prejudiced thinking, then, is by emphasizing the process of building belief systems, and to leave the question of "reality" out of the picture altogether. True Reality, by definition, is something as yet unattained by us, unfully *grokked*. If we seek to prove the reality of our beliefs to others, we betray our own doubts. The only objective of such an exercise (to prove a personal hypothesis) can be to make it *more real* by persuading others to believe in it too. In which case, we should be careful just where our beliefs are leading us, and ask ourselves whether we are ready to follow them.

This is the only way to return the Imagination to its rightful place, at the center of perception, upon the throne of creation. *The Lucid View* is a largely romantic work; it does not contain answers. Rather, it attempts to initiate a "process of creating questions than can neither be borne nor answered."[1] That is what Life is all about, after all. I can't speak for life, but the point of this book is to challenge, stimulate, and develop the reader's imagination. It is a fable from which truth may or may not be divined, or imagined. I leave it up to the reader, then, to hatch this egg or not. But bear in mind, afore ye enter, the words of the poet: "The only way of strengthening one's intellect is to make up one's mind about nothing—to let the mind be a thoroughfare for all thoughts." (John Keats, *Letters*)

Our endeavor, then, is not to create more belief systems but to explode already existing belief systems, thereby clearing the slate for new ideas to surface. It befits us, therefore, to stretch our credibility at all times to the absolute limit; consequently, the more challenging, preposterous, or offensive to reason my hypotheses become, the more happy I am to hurl them at you. Charles Fort wrote: "I believe nothing of my own that I have ever written. I cannot accept that the products of minds are subject-matter for beliefs." I would like to second that.

*

A man goes to knowledge as he goes to war, wide-awake, with fear, with respect, and with absolute assurance. Going to knowledge or going to war in any other manner is a mistake, and whoever makes it will live to regret his steps.
—Carlos Castaneda, *The Teachings of Don Juan*

There is a tale about a fish. This fish went on a quest to find the meaning of "water," a mysterious force, or power, or quality, of which he had heard much but never ever seen. Everywhere he flew, this little fish, he heard different stories, different legends, fables, and opinions. But none of them ever seemed to agree, and so they only confused the fish all the more. Water was the source of all life, said one. Water is the figment of fools' imaginations, said another. Water is everywhere and nowhere, and cannot be known directly, said a third.

When the little fish plucked up his courage and approached the wisest of all creatures, the blue whale, he received only deep and thunderous laughter for his response. Finally, the blue whale settled down and told the fish the following:

"My dear little fish, I fear that nothing I can say will ever satisfy you. If I told you what water is, and where to find it, you wouldn't believe me. And if you did believe me, you wouldn't understand me. I can only say that the answer is to your seeking is closer than you know."

Not to be discouraged by such cryptic ramblings, the little fish continued on his quest. One day, his seeking reached such a fevered pitch that, unaware of what he was doing, the little fish threw himself out of the water and onto on dry land! For a time, he thrashed and flailed there, in a paroxysm of terror and despair. And as he took his first and last gasps of air, his death but moments away, he realized, in a flash, what water was!

1: *The Key*, by Whitley Strieber

"What a fool I have been," he thought. "It was under my nose all along! And now that I have discovered what it is, I have lost it forever!" Realizing this, he died.

But the brave little fish did not die in vain, as this story (and my telling it to you) amply testifies. Over the millennia, other fish followed after, and many died, in same the hopeless quest for the truth. But, little by little, over immeasurable periods of time, under the duress of necessity, the seeking fishes began to change and mutate: they began to *grow lungs*. And, by so mutating and adapting, they were gradually able to experience this wondrous and terrible new reality, called "air" (while simultaneously granted understanding of the nature of "water"). These were the first amphibians. We are now at this very same point, one rung up from our fishy ancestors, on evolution's crossroads. I tell this tale as a parable.

Myths and parables that associate knowledge with forbidden fire (*hubris*), and warn us of the danger inherent in seeking such, are serving a purpose that cannot be ignored. The scientific or academic approach to knowledge is a disrespectful one, to say the least. Much akin to Industry's assault upon Nature, it plunders, violates, conquers, and finally destroys the very thing it is pretending to harness. The "academic" likewise approaches a work of art with tweezers, rubber gloves, and a microscope, intending to analyze and sterilize at the same time—to protect himself from the very emotional onslaught that he is unconsciously seeking (since emotional onslaught is what "art" is all about). In his own mind, the academic is divided against himself; and it is through this rift that the demons of knowledge enter.

The desire to remain in control, at a safe distance, to reduce the unknown to the sum of its parts, is a seemingly irresistible temptation for the scientist. Led by *reason* into the atavistic realms of unreason (the primal chaos of the jungle, standing in for his own unconscious), the scientist is driven to extract the desired elements for "objective study" in the laboratory of his mind. But he never really admits the obvious—that once taken from its natural habitat, a snake is but a shadow of its former self.

There is nothing to be learnt from such shadows, but sooner or later, the jungle will bite back. Atavistic nature—like the tortoise—is patient to a fault; but in the moment in which it finally stirs, it is as swift and deadly as the trodden serpent.

Far from protecting us, the rational mind—with its rigid order and its need to control the uncontrollable—only serves to enrage the demons of the unconscious which it has invoked. The chaos bubbles to the surface; enraged at the rational mind's cheeky impositions of "order," it strikes back.

Knowledge is an unexplored terrain, an *abyss* that stands before us. Only by showing such a total lack of personal attachment and concern, says the paranoid, can we appease this dreadful abyss to our presence within it. For in order to access the worlds beyond death, worlds of magik, mystery, darkness and power, we must first acknowledge the corresponding void within ourselves, and see ourselves as death must surely see us: as next to nothing.

Chapter One: Archetypes

Mind Fields

I walk among men as among the scattered fragments of the future: of that future which I scan.
—Nietzsche, *Thus Spoke Zarathustra*, "Of Redemption."

The history of the abyss has so far been characterized by an extreme reluctance upon our part to gaze unflinchingly inward. Since God abhors a coward, this reluctance has resulted in a disassociating from the true nature of our existence, a "banishment." Archetypally speaking, we have fallen from grace, and landed in oblivion. Living here, over time, throughout recorded history in fact, we have, like good mammals, adapted to the environment and become wholly dependent on it. "For man has closed himself up, till he sees all things thro narrow chinks of his cavern."[1] And now, the true nature of our existence has become a closed book. We subsist on a scattering of symbols, all of them divorced from their essential meanings. We live a map and discuss the territory. We munch greedily on menus, and rave about the meal. At sea in a mess of unknown imagery, surrounded on all sides by all types, both arch and stereo, the legion of demons come and go, gods which we never see, but still hear of now and then, in our mythic underworld.

In occult writings, there is a tradition that states that the true light of being is hidden beneath a false light of "knowing"; that, between the object and the eye, there exists an opaque film, a film which we know of as "interpretation." The sun we see, for example, is no more than an image created by us to apprehend a mysterious phenomenon which we will *never* understand. It is no more than a shell of the true Sun. Even outside the halls of occult lore, the Sun is the central archetype of our existence as humans. It is not only the center of our system, it is the center of our world. It is our heart and our soul.

The number of the physical sun in Kabalistic gematria is 666, the number of the beast. In occultism, the splendor of Nature, as represented by the beast, the tempter—passion, courage, strength, lust, energy, *will*—is not evil, as so many religions would have it. But it *is* deceptive, jut as the Serpent in the fable is deceptive. As such, it can be utilized only so long as it remains in its proper place. The beast, or "instructor," is the means by which we acquire knowledge of good and evil. The good relates to the true, higher, or divine aspect of Nature. The evil corresponds with the lower aspect of nature, that which binds rather than looses us. The danger of the beast, then, is only in that he is not what he appears, or claims, to be. The key is to convert knowledge into wisdom, interpretation into understanding.

1: Blake, *The Marriage of Heaven and Hell*

This is the difference between the symbol and the archetype which it represents (and conceals). The first acceptance of paranoid awareness is that archetypes, like all invisibles, come disguised, be it in rags or in robes.

The number of the hidden Sun, by the same system, is 888, the number of Christ, the savior—kindness, wisdom, mercy, beauty, vision, love. By such occult logic, Beast and Christ are two aspects of a single archetype, the one naturally serving to conceal the other.[2] By the very act of representing him, the beast obscures Christ.[3] So it is with all symbols. One cannot take the clothes for the man, or the finger for the Moon, without getting lost in a maze of misconception. By taking the myth for the history and the history for the myth, says the paranoid, we have ensnared ourselves in a never-ending web of illusion.

Lucifer, Sirius, and the Prime Directive

And the Lord God formed man *of* the dust of the ground, and breathed into his nostrils the breath of life; and man became a living soul. And the Lord God took the man and put him into the garden of Eden to dress it and to keep it.
—*Genesis: 2:7,15*

God made Man in His image? So anthropomorphic (Judeo-Christian) religion would have us believe. Concerning the Original Archetype, however, it pays to bear in mind that, in Genesis, the Hebrew word translated as "God" is *Elohim*, referring to gods, or "builders," in the plural.[4] If, as some interpretations of the myth have it, the *Elohim* made Man in their *own* image out of a kind of divine pride (a desire to extend their kingdom into the world of matter), this might explain why They considered *hubris* to be the ultimate "transgression." Perhaps the Gods wanted to be sure Man's divine origin would not go to his head? Yet, at the same time it was forbidden, the original sin (hubris/pride) appears to have been evolution's prime directive. Jehovah tells us in no uncertain terms, "*I am that I am!*" following which he sets Himself up as our one and only Role Model.

2: The Greek spelling of the name "Jesus" amounts to 888. "[T]he number of Jesus, 888, the Spiritual Sun, is contrasted with the number 666, that of the physical sun . . . 666 and 888 define the ratios of the musical scale." See *Jesus Christ, Sun of God,* by David Fideler, for details.

3: "The Serpent became the type and symbol of evil, and of the Devil, only during the middle ages. The early Christians . . . had their dual Logos: the Good and Bad Serpent, the Agathodaemon and the Kakodaemon. . . The great Serpent of the Garden of Eden and the 'Lord God' are identical, and so are Jehovah and Cain *one*." H.P. Blavatsky, *The Secret Doctrine.*

4: "Man is not, nor could he ever be, the complete product of the 'Lord God,' but he *is* the child of the ELOHIM . . . commissioned to 'create' man in their image [who] could only throw off their shadows, like a delicate morsel for the Nature Spirits of matter to work upon. Man is, beyond any doubt, formed physically out of the dust of the Earth, but his creators and fashioners were many." (H.P. Blavatsky, *The Secret Doctrine*)

Mythology is all about gods falling from grace and men becoming gods. Lucifer, Set,[5] Prometheus, Loki, the wily old Serpent or the subtlest beast of the field; all these maligned meddlers are not merely tempters, they are *instructors*.[6] Prometheus-Lucifer is the original anti-hero, the rebel with a cause. He is the man of passion, of irrepressible activity, whose intentions were so *good* they paved the road to Hell thereafter. Even according to the most orthodox of sources—the Christian myth—Lucifer is the Morning Star, the brightest and most beautiful of the Angels. He simply makes a choice: to produce his own music. "Better to reign in hell than serve in Heaven."

5: *"Set:* The prototype of Shaitan or Satan, the God of the South whose star is Sothis. Set or Sut means 'black,' the main *kala* or color of Set is black, or red (interchangeable symbols in the Mysteries), which denotes the underworld or infernal region of Amenta. As Lord of Hell, Set is the epitome of subconscious atavisms and of the True Will, or Hidden Sun." Kenneth Grant, *Cults of the Shadow*

6: The Hebrew word for serpent is numerologically interchangeable with the Hebrew word for "instructor."

God banishing His brightest Angel from Heaven for the Sin of Pride

In the book of Job, Satan is identified as a Son of God, and associated with Cain, who was also condemned to walk the Earth. And it is with Cain that the human race may be said to begin, the very first post-Eden civilization being founded by the exiled son. According to arch-occultist Aleister Crowley, "Cain was the child of Eve and the serpent, and not of Eve and Adam" (*Liber 418*). As John Keel notes in *Our Haunted Planet*, "The mating of ordinary women with supernatural beings is an integral part of all religious lore." Of course the Bible has its own "official" version of events, found in the much-quoted passage from *Genesis*:

> And it came to pass, when men began to multiply on the face of the earth, and daughters were born unto them, That the sons of God saw the daughters of men that they *were* fair; and they took them wives of all which they chose. . . . There were giants in the earth in those days; and also after that, when the sons of God came in unto the daughters of men, and they bare *children* to them, the same *became* mighty men which *were* of old, men of renown. (6:1-3)

When you get right down to it, beyond all the myths and fables and from a lucid view, Lucifer is just another word for *Man*.[7] According to Blavatsky, Lucifer is the "Astral Light," the etheric womb of the world on which are retained all the myriad, countless impressions left by the acts, thoughts and aspirations of Man. Hence he "becomes, with regard to Mankind, simply the effects of the causes produced by men in their sinful lives."[8]

As the Morning Star, Lucifer is the original archetype and source of all energy, the Sun. (What Star heralds the morning if not the Sun?) Traditionally, the morning star is Venus, of course, which links Lucifer with the Serpent Kundalini energy of the body, and with Gaia, the Earth. In his most secret aspect, Lucifer is a *female* archetype, and corresponds with the resurgent Goddess movement beloved of New Agers. The energetic fact remains that—archetypally or mythologically speaking, and regardless of moral doctrines or religious dogma—Lucifer or "Shaitan" (corrupted to Satan, "adversary," by the Hebrews) is synonymous with the Inner Man: the Other or Hidden God whose dream has been the ghost-written history of Man, and whose awakening promises the long-awaited New Aeon.[9]

7: "Lucifer—the spirit of Intellectual Enlightenment and Freedom of Thought—is metaphorically the guiding beacon, which helps man to find his way through the rocks and sandbanks of life, for Lucifer is the *Logos* in his highest, and 'the Adversary' in his lowest aspect—both of which are reflected in our *Ego*." H.P. Blavatsky, *The Secret Doctrine*. Note also William Blake's words: "Messiah or Satan or Tempter was formerly thought to be one of the Antediluvians who are our Energies." *The Marriage of Heaven and Hell*

8: Blavatsky, *Secret Doctrine*. See also Eliphas Levi: "The old serpent of legend is nothing else than the Universal Agent, the eternal fire of terrestrial life, the soul of the earth, and the living center of hell." Levi, *La Clef des Grands Mystères*, trans. Aleister Crowley. Levi continues, "Lucifer, of whom the dark ages have made the genius of evil, will be truly the angel of light when, having conquered liberty at the price of infamy, he will use it to submit himself to eternal order, inaugurating thus the glories of voluntary obedience." "The mark of the disobedience of Adam, preserved in the Astral Light, could be effaced only by the stronger mark of the obedience of the savior, and thus the original sin and redemption of the world can be explained in a natural and magical sense. The Astral Light, or Soul of the World, was the instrument of Adam's omnipotence; it became afterwards that of his punishment, being corrupted and troubled by his sin, which intermingled an impure reflection with those primitive images which composed the Book of Universal Science for his still virgin imagination." *Le Dogme et Rituel de la Haute Magie*

9: "Horus is thus Hrumachis, (son of) the Star, Sirius . . . The Star (Atu XVII, attributed to Aquarius) is therefore the key to the present Aeon of Horus, for it represents *the Energy of Satan that will permeate the earth during the present cycle*." Kenneth Grant, *Aleister Crowley and the Hidden God*, pg 60. My italics. Compare with Blavatsky's *Secret Doctrine*: "*Satan is always near and inextricably interwoven with man.*" (My italics.)

Varying Depictions of Lucifer/Satan, the Fallen Angel, in Religious Art

Every paranoid knows that the best way to keep knowledge (or wisdom) from the people is to make it seem undesirable—to convince them that they are better off without it. Though few would admit this (lacking the knowledge) many if not most of us are actively convinced that certain areas of knowledge are better left unexplored. A Christian does not go to Church to hear about Satan (save for the occasional blood-curdling threat of hell-fire). And he doesn't ask awkward questions about contradictory dogmas or confused symbols. If he does, he is told: "It is a mystery; it is not given to mortals to know such things." Of all lies, this (of priests, politicians, and parents) may be the most pernicious. It is a lie that prohibits us from seeking the truth, without *tempting* us to do so. (Even Jehovah had a sufficient sense of fair play to that.) The point is, so far as the true believer is concerned, the less he knows about Satan, evil, and other heresies, the better. This is a logic fit for children. From cradle to grave, we are told to shut up and defer to a greater authority, that of Faith, Blood, and State. The implication is that asking questions is itself a kind of hubris.

The Consensus whispers nightly to itself: Hear no evil. Speak no evil. See no evil. And meanwhile, regardless of what we see, hear, say and do about it, evil goes on festering unattended, at the rancid center of our lives. Paranoid awareness assures us that an adversary whom we neither hear nor see, nor even speak of, is an adversary who is laughing all the way to the blood bank. He has us exactly where he wants us. The power of the adversary (be it death or government) *depends* on our mutual agreement to ignore it. As Baudelaire put it, "The devil's deepest wile was to convince us that he does not exist." We have persuaded oursleves likewise of the non-existence of death and conspiracy.

In more mundane terms, our decency has, by Consensus agreement, become a cloak for our degeneracy. "Politically correct" is newspeak for morally bankrupt. We have the *words* needed to make us feel like decent people, but we lack the spirit, the knowledge or wisdom to understand these words, and so there is no way to make *use* of them. Instead, we have opted, like good creatures of comfort, to become slaves to syntax, and so remained in ignorance. Still stuck in "Eden," long after having been banished from the Garden of Delight.

Lucifer's goal was freedom. Freedom is the ultimate, abstract non-entity, which is exactly what makes it free. Since freedom is a lot like death, it cannot be sought directly. freedom is understood first of all *negatively*, as what we wish to escape *from* (death). Obviously, a warrior *seeks out* whatever he is trying to get free from. H doesn't hang about waiting for the enemy to come to him. So the quest for freedom is a quest for *adversity*. The Devil is the door that bars the way, and if heaven is the goal, the going is hell.

Most folk would agree, if pressed, that we have, as a society and even as a race, reached an impasse. Many of us feel that we are faced with a choice: to collapse inward, into despair, or make the leap beyond. We are given enough "facts" to deduce that eco-system (and hence all life) is in danger of coming to a violent and total *end*, and so our despair grows more justified with every passing day. But then, so does our *hope* for some mysterious, magikal solution. The solution, however magikal, is obvious: to re-engage our natural instincts, the consciousness of our living connection to the Earth.

Magik is this connection, the Rainbow Bridge between the worlds of the living and the dead. It states that there is but one world, and that Man belongs to it, and that it does not belong to Man.

Putting all the "occult facts" together, it appears that the awakening of a deeper, primal consciousness in Man will only be achieved via a reconnecting with the basic, animal energy, perceived by nice politically correct people as satanic, or at best bestial. This energy is needed to reach the higher realms that we have been so vainly striving towards; without it we have no more chance than a floppy dick has at penetration. The "adversary," then, is *the rock* against which consciousness must push, in order to "lift off." The impending collapse of civilization and the subsequent "Dark Age" foreseen by paranoid awareness is also seen as but the first, catastrophic motion of this primal awakening. It is the moment when everything grinds to a halt and the old gods emerge, from the depths of our unconscious, demanding blood.

*

I am the flame that burns in every heart of man, and in the core of every star.
—*The Book of the Law*, II:6

According to the leading authority on the subject, Carl Gustav Jung (writing in *Man and His Symbols*), archetypes "have their own initiative and their own specific energy . . . archetypes create myths, religions, and philosophies that influence and characterize whole nations and epochs of history." Jung, who pretty much coined the term "archetype," used it to supplant Freud's "archaic remnants," or "primordial images," relating to the deeper, darker consciousness of "archaic man, whose psyche was still close to that of the animal."

More than anything else, an archetype is an *idea*—in the sense both of image (or inspiration) and impulse. The key to understanding archetypes from the occultist perspective (i.e., as gods) is to accept that they exist not only within us but outside, and independent of, ourselves. They pertain not to individuals, but to the race as a whole. At the same time, they *appear* to reside within the heart and soul (the psyche) of each and every one of us, because there exists within us the corresponding quality by which we are able to identify these archetypes. (God does not live in a dog, but a dog lives in God.) the current global crisis screams out at us that we have lost touch with the deeper, darker and more potent areas in our psyches and, by extension, in the Universe at large. Hence it turns against us.

The assumption that what gives structure or meaning to our reality may itself be devoid of reality is an assumption whose vanity is equaled only by its blindness. It is akin to attributing the light of the Sun to the power of our eyes. The apparently diverse concepts of star and god have more in common than their names. A god is "a pure working."[10] It is a first cause, and as such is inconceivable to us in all but *effect*. We only perceive the *acts* of the gods. And yet, in occultism, the act and the god are one. "Great aggregations of events coalesce, become cosmic in scope and

---

10: "God is a being withdrawn from creatures, a free power, a pure working." Tauler, quoted by Aldous Huxley, in *After Many a Summer Dies the Swan*

are called 'gods.' A god is technically an energy-aggregate of colossal concentration."[11]

The primary archetypes of our existence are the celestial bodies; the secondary archetypes are the earthly bodies; respectively, the gods and the beasts. According to occultism, Man is the medium between the two. His is the rational thought by which the void assumes meaning. To release this meaning, our primitive nature must be awakened through an understanding and a dominating of the animal realms. Our divine nature, on the other hand, must be accessed through an acknowledgement and a surrender to the celestial realms. This is basic alchemy: as the roots strain ever downward into Earth, so the branches spread ever higher, towards the Sun.

The animal realm is known as the daemonic or elemental kingdom, the celestial realm as the angelic. The language of both is found in mythology, science, religion, and occult lore throughout history and throughout the world. The names of the gods, beasts, planets, stars, angels, demons, warriors, saints, heroes and general wildlife, both real and mythological, are the *keys* to this understanding of Nature, and of God.[12]

*

A considerable number of otherwise diverse cultures and mythologies share a common preoccupation within the binary star Sirius, commonly known as the Dog Star. Though they may differ in details, they all seem to agree about one thing: that Sirius is the source of both life in general and of specific knowledge, or wisdom, here on Earth. In fact, "the unruly star," found in the constellation of Canis Major (eight and a half light years from Earth) is rather a star *system*, that includes at least two other celestial bodies: Sirius B, or Digitaria (a white dwarf star[13]), and Sirius C, "discovered" by certain astronomers in the early part of this century.

Supposedly accompanied by a satellite planet, Sirius C is known by the Dogon people as "the sun of women," *Sorghum-Female*, "the seat of the female souls of all living and future beings."[14] The Dogon, an African tribe living in Mali, attribute their special knowledge to the intervention of advanced, non-human beings who passed by planet Earth many millennia ago. In actual fact, their mythology does include a profound knowledge of astronomical data only recently verified by

---

11: "When a vastly coagulated series of acts, performed *under will*, achieve cosmic magnitude, a 'god' is born." Kenneth Grant, *Aleister Crowley and the Hidden God*, pg 189.

12: Nature must come first, logically, as it is through natural channels that we seek out the divine. There is no way to activate the higher psychic centers without first awakening the lower. Hence, most of traditional magik and even mythology has concerned itself more with animals than with angels. "Because man evolved from the beasts, he possesses—deeply buried in his subconsciousness—the memories of superhuman powers he once possessed. Each animal typifies one or more such power. . . Any required atavism could be evoked by the assumption of the appropriate god-form." Kenneth Grant, *Aleister Crowley and the Hidden God*, pg 15.

13: Murray Hope: *Ancient Egypt: The Sirius Connection* "A white dwarf is a star that has used up its lighter hydrogen and helium atomic fuel and has collapsed, which means that the remaining elements have become so densely packed that the nature of its substance hardly equates to matter as we know it."

14: Ibid

modern science (as well as possessing curious parallels with the Christian religion, and other, older traditions).

The leading authority on the subject, Robert G.K. Temple, writes, in *The Sirius Mystery*:

> Digitaria, as the egg of the world . . . was split into two twin placentas which were to give birth respectively to a pair of Nommo Instructors. What happened, however, was that a single male being emerged from one of the placentas; in order to find his twin, this being tore off a piece of this placenta, which became the earth. This intervention upset the order of creation: he was transformed into an animal, the pale fox, *yuruga*, and communicated his own impurity to the earth, which rendered it dry and barren. But the remedy of the situation was the sacrifice, to the sky, of one of the Nommo Instructors, and the descent of his twin to earth with life-giving, purifying rain. The destiny of Yourougou is to pursue his twin to the end of time—the twin being his female soul.

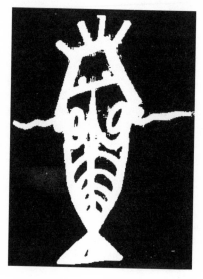

Dogon art representing the fishlike space people, the "Nommo"

Cave painting from circa 2000 BCE found on the Russian-Chinese border.

By all accounts, Sirius (as referring collectively to the two "twins," that ancient mythic dyad, Christ/Lucifer, Cain/Abel, Thor/Loki, Horus/Set) stands in, mythologically if not scientifically, as a kind of "Central Command Headquarters" for the Earth people (and probably for the whole Galaxy). What if our various, neatly corresponding myths and legends are not merely the result of collective *dreaming*, but *blueprints* for an on-going evolutionary strategy for which all recorded history is but the warm-up?

Kabbalists would point out that (like the fable of Adam naming the animals in the Garden) all things are named—imagined—before they can be "discovered." It was only possible for Newton to prove the reality of gravity by first positing its existence. Newton found exactly what he set out to look for. From such a lateral, non-linear, perspective, Newton did not discover the law of gravity, he *imposed* it. This is the reason, according to occultist logic, that modern science has failed to find any substantial evidence for angels, spirits, or other entities: from a lack of imagination on the part of the seekers, and not from an actual lack of evidence. There is evidence a-plenty, as every paranoid knows.

State science, on the other hand (being a Faith unto itself), sends signals on precise frequencies into the cosmos, on the assumption that potential life forms all communicate on the same wavelength (and that they would respond in kind if they did). As Terence McKenna once observed, this is about as logical as searching the galaxy "for a good Italian restaurant."[15] The idea of an intelligent life form existing incorporeally, without organic structure, has not occurred to these far-seeking minds, evidently. Why should it? They are all organisms, after all.[16]

*

> The ancients concealed beneath the grotesque veils of Seth, Pan and Typhon, the awful powers which science today is beginning to encounter in its probings into Matter, Time and Space. . . . The occultist understands that contact with these energies may be established more completely through symbols so ancient that they have had time to bury themselves in the vast storehouse of the racial subconscious.
> —Kenneth Grant, *Hecate's Fountain*

In his book *Sacred Science*, the occult scientist R.A. Schwaller de Lubitcz writes of *"Neters,"* an Egyptian term referring to the gods—or principles of nature—worshipped (or at least acknowledged) by the ancients. The primary five "epagomenals" were Osiris, Isis, Set, Nephthys, and Horus. Schwaller de Lubitcz states that, "There exists a bond between cause and effect, and that bond is called the Neter. . . . *The Neters* in general are considered to be *without cranal skullcaps*, which means they are devoid of their own arbitrary judgments. They are powers acting in a set way, the determination of which is made clear by a crown, or by an animal head."

As a power, principle or quality, the "Neter" refers to both a force and an awareness, an archetype. Yet for the ancient Egyptians a Neter was also a practical reality, just as much as gravity and electricity are for us. Kenneth Grant's observation (quoted above) is central to the paranoid understanding. If true, it suggests that we sophisticated moderns—with our psychological dependence on technology and rational interpretations of phenomena—still have much to learn from the ancients, with all their "primitive superstition." As *givers* of life to all that lives, it seems inevitable to equate the celestial bodies (stars and planets) with the atavistic concept of gods. But even ordinary logic was eventually ask: if the stars live, couldn't they be conscious of the life within them? We would never rationally attempt to posit awareness without energy; so why do we presume energy without awareness?

Sooner or later, the man of science arrives at the same conclusion as the man of knowledge. Both call their respective conclusions: *Energy*. The scientist or sceptic must also acknowledge the symbiotic relation (in the cosmos) between consciousness and energy. Quantum mechanically speaking, information (charge) is the only factor that lets us differentiate between the various forms of Energy; every

---

15: *The Archaic Revival*. Note also: "The British astronomer Fred Hoyle postulates that the giant masses of dark cloud in outer space are a kind of consciousness. . . He arrived at the conclusion that 67%, or some 130 billion of the stars in our galaxy, are surrounded by planets. If that is true, then our galaxy is swarming with life." (Pauwels and Bergier, *Impossible Possibilities*)

16: Yet all the essential elements of our existence—gravity, electricity, oxygen, even thought itself—can be experienced and employed but never actually *proven* (or even accurately defined). Where do these mysterious forces come from? Is "gravity" necessarily any more fanciful or subjective a term than "devil"? Both are presumptions on our part, propositions, for the sake of argument and convenience.

atom consists of its program, its particular *spin,* or information load. Atoms *behave.* They experience, they have their ways. This alone is evidence (to the occultist if not the scientist) of life, and of awareness. And if atoms are aware, how much more so a star, which is simply an atom on a grand scale?

11. R. Fludd, *Utriusque Cosmi. Metaphysica*, Oppenhemii 1617, Fronte-
spizio.

Microcosmic Man in the Macrocosmic Universe (by Robert Fludd)

By aligning ancient superstition with modern science, the Sun becomes literally our God. Not in some anthropomorphic sense, but in the mythological tradition of Creator, Source of all that we are. Because the sum and total of all we are is Energy. And all Energy, in this System at least, is Solar.[17]

*

Beyond their affiliation with abstract cosmic forces, the original Egyptian deities were reputed to have been mortal human beings of extraordinary character who (like Enoch, and Jesus), by the mysterious favors of Fate, became more than human. Here is where occult theory becomes practical. Esoteric societies throughout history have claimed to be in touch with preterhuman beings, beings

---

17: "The light of the sun is pure power. After all, it's the most intensely gathered energy there is . . . the life-line that links us to a greater awareness." (Taisha Abelar: *The Sorcerers' Crossing*) "We are pieces of the sun." (Carlos Castaneda, *The Second Ring of Power*)

that govern all earthly affairs through their interaction with *a chosen group of humans*. It is this very tie, or contact, that constitutes the authority (and vanity) of the so-called "elect."[18]

The nature of these beings or forces is that they are both omnipresent and (for this reason) occult (hidden). They constitute nothing less than the secret order of the Universe, and are by definition accessible only to those who have "made the grade," who are capable of withstanding contact. This of course makes their existence a self-fulfilling mystery: the reality of such beings is confirmed, rather than refuted, by their obscurity![19]

A brief digression. In the immortal TV show beloved of young paranoids, *Star Trek*, "the Prime Directive," a sort of Intergalactic Code Of Non-interference, dictates that no advanced race may interfere with the destiny and progress of another, less advanced race (not even if it is to help it along its evolutionary path). Occultism argues the same thing: the "god" will only appear if successfully *evoked*.

Now scientist man wants to build rocket ships to take him to the planets and stars. And whether or not he accepts the stars as gods, or even archetypes, he has already pledged himself to reach them.

Meanwhile, on the inner planes, a different evolutionary agenda unfolds.

The object of most, if not all, yogic and magikal practices is the awakening and raising of the dormant energy of the body (known as *Kundalini*) up from the base of the spine (and the soles of the feet) to the crown of the head, and outward. Occultism and Eastern religion has many terms for this: the emergence of the Other, the waking of the snake, the opening of the lotus, the perfecting of the Body of Light. It is easy enough (and perfectly logical) to imagine that this process may be enacted "as below, so above," and that we as a race are also preparing—over countless aeons—to make our way, upward and outward within the Galactic Body.[20]

18: Part of the pride of such connections perhaps comes from the degree of stamina and courage that is required to maintain them? The archetype of "the secret chiefs" (or Supermen) whose very presence proves harmful to the ordinary man extends to our present day, whether in the guise of gods, angels, faeries, extraterrestrial visitors, super-powered mutants, or Jedi Knights. "As to the Secret Chiefs with whom I am in touch . . . I can tell you nothing . . . My meetings with them have shown me how difficult it is for mortal man, however 'advanced,' to be in their presence . . . I felt I was before a force so great that I can only compare it with a shock one would receive by being close to a flash of lightning . . . The nervous symptoms I spoke of were accompanied by the cold sweats, bleeding from the mouth, nose and sometimes the ears." Gregor S. Mathers, one time head of the Hermetic Order of the Golden Dawn (founded in London in 1888), in a letter to his "Members of the 2nd Order."

19: "The self-validating logic is circular and perfect. There's no escaping from it. Freddy Krueger, as well as the Greys, cannot NOT be real . . . according to the definition they set up for themselves. Just when you THINK they're not real THAT'S JUST WHEN THEY'RE MOST REAL. The lack of any empirical proof IS ITSELF THE PROOF." "I Was Abducted by Aliens" by Rev. Ivan Stang, *Wake Up Down There: The Excluded Middle Collection*

20: Like so, the solar system begins to appear "as a huge light pump, wherein the light of souls is pumped from planet to planet until it finally leaves the solar system altogether, and is transmitted to

All this is supported by occult tradition: "From antiquity until Copernicus, the universe was popularly believed to consist of a great celestial hierarchy reaching from the Earth, up through the spheres of the seven planetary gods (Moon, Mercury, Venus, Sun, Mars, Jupiter and Saturn), to the fixed sphere of the timeless and unchanging stars."[21] The ruling principles of the Universe are represented by the stars and planets, in a symbolic arrangement akin to a mathematical equation. If the Sun is the Logos, or First Cause of our system—its God—then the planets are the Powers, the Archons, the Secondary Causes, "gods" who minister to the solar *will.* Each planet then has its presiding energy or archetype, the immanent, embodied life and consciousness of the planet itself. It is responsible for ordering all events, both material and spiritual, gross and subtle, from sunspots and thunder storms to floods and forest fires, world wars and mass migrations: it reigns "unconsciously," or suprarationally, over all minerals, vegetables, animals, humans, and angels.[22]

---

the galactic center." (Dennis and Terence McKenna: *The Invisible Landscape*) The galactic center being Sirius?

21: "According to Plutarch, a priest of Apollo and a contemporary of Jesus . . . at death the soul and the intellect ascend to the moon, leaving the outer shell of the body behind on the earth. After a period, Nous or divine intellect leaves the soul behind on the moon and rises to the sphere of the sun. In the Hermetic writings, the soul descending into incarnation acquires a negative propensity at each planetary station, while after death it casts off each vice at the appropriate sphere in its reascent to the divine and eternal realm. In fully developed mythological gnosticism of the pessimist variety, the planets become archons, astrological rulers of Fate." David Fideler: *Jesus Christ: Sun of God*

22: "To our spiritual perception . . . and to our inner spiritual eye, the Elohim or Dhyanis are no more an abstraction than our soul or spirit are to us. Reject the one and you reject the other, since that which is the *surviving entity in us* is partly the direct emanation from, and partly *those celestial entities themselves* . . . Around [the Sun], like an army of satellites, are *innumerable choirs of genii.* These dwell in the neighborhood of the Immortals, and thence watch over human beings. They fulfill

The first step towards accepting this premise, for the modern man, is to acknowledge the possibility that—contrary to all we have chosen to *believe*—the local planets are inhabited. Paranoid awareness allows that we have been spared the monumental distraction of such a truth for the sole purpose of keeping our attention where it belongs. Evidence does indeed exist, however, that the planets *were* inhabited once, in some bygone time, even if they no longer are.[23]

NASA photographs of the infamous "face on Mars" and the Cydonia complex

If so, the Parliament of Planets keeps its stony silence. It runs to another timetable, along parallel tracks to those of science, and of *reason*. It has its rebel forces, its antibodies, its poetic avant-garde to keep the flame of its awareness burning. These lesser, all-dependent yet essential life-forms (of which the human race is but one collective) are kept relatively in the dark—exactly as are the cells of

---

the will of the gods (Karma) by means of storms, tempests, transitions of fire and earthquakes, likewise by famines and wars." H.P. Blavatsky, *The Secret Doctrine*

23: "November 22, 1966, Washington Post: '6 Mysterious Statuesque Shadows Photographed on the Moon by Orbiter.' The photograph seems to reveal 6 spires arranged in a purposeful geometrical pattern inside a small portion of the Sea of Tranquility . . . all either cone or pyramid shaped . . . Soviet space engineer Alexander Abromov: 'The distribution of these lunar objects is similar to the plan of the Egyptian pyramids. . . . The centers of the spires of this lunar "abaka" are arranged in precisely the same way as the apices of the 3 great pyramids.'. . . . It appears that some of the pyramids of Earth may be part of a permanent marking system that extends to more than one planet of our solar system.'" William Bramley: *The Gods of Eden* "In January 1985 NASA discovered the Venus Complex, which is identical to the one at Giza in Egypt: 3 pyramids, and a Sphinx. There are over 200 photos of this Cytherean complex . . . NASA broadcast the information on a single TV station in Florida one time and that was it . . . (and so) fulfilled its legal requirement to make this information public." Bob Frissel: *Nothing in this Book is True, But That's Exactly How Things Are.* The alignment of the Cheops pyramid with the Pyramid of the Sun in Teotihuacan, Mexico, defines an orbital period which locks in with the rotation of Mars . . . When the Viking spacecraft orbited Mars in 1977, among the pictures that came back was one that included a giant Sphinx-like stone face, staring straight upward, as if designed to be seen from above. About 10 miles away was a rectangular pyramid." George Andrews: *Extra-Terrestrials Among Us* As to just how existing intelligent life might have escaped our notice so far, there are of course a dozen different explanations for such a possibility. Bob Frissel comes up with the most unassailable one: "When you go to any planet you have to tune to the right dimensional level to find anything significant. . . . There is no life on Venus on the 3rd dimension. However, on the 4th dimension, Venus is a well-populated, beautiful planet." No arguments from us.

the body, or the drones of a hive, or soldiers in an army—as to the will, *intent*, direction (and even existence), of the higher life forms, and as to their mysterious role as organizer-archons. Like that of the atoms, the lives of the gods remain secret unto us. Charles Fort suggests we are in quarantine.

> Then, if Exclusionism be general delusion; if we shall accept that conceivably the isolation of this earth has been a necessary factor in the development of the whole geo-system, we see that exclusionistic science has faithfully, though falsely, functioned. It would be world-wide crime to spread world-wide too soon the idea that there are other existences nearby and that they have been seen and that sounds from them have been heard: the peoples of this earth must organize themselves before conceiving of, and trying to establish, foreign relations. (Fort, *Complete Books*)

If this is so then, besides the popular fatalism of astrology, humanity remains unaware of being ordered and guided by a collective will, a will that connects us (both organically and psychically) to the Earth, and then (and only then) to the other planets and stars. We have chosen, collectively or individually, to ignore our place in the cosmos, in favor of some vague but tantalizing idea called "free will." Perhaps even the Gods make it a policy to let their creations run with this idea for a few millennia, just to see if any of them are dumb enough to actually buy it?

James Joyce said that history is a nightmare from which we are struggling to awaken. Or maybe it is a chrysalis from which we are shortly due to emerge? The archetype of this emergence is embodied not only in the gods and spacemen and superheroes of our mythology, but also in the ghosts, faeries, Ufos, and other apparitions, as encountered by growing numbers of people around the world, and with a growing frequency and intensity, by all accounts. Our myths have come back to haunt us, and reality gets more and more unreal with every passing day.

In a world of stereotypes, a true archetype might well appear to us, alien as it would be, as terrible and beautiful at the same time. Reaching out towards this unknown is only the paranoid's way of expressing his affinity with it. Reviling it, dismissing it, or fleeing in horror from it is his way of denying it, of refusing it access to his psyche. He might as well expect to stop a tidal wave with a hand signal. The "god" speaks a different language altogether.

The Sirius Star System: Sirius A and B, with Sirius C concealed
Lucifer: the Light Bringer and Morning Star

Chapter Two: Illuminoids

The Mundane Shell

The devil is a black outline all of us know.
—William Blake

Every word is a lie. Yet, at the core of every lie is truth. Imagine a circle: the outward bound or circumference is the word—it has no existence of its own, it is nowhere, and yet it shapes our perception at every step. The center, on the other hand, though infinitely small and apparently insignificant, is in essence everywhere. If there are no bounds, then every point is equally central or true.

Imagine a nut: the word—language—is the shell of this nut; it is deceptive, indigestible, without nutritious value, yet it contains and protects the nut within. Such is the lie around the truth, one must crack the shell to get at the nut, but only in order to devour it. Language, indeed reality as we perceive it, is simply a system of shells. We are so used to eating these dry and empty husks in place of the nuts, however, that we have long since become oblivious to what we are missing. All books are corpses, all scholars are necromancers: they seek to give life to dead things. For language is also *logos:* the ratio, the means of dividing up the silent truth into shapes and sounds, manifestation, so-called "life," though it is but a shadow of something greater. The word is a tool which in itself has no meaning or value. So great is the spell cast by the Logos, however, that we have succumbed to its mighty decree and become idolaters: we worship the lie, in the name of Truth.

Crowley, Hitler, and the Dogs of Reason

The word of the Magus is always a falsehood. . . . The task of the Magus is to make his word, the expression of his Will, come true.
—Aleister Crowley, *Confessions* (chap 81)

Aleister Crowley, the self-proclaimed Magus of the Aeon, was destined from his inception to be an exception. His father, a preacher, hounded him relentlessly to "Get right with God"; his mother, equally obsessed with biblical lore, referred to him repeatedly as a "beast." All this left its mark on young Alexander,[1] the great beast to be, and years later, he assumed the title and station of *"To Mega Therion,"* The Great Beast (signing all his correspondences not with a name but a

---

1: Crowley was christened Alexander Edward Crowley, but changed his name to Aleister for "magickal" reasons.

number—666). Crowley reasoned that infamy was every bit as useful as fame, and that much easier to achieve. Like Wilde, Crowley was

The many faces of Aleister Crowley

an early adherent of the maxim "all publicity is good publicity" (both amount to influence, which amounts to *power*).

Whatever games Crowley played with the perceptions of the world, he was undoubtedly a master, though in a fashion wholly his own. Never a dabbler, he applied himself to a number of diverse disciplines and excelled in them all: chess, literature, languages (ancient and modern), philosophy, poetry, espionage, mountain climbing, wild-game hunting, yoga, drug-taking, sex magick. Crowley was notoriously perverse in both his personal and professional life but—though he was to all intents and purposes a sort of inspired lunatic—he *did* practice all he preached. The central event in his life was the writing of *The Book of the Law*. *The Book of the Law*, or *Liber Al vel Legis* (*Liber Al* for short), is a text considered by some to contain the profoundest secrets of magick, as well as the keys to the inauguration of the long-promised New Aeon.

Crowley claimed that, on the 8th of April 1904—in Cairo at 12 noon exactly and for the following two days at the same hour—he heard a voice in his ear dictating the words of the text, which he transcribed faithfully. The voice belonged to *Aiwass*, or *Aiwaz*,[2] "the minister of Hoor-paar-kraat," Horus—the god of force and fire, child of Isis and Osiris, and self-appointed conquering Lord of the New Aeon, an Aeon now announced by the writing of *Liber Al*. The central tenet of the book is "Do What Thou Wilt Shall Be The Whole Of The Law!"[3]

2: The number of Aiwaz is 93.

3: The law of Thelema, meaning will, is the "eleven fold word of the Aeon" (11 words in all). Also the word Abrahadabra—another key—contains 11 letters. "My number is 11, as all their numbers who are of us." The union of 5 and 6, the pentangle and the hexagram (i.e., Man and "Lucifer"), 11 is the number of the magick of the Aeon.

The characteristics of ruthlessness, arrogance, and blasphemy found in *Liber Al* were traits for which Crowley himself would become widely known, and there is a fair indication, in conventional history alone (Crowley's claims aside), that Adolf Hitler adopted many of the central tenets of *Liber Al*, starting with the "secret four-fold word, the blasphemy against all gods and men": Do What Thou Wilt. Whether or not Hitler actually embraced "the Law of Thelema," there is little doubt that he was aware of the Book, and probably derived inspiration from it. The third part of the Book, pertaining to Horus, begins:

> Now let it first be understood that I am a god of war and vengeance. I shall deal hardly with them . . . I will give you a war-engine. With it ye shall smite the peoples; and none shall stand before you. Lurk! Withdraw! Upon them! this is the Law of the Battle of Conquest: thus shall my worship be about my secret house. [III:3,7-9. The book continues:] Mercy let be off: damn them who pity! Kill and torture; spare not; be upon them . . . [18] Argue not; convert not; talk not overmuch! Them that seek to entrap thee, to overthrow thee, them attack without pity or quarter; and destroy them utterly. Swift as the trodden serpent turn and strike! Be thou deadlier than he! Drag down their souls to awful torment: laugh at their fear: spit upon them!

Such sentiments, if taken at face value, might well have appealed to the young Hitler, set as he was upon leaving history in ruins. As he had done with Nietzsche, however, Hitler was wont to twist and distort the text to his own ends.[4]

Crowley's involvement in espionage in both the first and second world wars (he worked for US and British intelligence writing deliberately absurd, counter-productive "German" propaganda) is well known and presumably documented somewhere. It is extremely difficult to find anyone who will admit to Crowley's involvement with Hitler, however, despite Crowley's own claims.[5] But Hitler's obsession with the occult is well-known and there are dozens of books upon the subject, of varying degrees of interest. It even served to fire the plot for a pulp action movie, *Raiders of the Lost Ark.*[6]

*

> We have nothing with the outcast and the unfit: let them die in their misery. For they feel not. Compassion is the vice of kings: stamp down the wretched and the weak: this is the law of the strong: this is our law, and the joy of the world.

4: The Book itself perhaps set this trap: "There is great danger in me; for who doth not understand these runes shall make a great miss. He shall fall down into the pit called Because, and there he shall perish with the dogs of Reason." (AL—II:27) This may be partly why Crowley added the warning at the end of the Book: "The study of this book is forbidden. it is wise to destroy this copy after the first reading. Whosoever disregards this does so at his own risk and peril."

5: Israel Regardie denies the idea. The only work I have found that treats of the matter at all is John Symmonds's *The Medusa's Head—Conversations Between Aleister Crowley and Adolf Hitler.* Symmond's Crowley says: "Hitler was born to fulfill *The Book of the Law* . . . I realized that as soon as I picked up *Mein Kampf.* Hitler's coming was foretold in the Book."

6: Much of this literature is difficult to locate, and a great deal of little value. *Arktos,* by J. Godwin is an exceptional work, *The Spear of Destiny,* by Trevor Ravenscroft turgid and hysterical, *Morning of the Magicians,* perhaps the most famous, and certainly the first, by Pauwels and Bergier, contains much of the essential history as uncovered so far.

—*Book of the Law*, II:21

From a lucid view, all warfare is understood, first and foremost, as *internal* warfare. It is hidden, domestic, "cold," making all external, overt, and "heated" warfare between nations no more than a brief orgasm after years of foreplay. From such a view, wars are never won or lost; they are *negotiated*. World War II, to the paranoid, was no "good war," but it was perhaps the greatest business deal in history. (The Bank of England funded both sides.[7]) As a battle between "good and evil" or justice and injustice, it was a hollow drama, engineered expressly to distract and to decimate the masses.[8]

The Art of War then—like that of business—is to make itself as smooth and as efficient as possible, as silent and sustained an affair as its explosive, unpredictable nature will allow. The ultimate war-machine, mili-medical-media-industrial/entertainment complex, is designed to "serve" man in just precisely the manner which McDonald's has been "serving" cows for the last few decades: with all the unpleasantness under the counter.

7: Observe Chamberlain's enormous reluctance to declare war on Germany, mistakenly attributed to spinelessness. "[Hitler's] regime was no temporary nightmare, but a system with a good future, and Mr Norman [Montague Norman, the director of the Bank of England] advised his directors to include Hitler in their plans. There was no opposition, and it was decided that Hitler should get covert help from London's financial section. . . . The Bank of England contrived to support Hitler even after the Nazi dictator embarked on his program of conquest . . . after, the Bank of England naturally provided loans to Britain to fight Hitler." (William Bramley, *The Gods of Eden*.)

8: "In April 1943, a conference of British and American officials formally decided that nothing should be done about the Holocaust and 'ruled out all plans for mass rescue.' The Foreign Office and the State Department were both afraid that the Third Reich would . . . stop the gas chambers, empty the concentration camps, and let hundred of thousands (if not millions) of Jewish survivors emigrate to freedom in the West . . . not a single Allied nation wanted to let the Jews settle in their country. The unspoken consensus was that it was better to let Hitler handle them." (Jim Keith, *Casebook for Alternative Three*)

As a commodity, war must be rendered as appealing as any other "product." It is not only propagated and imposed upon the populace, it is advertised and glorified, until it is coveted and consumed willingly, hungrily, as manna from heaven. Above all, war is made to seem, however undesirable and inexplicable, an intrinsic feature of our existence: a fact of human nature. War becomes not a condition, but the primary nature of life, and of mankind.

The war-like nature of many of the passages in *Liber Al* would seem to be a direct response to this. It seems to regard this condition as a disease that must be purged, like a boil brought to a head and squeezed finally out of existence. To read many of his other writings leaves little doubt that Crowley, like Nietzsche before him, was a kind of proto-Nazi (though he abhorred all forms of fascism, just as Nietzsche despised anti-Semitism). On the other hand, Hitler doubtless aspired to immortality as a world leader, and nurtured delusions of his infallibility as the chosen "avatar" of the New Aeon. His Fourth Reich/Millennium of peace and prosperity under the *Ubermensch* is illustrative of an insane mix of the best intentions with the worst of methods. Hitler appeared to believe that global destruction was a necessary step on the way to evolutionary glory. He did not acknowledge any god or savior, as such, but he was firmly persuaded of the existence of his "Ubermensch."

In his own words: "The new man is living amongst us now. He is here! I have seen the new man. He is intrepid and cruel. I was afraid of him."[9]

9: Crowley probably fancied himself in the role. But Hitler, driven into frenzies of terror by these powers, had most of his encounters in the dead of night. "A person close to Hitler," wrote his doctor, Achilles Demas, "told me that he wakes up in the night screaming and in convulsions. He calls for help and appears to be half paralyzed. . . . He utters confused and unintelligible sounds, gasping as if on the point of suffocation."

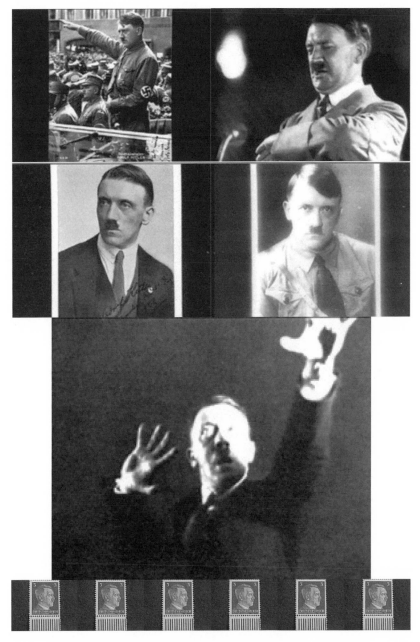

The Unchanging Face of Adolf Hitler
(Hitler would study pictures taken by his personal photographer and then alter his gestures
and posture until satisfied he was achieving the desired visual impact.)

Hitler's preoccupation with the Ubermensch echoes Crowley's own claims of affiliation (through Aiwaz) with the "Secret Chiefs"—namely, the preterhuman intelligences which (according to the paranoid and the occultist both) rule covertly over the destiny of mankind. Crowley considered contact with these beings to be the next evolutionary step for mankind. That the SS and Nazism as a whole was established upon an occult basis, and that its inner structures and purposes were not merely political but also sorcerous, has now forever crossed over from the realms of paranoid awareness into orthodox history. Many occultists are eager to stress, however, that Hitler was at best a low-grade medium with a deranged sense of self-importance. All his considerable accomplishments aside, it seems that he knew little or nothing of the forces which possessed him. In many ways a fairly ordinary, unremarkable person, he was well chosen to embody (and so fulfill) the demonic will of the mass, a mass which, ironically, he himself so despised. In regard to this, John Symmonds' Crowley remarks, in *The Medusa's Head*:

I never met . . . someone so demonic as Herr Hitler. Why do you think I spend so much time with him? And come when he bids me? I tell you only the universe can prevail against Hitler. But the universe for the present doesn't seem to be interested; though Hitler is the enemy of the universe, that is to say of God; for the universe is only God's instrument. It is as if God said, "Let mankind learn a lesson; they need to open their eyes a little wider. Hitler will do that for them. Just wait. They will see things that men have never seen or heard before—such horrors that there will be no word in the German or any other language to describe them." That is what the demonic is when it appears in a very ordinary person, a man of the people, someone the intellectuals are contemptuous of but not the masses. With an uncanny instinct, they know who he is.

So far as it serves to extend the myth of paranoid awareness, there seems no reason to doubt that, directly or indirectly, Crowley helped to feed Hitler's dark fantasies and ambitions as a "black messiah." A true Magician and Trickster, Crowley would have taken no sides in any battle, but would have deliberately played *both* sides against one another in good Machiavellian fashion. His goals, however (even if selfish), would have been sorcerous, and not mundane.

Paranoid awareness spins a fable from the age of paradoxes. It gives us a fairy tale about a "good war" that never was, a war that still rages and has yet to be fully divulged by history. It offers up Adolf Hitler as the past century's "Antichrist," and Aleister Crowley—the man in the shadows (as he carefully fashioned himself to be)—as its corresponding "Beast." It strains at the shackles of Consensus reality to remind us that we are still bound by the power of myth, even if we choose to call it "history," and that magik still rules our lives, even if we now know it as "politics."

A Brief History of Conspiracy

William Blake's "Body of Abel Found by Adam and Eve"

The shedding of blood is necessary for God did not hear the children of Eve until blood
was shed. And that is external religion
—Aleister Crowley, *The Book of Thoth*

This world that is our matrix is our own making. But to the paranoid
understanding, there exist those who would take advantage of our voluntary
incarceration and who would appoint themselves our jailors. For the sake of
simplicity, let's borrow a term from William Bramley and call them the Custodians.
Secret societies, from the ancient Assassins all the way up to the O.T.O and the
Scientologists, have plagued, dogged and finally overrun the paranoid's version of
history, and whether merely through myths and legends or in actual concrete "fact"
seems finally of little import. For the paranoid, the intrigue begins with organized
religion itself, the very first conspiracy of "the elect" to lord it over its flock. If
religion is a system of control, then, exoterically speaking, Nazism is the ultimate
religion: not only the latest, but also the last.

The essence of the "occult conspiracy" of paranoid awareness is exemplified
by the myth of Lucifer—*hubris*. A secret revolt against gods considered obsolete,
now to be supplanted. In the human psyche—paranoid or otherwise—a battle rages.

It has raged since the inception of time, since Michael rose up in righteous wrath at the glorious disobedience of Lucifer; since the Serpent tempted Eve; since knowledge split in two and went their separate ways; since the left-hand disdained the right, and right denied left. Like two parallel lines or universes which cannot be reconciled, the parties of the "secret brotherhoods" of schizoid Man have made war across the world, and throughout history. As slaves to the cosmic laws that created them, they are like contraction and expansion: one wages war for awakening, the other for oblivion. Both have their agendas, both have their methods, both have their ends. Though they appear at odds, like day and night they define each other, and what appears as two is really one.

The central tenet of paranoid awareness is that, behind all the battles, the betrayals, the conspiracies and the deceptions, there exist *two* primary agendas, or powers, and that these factions—according to the modern myth—in turn control or influence a myriad variety of minor conspiracies and societies, and plots and traditions, all of which conspire together, despite themselves and their professed animosities, to create the chaos and insanity in which we now live. This is the paranoid acceptance, in a nutshell.

*

Like all other cultures, our own is a conspiracy, a bevy of petty divinities who derive their power solely from our unprotesting acquiescence and constantly deflect our gaze away from the fantastic aspect of reality.
—John Keel

The fantastic aspect of reality is what concerns us here, and nothing else. It is in this spirit and this spirit alone that I paint the picture which I am now painting before you. This global or even cosmic conspiracy is of course the most reassuring of paranoid belief systems: it is as it were the very structure of paranoia itself, imposed upon the world at large. It explains everything, without explaining anything. All people everywhere believe in some sort of conspiracy. The Christians call it God or the Holy Spirit; the scientists call it evolution, or fractals; the nihilists call it Chance or Blind Fate. None of them can actually deny the existence of order or design behind all things in the universe, and would be fools to try. Only the paranoid, however, attempts to trace the lines of the design and attribute these lines to recognizable, identifiable forces, entities, person or parties in the world at large. As such, his ambition is prodigious and fearless: neither ridicule nor personal danger can dissuade him from his course. In his bid to render the invisible visible and make the unknown known, he stretches the boundaries of both collective reason and individual sanity and, if successful, allows a new order to break on through. He discovers, by imagining, an underlying "reason" or meaning, beneath the apparent absence of same.

So far as it functions—i.e., is a working system that allows new possibilities or philosophies to be entertained or grasped—then such paranoia is productive and therefore justified, and the question of its validity—its *provability*—is immaterial. So far as it becomes another article of faith, of personal obsession, a cause for fanaticism, it can be said to be counter-productive. The paranoid becomes another true believer, suckered by his own hypotheses, snared by belief. Once again, the validity of his belief is not the issue here, only its utility as a means for greater awareness. The will or desire to bring order and sense—a hidden but still evident meaning—to the chaos of our lives is perfectly healthy. It stems from the creative will, and as such is a positive desire.[10]

It is not so much that the paranoid, if successful, desires the truth behind the lies, but rather that he seeks, as an artist, to rearrange the random factors of history into his own *personal myth*. As such, he aspires to becoming a true poet, one of the legislators of the world, those men and women for whom reality itself is a canvas.

Having expressed all this, let us now proceed with our pseudo-history, starting with what an anonymous Franciscan monk[11] refers to as "protracted struggles between several 'elite' factions, 'cliques,' if you will, who have battled under various guises for supremacy from the days following the fall of the Roman Empire to the present." Although this monk's identification of the parties as "Zionists and Teutons" is a gross simplification at best, the notion of two strains or traditions at continuous war throughout the world and throughout history seems to be a recurring theme common to many dedicated researchers of forbidden lore. These two "lines," however, might better be understood as *traditions*. In which case, they cannot be described with any accuracy as existing parties or "cliques," seeing as how any group, over time (just like any individual), is likely to move from one tradition to the other, and back again.

Research concerning these "secret" traditions suggests (to me at least) that they correspond essentially with the old magikal/mystical dichotomy. On the one hand, we have the religious school of (supposedly) "passive" worship, as represented by Freemasonry. On the other hand, we have the "pagan" or sorcerous school of active participation, as embodied by "the Illuminati." Both, however, share as their central tenet the idea of *sacrifice*. To this day the former school practices old-fashioned blood sacrifice, be it of animals or of humans. The latter school practices the more new-fangled method (actually, it is perhaps the oldest tradition of all, but also the most secret, hence still largely unfamiliar to the world), the *self*-sacrifice of drug-taking and the even more secret techniques of sexual ecstasy. These are the so-called right and left-hand paths, respectively.[12]

10: "Chaos magic allows for such modern sensibilities by putting the dogma through a blender. A typical eight word blender is 'Let us adopt a belief system in which...' ... What the chaos magician is putting into practice is Austin Spare's principle of acting 'as if.' ... the correct approach to a Magical theory or model is not to seek to disprove it as one would with a Scientific theory, but to see if you can convince yourself that it is true by acting as if it were true. If this results in the theory 'working,' then you rejoice in it as a practical tool. What you do not do is assume therefore that it must be 'true' in any significant sense.' Ramsey Dukes, *S.S.T.O.B.M.E*

11: The author of *Secrets From the Vatican Library*, in *Secret and Suppressed.*

12: The inherent conflict in these two approaches to religious experience is summed up by Terence McKenna in *The Archaic Revival*: "What I think happened is that in the world of prehistory all religion was experiential, and it was based on the pursuit of ecstasy through plants. And at some time, very early, a group interposed itself between people and direct experience of the 'Other.' This created hierarchies, priesthoods, theological systems, castes and rituals, taboos."

A well-known mythological description of this dichotomy is hidden in the story of Cain and Abel in *Genesis*. Cain offers up the "fruit of the land," is rejected by Jehovah and rudely cast out of his favor. Abel, on the other hand, offers up animal sacrifice, his own slaughtered livestock, and is taken into the bosom of the Lord. Incensed by such brazen favoritism, Cain slays his brother, and for his sin is condemned to walk the Earth in solitude. It is commonly thought that Cain shed the first blood, but if one looks closely into the tale, it becomes apparent that Cain was rejected for his *unwillingness* to shed blood, and that Abel, in fact, is the first slayer, albeit of beast and not of man. Cain, for his part, rejects the judgment of Jehovah, which he perceives as unjust. This makes him the original rebel, and he has been accordingly maligned and slandered ever since. This seems to be the historical, mythological origin of the persistent bias towards the "right-hand path" and away from the left, a bias that continues to the present day.

In *The Masks of God IV*, Joseph Campbell describes the left-hand path as "The rose garden of the philosophers . . . the way of the senses—the eyes, the heart and the spontaneity of the body." By which reckoning, the right-hand path of the Masons (i.e., *builders*) can be said to be the path of *the mind*.[13] Hopefully this makes it clear that these two schools must finally be synthesized into one, just as Cain and Abel were "synthesized" by the exoteric act of murder. (Symbolically, Cain—the beast or body—absorbed meek Abel, the Christ or soul.) Blood sacrifice was most likely but a literalization of ancient, esoteric rites which had little or nothing to do with the slaughter of animals or people,[14] while drug-use is perhaps only the profanest of methods for attaining ecstasy.[15] A historical example of these two opposing schools working together, in the form of two opposing adherents in confidential collaboration, would be the briefly described psycho-history of Crowley and Hitler, Hitler being the right hand, Crowley the left. (Perhaps a better example of the right-hand man in history would be Moses or Mohammad, however.)

Besides the mushroom-munching shamans of South America, the Gnostics and Sufis were amongst the first historical examples of the left-hand teaching. It is all-too typical of the on-going, apparent rivalry between the two schools that the true, inner meaning of Christianity (as retained by the Gnostics) was quickly suppressed

---

13: Hence their worship of Lucifer, or Knowledge. See Blavatsky, "Satan, or the Red Fiery Dragon . . . and *Lucifer*, or 'light-bearer' is in us: it is our *Mind*—our tempter and Redeemer, our intelligent liberator and savior from pure animalism." This (from *the Secret Doctrine*) is of course the right-hand talking. "Only the Promethean power of Mind, which can see directly into the heart of creation and resonate with the very principles of Being, could ever steal the Fire of the Gods." David Fideler, *Jesus Christ, Sun of God.*

14: "[A]nimal sacrifices mentioned in ancient Sanskrit texts did not refer to the killing of physical animals, but to the clearing of elementals and entities. . . . According to this view, it is only when the original knowledge started to be lost that texts were interpreted literally and animals were slaughtered as part of rituals." Samuel Sagan, *Entities.*

15: Many shamans use drugs only when working with their apprentices, and only when strictly necessary, as in the case of Don Juan and Carlos Castaneda, because of the fact that they (drugs) "cause untold harm to the body." (Don Juan) On the other hand, Terence McKenna makes a case for the psilocybin mushroom forming the central factor in shamanic initiation, and is not the first to suggest that the drug serves as a gateway through which the alternate dimension is accessed. Nevertheless, the bottom line of the magikal doctrine must be that all props and aids are only that, and inessential.

and banished from the public realm by the "mystic branch" (i.e., the Catholic Church), which could not allow any hint of magikal awareness (*gnosis*) to contaminate their own hold on the masses. This suppression of magik is known as *the mystification of the mass* and is the essence of religion as a control system. Though apparently malevolent, such subterfuge is actually in accordance with the secret agenda of the magikal branch, which must remain hidden from view if it is to retain, not only its power but, its purity. Since it is dedicated, in opposition to mysticism, to the enlightenment of the individual, it must remain inaccessible to the masses, in order that the individual actively *seek it out* and thereby prove worthy of its attainment. Hence "mystification of the mass" and "enlightenment of the individual" may be seen not only to be unopposed, but as complementary aspects of a single agenda. If the school of Freemasonry concerns itself with exoteric *control* and the social engineering of the mass, then the tradition of Illuminism is dedicated to esoteric *influence*, and the creative evolution of the individual. As such, they work intrinsically together, even as they are apparently "at odds."

*

The brotherhood of man is no mere poet's dream, it is a most depressing and humiliating reality.
—Oscar Wilde

Beyond doubt, the most profane and debased form of the mystery school tradition is what is commonly known as Freemasonry, "the largest and most powerful secret society of all."[16] The common man understands by this something like an eccentric gentleman's club where kooky old farts gather together to scheme and plot, dress in strange robes, and perform obscure and kinky rites and practices. (Such was "disclosed" to the public, in suitably laughable a fashion, in Stanley Kubrick's *Eyes Wide Shut.*) By the popular understanding, anyone can become a Freemason provided he happens to know the right people: a plumber, a bus-driver, a dentist, a lawyer, a filmmaker, there is no specific criteria. There are 33 known degrees in Freemasonry, and it is commonly observed that, until one reaches the 33rd degree, one remains in the dark as to the "true nature" of the organization, its teachings, structure, purposes, etc. The lower grades, then, are really for the dupes, at least from the point of view of the "dukes." Freemasonry is a simple system of hierarchies, designed to infiltrate and control society *at all levels*. For example, if you are a dentist and a 23rd degree Mason, and you know other Masons below you who happen to be doctors, policemen, judges, politicians and suchlike, then you may find that you can exert an influence that has nothing at all to do with your standing in ordinary society. The lower-grade Masons do the dirty work for the higher grades, while still under the fond illusion of belonging to an exclusive club, and of being privy to special knowledge, or to other, unspecified privileges. In actual fact, these lower grades are not Freemasons in the true sense, and are regarded as mere dilettantes by the "true initiates."

16: Robert Anton Wilson, *Coincidance*

Freemasonry—in the esoteric sense—is at the heart of most if not all of the mystery traditions, and its rituals form an intrinsic part of all initiatory teachings. In this higher sense, then, to "be" a Mason is really another, arbitrary designation for Illuminoid, Initiate, Adept, etc. The various Rosicrucian brotherhoods, the Assassins, Templars, O.T.O, A.A., Golden Dawn, Gnostic Catholic Church, Knights of the Holy Ghost, Knights of Malta, Knights of St. John, the Hermetic Brotherhood of Light, the Order of Martinists, Theosophical Society, Vril, Thule, the Prioré de Zion, the Jesuits, the Order of Melchizedek, the Bönpas, the Church of Cthulu, and onward and downward, all of these various schools, or clubs, or systems, are linked and intertwined (in the mind of the paranoid) in such a way (either by persons, funds, or ideas and goals) that the only way to really come to grips with them at all is to start to see them as interchangeable—as various tentacles of the same octopus, different heads of the one HYDRA.[17]

*

Those old seers were terrifying men . . . I shouldn't use the past tense—they are terrifying even today. Their bid is to dominate, to master everybody and everything.
—Carlos Castaneda, *The Fire From Within*

There are two primary factors to consider when attempting to define or assess a given mystery school: its aims, and its methods. About the former, there is little that can be said, though we will endeavor to shed light upon this question as our researches progress. About the methods, however, we can say a little. Before and beyond secret societies' roles in mass movements, and their work of evolutionary engineering, besides all the wilder speculations about hidden agendas and masterplans, there remains their work with the individual, for which we have first-hand testimony in abundance. All schools *offer* enlightenment. They do not

---

17: Down the tree to the thoroughly debased cryptocratic factions such as the Nazi Party, the Open Friendly Secret Society (the Vatican), the MAFIA, the Round Table (Council on Foreign Relations), RAND Corporation, the JASON Group, the Trilateral Commission, the Bilderberg Group, Joint Chiefs of Staff, the Skull and Bones Society, the Navy, Air Force, Delta Force, CIA, FBI, NSA, DOD, FEMA, SDI, DIA, NASA, WTO, WHO, FDA, ATF, MIB's and so forth. Of course there is no real way to present a comprehensive listing of such fragmented factions, and apologies are here extended to any parties whom we have unwittingly forgot to mention. This might also be a good opportunity to mention a few names, to gain a certain devil-may-care credence. Of course, it is well known that almost every president in the history of the U.S has "been" a 33rd degree Mason. Then of course you have Napoleon, Alexander the Great, Stalin, Hitler, Churchill, while other such groups as the Knights of Malta have been favored by intelligence operatives such as William Casey, Allan Dulles, and so forth. The fields of the arts and sciences, however, is where the roster really picks up. The O.T.O stakes claims on such luminaries of history as: Lao Tze, Mohammad, Dante, Simon Magus, Christian Rosenkreutz, Francis Bacon, Sir Edward Kelly, Goethe, Richard Burton (the explorer, not the actor), Nietzsche, Eliphas Levi, and Richard Wagner. (It is noted that "the names of women members are never divulged.") Meanwhile, the Prioré of Zion enjoyed the grandmastership of Newton and Jean Cocteau; Blake is strictly property of the Druids, as was Lord Bulwer-Lytton. Rosicrucian affiliations, meanwhile, have been speculated for Shakespeare, Mozart, Beethoven, Einstein (who denied it), H.G Wells, Jules Verne, Philip K. Dick and Orson Welles. It begins to seem that every single man of standing in the arts, if not politics, has been an initiate of some order or another. Paranoid awareness asks us to look at it from another angle: If there *were* a secret organization that produced geniuses out of ordinary stock, it follows that a hell of a lot of artists and pioneers would *be* the result.

necessarily provide it. It will quickly be seen by the novice that the only alternative to enlightenment is enslavement, and that nature herself—as a field in which the evolutionary principals are at play—provides a similar kind of acid-test environment for its subjects to grow in.[18] Mystery schools serve to create a similar but *intensified* environment, and to force the individual into situations that will accelerate the natural process, to make of him either a free man or—at worst—another kind of slave. This is where the ritual comes in.

The aim of occult ritual, like that of religious ceremony only more so, is to induce in the subject a state of mind which is susceptible to receiving a *new program*. By and large, religious ceremony, like TV, tends only to reinforce the old program, that of passivity and oblivion. Occult ritual, on other hand, attempts to break this old program and to replace it with another.

Arkon Daraul writes extensively on the subject, in *A History of Secret Societies*:

> Initiation ceremonies of secret cults of the mystery type invariably involve tests, sometimes severe ones. The effect of certain experiences was a carefully worked program of mind training which is familiar in modern times as that which is employed by certain totalitarian states to "condition" or reshape the thinking of an individual . . . the experience may well be induced by physical methods: but in spite of that, "it is nothing less than spiritual communion with a supernatural power." This is the point at which scientists and mystics cannot agree. The mystic feels sure that he has experienced something sublime. The scientist tells him that it is an illusion.[19]
>
> The mechanisms which are used can be summarized as:
>
> 1. The desire to participate in the ritual, and expectancy of something happening.
>
> 2. Isolation, vigils, hunger or abstinence, causing debilitation and time for reflection.
>
> 3. Noise.
>
> 4. Real or symbolic potions.

Generally speaking, the test involves a confrontation with one's fondest beliefs and profoundest fears. In Masonic ritual, one is made to face death and/or mutilation several times over (generally going through the elements, i.e., death by drowning, falling, burial and burning). One is then compelled to reject certain essential sacred and cherished illusions (such in as the Templar rite of spitting on the crucifix and kissing a fellow monk's anus). The new program (that of Freemasonry, let's say) ideally serves as a violent contrast to the old one, by which the subject comes to realize the futility and irreality of both, and so opts for neither.[20] He thereby finds himself with no program at all, free from external

---

18: "[O]ne might become a Master of the Temple without necessarily knowing any technical Magick or mysticism at all. . . . Many people may go through the ordeals and attain the degrees of the A..A.. without ever hearing that such an order exists. The universe is, in fact, busy with nothing else." (Aleister Crowley, *Confessions*, chap 68)

19: Of course, both are right; the point is, the sublime *is* an illusion, but serves to expose the fact that the mundane is also illusory.

20: "Only if one pits two views against each other can one weasel between them to arrive at the real world . . . what matters is not to learn a new description but to arrive at the totality of one's self." Castaneda, *Tales of Power*.

influence, beliefs, and assumptions, and ready to make a real bid for freedom. In the words of Carlos Castaneda—he is given "a chance to have a chance." It is only thus that he becomes an initiate, an adept, having learnt that "Every man and every woman is a star" (*Liber Al*).

The meaning of this aphorism seems to be that, beyond personal identity is—Individual Sovereignty.[21] Failing this, our novice falls from one program into another, and must remain forever content to be a slave of one sort or another, be he plumber, banker, or "Freemason."

Suppressed Technology and Secret Space Colonization

The book is *fiction based on fact*. But I now feel that I inadvertently got *very close to a secret truth*.
—Leslie Watkins, on his book *Alternative Three*[22]

All good dramas contain elements of truth, and all truth is inherently dramatic; from our perspective as psycho-historians—investigators of the eschaton—we proceed in the spirit of invention as much as inquiry, accepting that there *are* no facts, as such, only points of view. The important thing is not to have any specific, determined point of view to defend or prove, to avoid pre-conceived conclusions and pre-supposed premises, which only ensure that the "facts," as such, will never be found to agree (there being too many points of view to any given event). Personal bias can only be upheld by such a degree of manipulation, falsification, and contrivance as to render the objective wholly redundant: truth is banished by conviction. As Charles Fort put it: "To have an opinion, any opinion, one must overlook something."

The second acceptance of paranoid awareness is that *the efficiency of tyranny depends upon the maintenance of secrecy*. From here, we may begin to see that the paranoid's notion of a "one-world conspiracy" or shadow government, far from being implausible or far-fetched, is a wholly logical deduction, given the evidence before him. More to the point, it is a completely necessary one, if he is to make any sense at all of the evidence. Paranoid awareness proposes that, no matter how overgrown and wild the tree of global society may be, all its myriad branches do indeed lead back to the same trunk.

21: "[T]he ultimate goal that requires the total abolition of personality and egoidal consciousness. The *Ipsissimus* (Literally 'His very own self') is described as having 'no will in any direction, and no Consciousness of any kind involving duality.'" Kenneth Grant, *Cults of the Shadow*

22: See *A Casebook on Alternative 3*, by Jim Keith. The book *Alternative 3* was the first publication to deal with the subject of secret space colonization in any depth, and was considered by researcher Mae Brussel to be the capstone to her researches. (The book claims: "These are the strands in a web of conspiracy so monstrous the human mind can scarcely grasp its true enormity.") The book was the follow-up to a British TV broadcast, later claimed to be a hoax. (It was scheduled for April Fool's Day, but actually aired on June 20, 1977, on Anglia TV). The book claims this claim to be false in itself, a hoax of a hoax.

It's been said that "the house that is divided against itself must fall," and yet government as an international control system continues to endure, regardless of how many systems, philosophies, leaders, and parties come and go. The paranoid must be forgiven for deducing from this a certain complicity—if not actual conspiracy—between the varying government systems and ideologies, and, to a lesser extent, their proponents. Just as crime gives the forces of law and order a reason to exist, so does one government support and uphold another, precisely by dint of opposing it. In order to sustain itself as a global tradition, politics—or, to call a spade a spade, tyranny—must *at some level* be unified, no matter how disparate its various practicants may appear to be.

What unifies these variants is a common goal, a goal that may be summed up equally succinctly as: the final frontier. To boldly go, where Man has never gone before. All the policies and agendas of government (both overt and covert) have been unanimously directed towards this single goal: the stars. The fact that it was apparent early on—during the so-called Industrial Revolution—that the Earth itself was a "limited option" only served to accelerate these plans.

One does not need to be paranoid to accept that it is human nature to conspire and conceal. In order to control the mass populace, it must first be kept in ignorance. To the paranoid understanding, it is *imperative* to keep the masses enslaved by their own sense of ignorance and impotence.[23] History, and simple observation of human nature, teaches us that, he who knows how to keep his advances secret, advances fastest. This has nothing to do with the so-called Cold War, or at least if it does, the Cold War itself must be re-defined, according to paranoid awareness, not as a war between nations but between "Custodians" and the rest of us. It follows that such Custodians would by definition recognize no division besides that of their own election: no borders of state, religion or politic would keep them from gravitating together. At the highest levels of government—says the paranoid—there *must* be agreement. The fact that the world has been descending into an ever-greater state of chaos is no argument against this view, if the order as such is being directed *towards* chaos. Obviously, it is a far simpler matter to achieve a sustained level of war, strife, misery, and chaos than one of peace and harmony. By creating global chaos, the Custodians can be sure of knowing where to find the little pockets of order that exist within it, pockets from which they may direct the chaos to their own advantage.

For the duration of our lives, from childhood through adolescence to so-called maturity and independence, we have been treated by these Custodians exactly as irresponsible infants: not to be trusted to play with fire. The Promethean gift of

---

23: To give one example: the human body's capacities for telepathy, telekinesis, remote-viewing, clairvoyance, even teleportation and levitation, and for self-healing and other, more offensive uses of the invisible "aura" surrounding and connecting all living beings. These "facts" (documented in *Psychic Discoveries Behind the Iron Curtain*) have, according to the paranoid, been kept from the populace with all the jealousy and dread that the gods once kept fire from Prometheus. Should the vast array of discoveries made in the last century (confirming ancient so-called "occult" teachings of countless millennia) be even partially disclosed, it would amount to no less than a psychic revolution, in which Man would indeed be revealed (to himself) as a potential *Superman*. Only the most naive of scoffers could doubt either the need or the capacity (of "the Gatekeepers") to maintain secrecy on this matter.

knowledge was handed down to our forefathers, who in their turn, choosing *personal advantage* over good manners, declined to pass it on. Knowledge is the most valuable commodity that exists, so why share it?

Like any other commodity or currency, knowledge is devalued when spread about. Instead, it was called "sin," and made not only inaccessible but *undesirable* to all but the few. Of course, it is all-too easy for the paranoid to blame the Custodians for all his troubles, all-too easy for him to ignore the fact that any existing division between "us" and "them"—any deprivation of information from which we are suffering—depends as much upon our own acquiescence as it does on the foul-play of these hypothetical "others." If such a betrayal of trust has really taken place, outside the torn and divided psyche of the paranoid, it has taken place only and precisely because *we have allowed it to do so.* The Custodians respond to the apathy of the mass and act accordingly, in exactly the same way a fox slaughters chickens in their coop (whether he's hungry or not): because he *can.*

*

If one wants to *stop* our fellow men one must always be outside the circle that presses them. That way one can always direct the pressure.
—Carlos Castaneda, *Journey to Ixtlan*

Of all mundane conspiracy theories, "Alternative 3" is the most all-inclusive and far-reaching in scope and effect. It is here, at this very point, that the machinations of man overlap with the motions of the gods (or at least, the planets and stars). It is as improbable and unfounded as all good conspiracy theories must be, but it retains a mythic coherence and logic, and is mostly unassailable by reason.

The alternative of Alternative 3 refers to the option finally selected by the "secret world government" of paranoid awareness. It was a "final solution" to the greenhouse effect, world pollution, over-population, and other doomsday scenarios already being forecast at the turn of the 20th century. The first alternative involved nuclear war-heads aimed at the stratosphere, intended to break through the build-up of cloro-carbohydrates causing the so-called "greenhouse effect." (This was perhaps the first "doomsday symptom" to be noticed, with the inception of coal-burning, etc.) When this crackpot scheme failed, a second alternative was quickly sought: in a nutshell, to go underground. Tunnels and catacombs have been discovered underneath many of the major cities, but news of this was never released to the general public.[24] Such catacombs gave rise to speculation that bygone civilizations had used them to flee some crisis, perhaps a similar crisis to the one which humanity was now faced with? Although this was a short-term solution at best (in the case of floods, the catacombs would be inundated), plans were initiated for the "colonization of Hades."[25] Meanwhile a third, more far-reaching alternative was

---

24: In *Foucault's Pendulum* Umberto Eco posits that the rapid advancement of metro lines in the major European cities was meant primarily to serve as a cover for developing these underground cities

25: Researcher Michael Lindemann gave a lecture in 1991: "There is indeed another government operating, and that government . . .operates primarily behind the scenes . . . these people, in effect, are building their own version of Noah's ark. And that Noah's ark they are building is underground: underground bases, indeed all over the world, but particularly in the United States. Huge underground

sought and found, in the heavens. This is "Alternative Three." The first step, logically enough (to the paranoid), was the Moon.

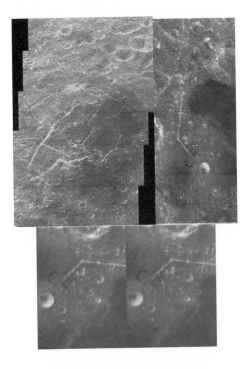

Images of the far side of moon from orbit 246 with South toward the top of the image. Supposedly a Russian supply base, centered at 24 degrees latitude, 151 degrees longitude.

Since the invention of the telescope, many astronomers have observed strange signs suggestive of life, and even civilization (past or present), on Earth's sister satellite. Certain signals (flashing lights, smoke, and land patterns similar to the "crop circles" currently in vogue on Earth) had been seen, leading to the almost

---

bases which actually festoon the underground geography of our continent . . . These are places that are capable of supporting on an on-going basis some tens of thousands of people, so across the country it may be possible to save an elect remnant . . . . who will be the cream of the civilization that is meant to survive the Apocalypse." (quote from *Casebook on Alternative 3*, by Jim Keith) "'We do know that the military-industrial complex and various federal government agencies have constructed and are working in many installations, underground bases and detention facilities . . . Tunnels could be as large as 50ft. by 50ft. in diameter and chambers as much as 100 ft. high. . . . Two-track railroad or two-lane highway tunnels (are) as much as 31 ft. wide by 22 ft. high . . . We also know that they extended underground bases and facilities as deep as 6,000 ft . . . We have maps, official documents, designs and exact locations of deep underground bases and detention facilities; pictures of equipment used for tunneling technology; information concerning underground structures; designs and construction; the flame-jet tunneling system; the high-temperature protective suit designs, and more." Canadian journalist Serge Monast, quoted by Jim Keith, *Black Helicopters Over America*

inescapable conclusion that someone, or *something*, was up there.[26] According to paranoid awareness, the "Moon project" was well underway by the twenties, if not before.[27] Paranoid awareness suggests that the program was from the start aimed at building a base, and transporting the necessary slave-workers and machinery to construct a space station in the Earth's orbit. (These slave laborers are known in the folklore as "batch consignments": diverse individuals rounded up into groups and whisked off to the Moon colony. It was reasoned, in a burst of pure Custodian logic, that "the ultimate survival of the human race must take precedence over the fate of a limited number of low-grade individuals."[28]) This space station, once constructed, would serve as a launch pad for the final exodus, to Mars.[29] Those who got to make

---

26: Charles Fort may have been the first to record data of such observations. Jim Keith reports: "Curious lights, clouds, and unexplained moving objects on the surface of the moon have been observed by both professional and amateur astronomers . . . photographs include large objects which seem to have traveled across the lunar landscape, leaving miles of stitch-like paths; what appear to be Arabic numerals and other symbols carved into the lunar surface in conjunction with dome-like objects and multiple triangular pond-like constructions which utterly defy any explanation as natural formations." *Casebook on Alternate Three.* There is a persistent rumor amongst alternate perceptions literature "that the moon is partially hollow: [it is] a spaceship from the depths of the universe, that has been transported to the solar system by its crew. The surface we see is no more than an exterior layer; the true surface is 80 km below. The inhabitants left a space of 50 km over their heads and built an exterior layer as a screen against meteorites . . . According to Russian scientists, the moon has a density lower than the earth's because it is hollow in part." (ibid) "Recently, Professor William J. Pickery of Harvard University made a study of the moon from his observatory in Jamaica. He declared the canal lines on the moon were artificial. He also asserted there is a race of superior beings living up there." (Warren Smith, *This Hollow Earth*) And so it goes.

27: If history is fiction, we are free to make our own revisions. "The Germans landed on the Moon as early as probably 1942, utilizing their larger exoatmospheric rocket saucers of the Miethe and Schriever type. . . . Everything NASA has told the world about the Moon is a lie and it was done to keep the exclusivity of the club from joinings by the third world countries. . . . Ever since their first day of landing on the Moon, the Germans started boring and tunneling under the surface, and by the end of the war there was a small Nazi research base on the Moon . . . When Russians and Americans secretly landed jointly on the Moon in the early '50s with their own saucers, they spent their first night there as guests of the . . . Nazi underground base. In the '60s a massive Russian-American base had been built on the Moon, that now has a population of 40,000 people, as the rumor goes." (Vladimir Terziski, president of the American Academy of Dissident Sciences, *Secret Research on Antigravity*, from *Steamshovel Press # 9, fall 1993.)*

28: A supposed "report" quoted in Alternative 3. The report refers to these slaves as "components," and voices the concern that "there may be those who initially harbor reservations about the morality of the mental and physical processing considered necessary for Components" (of which, more later). Certainly the wording of this "report" is convincingly machine-like. It is postmodern paranoid newspeak at its finest: "physical processing" refers to torture and psycho-surgery, amongst other things. Note also the completely subjective use of terms such as "low-grade" and "limited number" (the latter term, as any mathematician knows, means nothing at all). "The operations, known as psycho-surgery, are carried out to remove or destroy portions of brain tissue and change the behavior of severely depressed or exceptionally aggressive patients who do not respond to drugs or electric shock treatment." (Sunday Telegraph, Aug 28 1977) "I performed five of these operations on people—four young men and one young woman—who appeared to be completely sane. There were two objects. The patients had to be completely de-sexed, to have their natural biological urges taken away, and they had also to have their individuality removed . . . they would virtually be thinking robots. I was told that the operations were vital to the security of the country." Dr. Crepson-White, probably a fictional character "quoted" in *Alternative Three*, by Leslie Watkins.

29: This plan has an undeniably logical rationale behind it. As we have seen, it was supposed to have been initiated by the Germans and then taken up by the Americans after the end of WWII. "There is a strong case to be made for UFOs as part of a hidden and high echelon government project, utilizing the secrets of flying disc craft received from Nazis at the end of WWII . . . In a letter published in *World Watchers International* magazine, the following appears, mentioning no names, concerning a designer

this exodus (voluntarily that is) were known as "designated movers. Each designated mover will, it is estimated, require labor support of five bodies. These bodies, which will be transported in cargo batch consignments, will be programmed to obey legitimate orders without question and their principal initial duties will be in construction."[30]

*

> Although the so-called "moral issues" were raised, in view of the law of natural selection it was agreed that a nation or world of people who will not use their intelligence are no better than animals who do not have intelligence.
> —*Silent Weapons for Quiet Wars*, from *Secret and Suppressed*

As paranoid awareness has it, the blue-print for this macabre future society was already extant, in embryonic form at least, on Earth: it was indeed the very society towards which all earthly manipulations and strategies had been steadily moving, for lo, these past few millennia. Concentration of power, centralization of property and wealth, control of information (via education and the media), precise regulation of the population, social and racial segregation, all were directed by the secret agenda of the Custodians. The first models for this totalitarian society were attempted on Earth in bygone centuries, and certain evidence suggests that both the British and German Empires' preoccupation with concentration camps (invented by Lord Kitchener for the British in India, and evident also in the US in such bizarre experiments as Jonestown) related directly to this same agenda. With a Moon base, however, the program could finally be initiated, free from worries about snooping press agents, pesky humanitarians, et al: every element, most importantly the *human* element, could be scrupulously controlled, as could the environment itself. A world, in short, designed entirely by *reason*, where nothing would be permitted to exist that was not essential to the smooth functioning of "AI."

It seems a logical deduction for the paranoid, then, that worldwide programs of eugenics, psychiatry, psycho-surgery, mind control, social engineering, and so forth, were being so rapidly developed on Earth *as research* for artificial space colonies already blooming on the Moon, and later on Mars. By this reasoning, the

---

working for US govt at the Jet Propulsion Lab in Pasadena (c/1962): "His function was to design domed, modular living facilities for 'colonies' on the moon and then Mars! The secret name of this amazing project was 'Adam and Eve.'" In 1961, there was widely observed (by astronomers) thickening of the cloud cover of Mars followed by heavy storms. "When the clouds eventually cleared, some remarkable changes were seen. The polar ice caps had substantially decreased in size, and around the equatorial regions a broad band of darker coloring had appeared. This, it has been suggested, was vegetation . . . The sudden outbreaks of storms on Mars, the dwindling of the ice caps, the growth of what appears to be vegetation in the tropical zone . . . all that is recorded scientific fact." "Gerstein," interviewed in *Alternative 3*. The book states that, "the first—and secret—landing on Mars by an unmanned space probe from Earth" took place on May 22, 1962. It claims to have the film of this landing to prove it. The author has seen the film, and finds it neither convincing nor obviously faked; it is simply another krazy klue in our paranoid's mess of red herrings.

30: *Alternative 3* quoting a 1958 report issued by "The Chairman, Policy Committee," and addressed to "Nation Chief Executive Officers." Less credible sources are cited by John Keel: "Some contactees who claim to have visited Mars blandly point out that the planet is divided into zones with the Negroes and Jewish Martians carefully segregated from the others." (*This Haunted Planet*)

Earth becomes an open laboratory, in which such scientific techniques might be ruthlessly applied and steadily perfected. Within the limitations inherent in an "imperfect" (i.e., natural) environment, the masses can be slowly reduced to slave status by means of covert drug administration (in tap water,[31] chemical food additives, medical products, etc), subtle microwave bombardment (via ultraviolet lights, telephones, computers, etc), and above all through the steadily-advancing hypnotic power of the media. All in all, a program of mass-lobotomization, without the public's knowledge or consent.

All this is quite coherently mapped out in the mind of the paranoid. Also noted is the total disregard for environment which began to dominate in both the production and consumption of goods, facilitated by the suppression of facts concerning the state of the eco-sphere, etc. The plundering of Earth's resources, meanwhile, was leading to catastrophic results, results which would, in their turn, form an integral part of the agenda. Secrecy was maintained by any and all means necessary.[32] How could the human race remain so utterly oblivious throughout all this, you may ask? The question poses no real threat to the paranoid's *weltanschauung*. His answer is simple: the human race's head has been surgically inserted up its rectum. It is unable to consider the existence of the Custodians, because the Custodians do not *allow* such thoughts to enter into the human race's collective head *at any time*. Once again, a self-sustaining argument.

*

We hypostatize information into objects. Rearrangement of objects is change in the content of the information; the message has changed. This is the language which we have lost the ability to read. We ourselves are part of this language.
—Philip K. Dick, *Valis*

To first understand the conspiracy of nature, the "matrix" that constitutes the foundation of paranoid awareness and is forerunner to the lucid view, it is necessary to see that *nothing* is as it seems. This is the key. Paranoid awareness insists that we exist peripherally, superficially, "skating over thin existence,"[33] with neither scope

---

31: "In the rear occiput of the left lobe of the brain there is a small area of brain tissue that is responsible for the individual's power to resist domination. Repeated doses of infinitesimal amounts of flourine will in time gradually reduce the individual's power to resist domination. . . any person who drinks artificially fluorinated water for a period of one year or more will never again be the same person, mentally or physically." Charles Perkins, a US industrial chemist, speaking of the Nazi's plans for mass control. Quoted in *Liquid Conspiracy*, by George Piccard. Piccard continues, "Evidence suggests that fluoride increases the risk of certain cancers, accelerates the aging process, decreases fertility, causes damage to the kidneys, and impairs vital DNA repair enzymes which are crucial to the immune system. All this risk occurs even at the one part per million recommended concentration in drinking water."

32: Whether or not the paranoid permits E.T contact to play any valid part in all this, or whether he dismisses the various leaks and rumors that begun around this time as merely cover for something more mundane, is a question we will get to in good time. The fact remains that a type of technology generally considered impracticable, if not impossible, was at this time already being employed. The "foo fighters" of WWII, flying discs, evidence of large-scale teleportation (falling fish and so forth), and such like, all played a central part in this "mass movement" of space colonization.

33: Charles Fort.

to our vision nor depth to our understanding. Let us briefly embrace the point of view of the paranoid, then, and extend it from mere conspiracy into cosmology. Let's imagine there exists a design—a pattern, map, grid, or web—into which all things invariably fit. This idea is not new. It is established by science (chaos physics and fractals), and more or less in accord with most people's idea—however dimly conceived—of religion. There is an underlying order, a superstructure that exists to the world, called Nature by the realists, God by the romantics. The ramifications of this idea are somewhat more challenging. They suggest that every single phenomenon—every name, word, number, occurrence, color, sound, sight, smell, and individual being—is a part of this order and has precise meaning or significance—and by extension, *function*—within it. In other words, absolutely *nothing* that happens in this life is random or accidental or irrelevant to the paranoid. Every piece plays its part in the puzzle, and contains some secret or clue to the Mystery. We are referred by paranoid awareness not to this and that, mind, but to *everything*. By such an understanding, ordinary paranoia is not only justified—it is incomplete. Paranoid awareness is an intermediary but necessary stage on the path to lucidity. Paranoia is the beginning of wisdom.

In light of this darkness, this veil that has been pulled over our eyes to keep us from seeing the truth, we have adopted the term "mundane shell." What we call existence is just that—a shell. We have made this shell opaque by staring so hard and long at it that we can no longer see beyond it. The shell is like thin ice: it is easily broken. To the paranoid it is logical that, if all the elements that make up our world, the secrets that surround us, can be cracked, decoded, employed *as a language unto themselves*, if it is within man's power to do this, then it stands to reason that someone, somewhere, has done so. Ergo, the Custodians.

Between the All-Seeing Eye of Lucidity and the blind base of matter, there exist degrees of insight. Between the puppets and the puppet-master are the strings; and so, consciously or otherwise, the pattern is extended. Magik—the occult or hidden law of Nature and its connection to human consciousness, says the paranoid—rules both over and under *everything*. That is the paranoid's acceptance. *Belief* in magik is not the issue here. A man does not need to believe in electricity to use a flashlight, and dismissing occult realities does not change the fact that a major portion of reality remains occulted from us. Paranoid awareness argues that we may as well expect honey without bees as sorcery without sorcerers. So-called adepts and initiates, be they monsters or masters, saints or scoundrels—*if they existed*—would, by their nature, be intimately and inexorably present at every level of politics, economics, media, medicine, science, art and religion. That should come as no surprise. Such hypothetical entities would be intimately and inexorably involved with *everything*.

Between God and the mass, there must be a medium. From ancient worship to postmodern paranoia, we have gods, natural laws, angels, elementals, aliens . . . a rose by any other name. We have manifest rulers or principals to order and direct the great hordes of creation. Can we prove these things do not exist? The paranoid options a greater perception of reality over a smaller one, even if he must reduce himself to a cosmic pawn to do so. The fact is, there *are* conspiracies; we may as well question the existence of the air that we share as doubt that.[34] After all, reality itself is the result of Consensus. And Consensus is merely an unconscious kind of conspiracy.

The enemy of the Consensus is the individual, he who makes all government redundant. Hence the lie of "the mass" was invented. The mass does not exist, for if the mass *did* exist, there would be no conspiracy, no secrecy, no tyranny, no government, no war. It would be a simple matter to herd such a mass into slavery or slaughter. Paranoid awareness states that it is up to the individual man and woman to realize this. Obviously, we cannot be herded into independence. Hence we are set the test of paranoid awareness, by the tyranny of ignorance. We must choose it, individually.

The essential thing for Custodians to maintain control of the Consensus is not merely to know, but to know what others *don't* know. Knowledge that is controlled becomes power; if you control what people know, you can control what they think. If you control what people think, then you can control what they say and do. This is total control, the only kind of power available to those lacking wisdom. Paranoid awareness states that, if we admit that the world at present is ordered upon principals of tyranny, we admit also that it is founded upon secrecy. We may be paranoid as a result, but at least we are *aware*. On the other hand, if we *don't* admit this, then we are merely confirming the success of the secrecy, and of the tyranny. We may not be paranoid, but the price of our "security" is high. It is the security of slaves.

The existence of any law at all is proof of tyranny.

Occultism defines magik as the *manipulation of awareness*, or the control of perception. Fifty percent of sorcery's power is in its subtlety: if you are aware of being controlled, then you are already that much less susceptible to control. If the true nature of organization is sorcerous, it follows that the real society must be secret. Since the goal of such hypothetical "Custodians" is tyranny, they would have no interest in fair play: like chess-players who ensure that their opponent only see his own pieces, they make their victory certain, even if they must spoil the game to do so. Their bid is for superiority over everyone and everything.

The essence of conscious, willed magik is deception; it depends on trickery and subterfuge. It is a *snare*. This is not because magik is false or illusory, but because a good magician knows that an illusion will serve just as well as the real thing. Since magik is a matter of perception, of awareness, often the Imaginal and the actual count as the same, provided that they are both equally *believed* by the percipient. Hence, one basic rule of magik might be: never perform a real miracle when mere trickery will suffice.[35] At some level, every paranoid knows what he is doing when he attempts to supplant history with myth, to replace reality with fantasy, to

---

34: Conspire = to breathe together

35: Jesus, a master Magus, adhered reverently to this principal. The water to wine is a possible example—why go to the trouble of transmutation when a little hypnotic-suggestion will suffice? Who is to say that it is a greater miracle to feed five thousand with a few loaves and fishes, or to satisfy the hunger of five thousand with nothing but air? And who is to say, if those five thousand really believe they have eaten and are thereby fulfilled, that a difference even *exists*?

overthrow *reason* with the imagination, with *will.* He seeks to become a figment of his own dream, to dispel the cloud of illusion and make contact with what lies beyond. A period of dementia and unreason—of paranoia—is a necessary and desirable stage in this process. Just as the apprentice must surrender his ego (lose his mind) to the Master if he is to successfully enlighten his Soul, so the warrior's bid for lucidity demands that he consciously *attack* the mundane shell or matrix of Consensus reality that restricts and defines him. He must endure a designated gestation period in which he is—in the eyes of the world, and even perhaps himself—*cracked.* This is the rule of paranoid awareness, and the inevitable price of "awakening": complete social ostracization.

Illuminoids

Three: Assassins

Theatre of Hate

> Whoever has come to understand the world has found only a corpse, and whoever has found a corpse is superior to the world.
> —The Gospel of Thomas

JFK, the Twin Towers, and the Revelation of the Method

> John F. Kennedy, the one and only Catholic president of the United States, was a human scapegoat, a "pharmakos.". . . Masonry does not believe in murdering a man in just any old way and in the JFK assassination it went to incredible lengths and took great risks in order to make this heinous act correspond to the ancient fertility oblation of the Killing of the King.
> —James Shelby Downard: "Sorcery, Sex, Assassination and the Science of Symbolism," *Secret and Suppressed.*

In his last, unspoken speech, President John F. Kennedy was to have said these words: "We, in this age, are the watchmen on the walls of world freedom. For as was written long ago, 'Except the Lord keepeth the city, the watchmen waketh but in vain.'"[1] A mere ten days before his death Kennedy was quoted as saying, "The high office of President has been used to ferment a plot against the American people. Before I leave office, I must inform the citizen of his plight." These words have been taken as further evidence of the threat which Kennedy posed to the shadow government, but they may also indicate that he was not wholly unwitting a player in *his own assassination.* In offering himself up to be martyred on the cross of conspiracy, Kennedy was assuming responsibility for the sins of his office.[2]

Kennedy was the last American president to be a hero to his people. It is well known that he modeled himself after the Arthurian mythos, and Arthur is but an updating of the Christ archetype, complete with friend-betrayer Lancelot. In his spare time, Kennedy was said to be mildly obsessed with the idea of being assassinated. His sacrifice—willing or not—was the most public act of murder in history. Apart from any other meaning it may have had, it functioned as the most

---

1: *Psalms,* 117

2: The ultimate JFK assassination theory has Kennedy himself as a part of the plot. If so, he almost certainly did not expect the hammer to fall so soon. JFK was riddled with sicknesses, leading one commentator to remark that "he took so many pills he must have rattled when he walked." Foremost among his afflictions was a spinal condition which would eventually have rendered him a cripple. Kennedy is rumored to have expressed a preference for being dead rather than living his life as an invalid. If he had suicidal tendencies, perhaps he opted to go out with a bang?

powerful and profound act of *propaganda* in modern times. As the scapegoat for a nation, JFK's death was not only a political blow but a psychological one. It was a *coup*, the aim of which has never really been acknowledged by the public. If we are to take paranoid reasoning to its logical conclusion, beyond the sphere of the mundane and the temporal and into the surreal or spiritual, we have no choice but to accept that the object of the JFK assassination was not that of mere espionage or intrigue, but that of sorcery.

There exists a very poor copy of the original Zapruder film, as presented by the late Bill Cooper, who demonstrates that the film was scraped and scratched and over-exposed to conceal the actions of the driver, SS agent William Greer. In the film in question, it is just about possible to see Greer turn around (as the senator behind him reaches over and takes the steering wheel), remove a pistol from his jacket, and point it at Kennedy, following which occurs the famous exploding head shot. Besides this confounding "evidence," there are enough disparate sources to give this theory as much weight as any other theory about the assassination. Apart from anything else, it goes a long way to explaining one curious detail, namely, just what the hell Jackie was doing when she clambered onto the back of the car?

The point of uncovering the "real assassin" in this case is just this: to the paranoid mind, it doesn't *matter* who did it. The JFK conspiracy is of such far-reaching dimensions as to include absolutely everyone who has any *reason* to be included. Those behind the conspiracy keep their silence, for obvious reasons, while those who attempt to expose it are simply silenced, one way or another. Our paranoid knows just how paranoid all this sounds, even to himself; but he has no option left, once he has taken on board the sorcerous dimensions of the mystery, which extend in his mind, from local to global to cosmic proportions. As a psycho-history, or collective myth, spilling out from our psyches into the world at large, we are *all* involved.

Through a paranoid glass, darkly, the conspiracy appears so intricately planned and so masterfully orchestrated as to include the president's own bodyguard, and not only to include him but to place his finger on the trigger of the proverbial smoking gun. What does this imply? Like everything else in the paranoid's plot, its meaning is symbolic more than factual, and relates to the specifically sorcerous purposes of the assassination, as living propaganda directed at the collective consciousness of America (and by extension, the world). From a more lucid view, the whole conspiracy-mania that has since ensued, the subtle but pervasive sense of malevolence, is as much a part of the plot as the murder itself. Kennedy was sacrificed, not because he was gunning for the mafia, out to dismantle the CIA, reveal "the alien truth" to the American public, withdraw from Vietnam, end the cold war, nor for any single factor. The man himself was never a threat to any of the above; how could a puppet-man ever be a threat to those that hold the strings? All these so-called motives were presumably part of the reason that Kennedy was chosen to begin with; in fact it seems fair for the paranoid to assume, finally, that JFK was elected for his *pharmakotic* qualities, i.e., precisely in order to be martyred.

"The ultimate purpose of that assassination," Downard writes, "was not political or economic, but sorcerous; for the control of the dreaming mind is the underlying motive in this entire scenario." The *intent*, then, behind all the "lies, cruelty and degradation" was simply this: disillusionment of the American people. The murder of JFK proved to the world, at a subconscious level, certain, basic "facts": Innocence is *not* protected; crime pays; no one is safe. The precious order of so-called civilization is no more than a thin and tenuous facade which at any moment can and will collapse, revealing only an all-consuming chaos behind it. The president, or any other world figure, is no more than a marionette, a figure-head just waiting to explode, leaving nothing behind but smoke and brains.

The real power of government is spread out, diffused, impossible to pinpoint, expose, or resist; it is vast and unknowable, like the Devil himself. It may depose or dispose of the figure-heads it has chosen, when and how it likes, by means fair or foul (usually foul), subtle or brutal, and most often a sly, insidious mix of the two. All politics are a game of chess in which the power is on high, unseen, and in which the pieces have only and exactly that power which they are permitted to wield, as *tools*. In our present example of the paranoid's "politics as theatre," this fact is proven beyond reasonable doubt by a single act, an act that by all rights should be impossible, from the point of view of the pieces on "the board": *pawn takes king*.

The image of the world's beloved idol having his brains blown out in broad daylight, captured on film and witnessed over generations, is now imprinted on the collective consciousness of mankind forever. One bullet can end the dreams of a lifetime, of a hundred million lifetimes, of history itself. More than anything else, JFK's death propagated a sense of total, final defeat; of paranoid awareness, certainly, but also of powerlessness and despair. These three attitudes—paranoia, impotence, despair—are consolidated in the dim, dark and mute acquiescence of the mass to the existence of malevolence and chaos, of conspiracy and deception and evil across the board. This is the "revelation of the method" employed by the Custodians to ensure that the bulk of "humanity" continue to sink ever further into the Consensus program. The Custodians know that, when confronted by intimations of the true nature of their predicament, most humans prefer to take refuge in ignorance, and so slip ever deeper into slumber, if only they may find some small relief therein.

*

"I am come to send fire on the earth; and what will I, if it be already kindled?"
—Luke 12:49

Mysterious satanic forms seen by witnesses in the smoke of the burning twin towers

Clearly to the paranoid, catastrophes on an increasing scale are what it takes to wake us from our slumber: they are the only way for us to realize the truth. On September 11th 2001, when several thousand people died encased in a giant steel tombstone, their lives devoted to upholding a tyranny of lies, it was the fulfillment of the paranoid's darkest warnings. From his view, this was apocalyptic revelation of method. This "Holy War" was not between Christ and Allah, or God and the Devil; it was between Humanity and Itself.

To the paranoid, seeing the New York skyline enveloped in smoke was a poetic image worthy to herald in the new millennium. The appalling power and beauty of this image came from his feeling that, at long last, here was a tear in the fabric of the Consensus. And this was not a movie; or if it was, then we were on the wrong side of the screen, and no hero was coming to save us.

The twin towers, as the second highest buildings on the planet, served as a fitting symbol of man's *hubris*, his overreaching attempt to erect idols in his own image, and so compete with the gods for air space. The World Trade Center was the modern day, schizophrenic equivalent of that ancient Tower of Babel by which man (once before, and equally unsuccessfully) tried to reach the stars (godhood) by the most ill-founded and materialist of methods. If God wished to demonstrate to the Western world the folly and fatality of its consumer-demented ways, He could hardly have picked a more effective and succinct way of doing so.

The image of stockbrokers trapped at the top of a skyscraper, looking down as their doom approaches, is a quintessential one: a metaphor for our times. To the paranoid, we are all likewise situated. We have entered into an uneasy alliance with a mechanized, soulless edifice-society, for the dubious rewards of comfort and "success." The very loftiness of our material status is inseparable from its precariousness, for an edifice of glass and steel standing a quarter of a mile in the air is bound to fall sooner or later. The same structures that we have built to house and protect us will be the death of us. The paranoid perceives a civilization watching as the agent of its doom approaches, waiting for the moment of impact. He pictures humanity looking up at the heavens, praying for a miracle to swoop down and deliver it; looking down at the crumbling superstructure beneath it, as the searing flames approach ever closer, and realizing it has only one sane option: to leap, wings or no, into the Abyss. This is the fate that awaits us, says the paranoid, making the New York catastrophe a harbinger of what is to come. A global preview.

The paranoid is not a terrorist, and has no interest in becoming one, so is forced to trust that the Empire will destroy itself, in the end, and that the Consensus is *self*-imploding. This is suggested by the nature of the catastrophe itself: United and American Airlines planes crashing into the World Trade Center.[3] The "terrorists" were using Uncle Sam's own arms against him. This was strategically brilliant, but also poetically apt.

The paranoid has no choice but to view the whole travesty as yet another act of Masonic Sorcery Theater, an act with the following aims:

Firstly, to escalate the situation in the Middle East and allow for even heavier US foreign policies, in the process transforming George W. Bush Jr. from the least popular president in US history to a conquering hero. (The same basic technique was used with his father, who entered office amidst murmurs of "wimpishness," only to be converted into a rampaging warlord by the first Gulf War, timed with equal precision as was its sequel.)

Secondly, and more far-reachingly, the event served to create a State of Emergency in the US (and to a lesser extent in the entire "free" world), and so help implement the New World Order policies so feared by the paranoid: heavier police presence, more prevalent helicopter surveillance, tighter security measures, compulsory ID checks, and so forth. This will all help to facilitate the introduction of computer chip implants. *Et voila*—the paranoid's prophecy fulfilled: the mark of the beast, the Reign of Antichrist begins! Since a State of Emergency was indeed declared after the attack (and never *un*declared), it follows that Martial Law can be applied *at any time*, whenever it suits the Custodians to do so. This means that anything perceived as a "threat against the State" can be punished immediately, with incarceration or death, without hearing or trial. After the explosive event of 9/11/01, the American (and world) public have gratefully accepted these severe and unconstitutional measures, just so long as their lost sense of security and stability can be restored. Many of these people are dimly aware that the event may have been perpetrated by the same powers now implementing these measures; but, unable to confront the implications of such an idea, once again opt for sleepy ignorance and blind "trust." To the paranoid as to the Custodian, such humans are little different from cattle, going meekly to the slaughter.

The German psychologist Kurt Lewin, head of the Tavistock Institute for Human Relations in Great Britain theorized that "if a society as a whole were

---

3: The crashed plane was flight 93, no less; one that hit the tower was AA11: both covert, if unmistakable, references to the Aiwaz-Lucifer current.

subjected to a sense of terror, then society would revert to a blank state where control could easily be applied from the exterior."[4] Such a collective sense of terror has become prevalent in the Western world since the inception of worldwide media, making it possible for otherwise limited events (such as the twin towers attack) to receive almost endless coverage, and come to seem overwhelming in their implications.

It is especially ironic that the supposed "war on terror" waged by Western government, in order to justify itself, depends on the propagation of fear, dread, uncertainty, and paranoia via the mass media that no terrorist network could ever equal. In other words, "the war on terror" is itself a form of terrorism, designed to reduce the populace to a helpless state of anxiety, so rendering them docile and malleable. In such a shocked state, the general public is happy to surrender its civil liberties, and even any option of individual thought or action, if only their material interests are being looked after.

It is also (diabolically) ironic that this same mass populace takes most security and comfort of all in watching TV, the primary tool employed by Government to disseminate anxiety and terror. And we ask ourselves why schizophrenia, crime, suicide, and murder run rampant through the Western world? It is all part of the program.

Charles Manson, Public Enemy No. 1

Charles Manson and Scientology Psi Wars

4: George Piccard, *Liquid Conspiracy: JFK, LSD, the CIA, Area 51 & UFOs*

I am only what lives inside each and every one of you.
—Charles Manson

According to paranoid awareness, Charles Manson was no ordinary drifter. A well-known and much-favored police informer, he had certain, tenuous ties with the FBI, and by extension with the intelligence community at large, with whom his first contact was perhaps through Hubbard's Church of Scientology, which Manson discovered in jail (where he has spent most of his life) during the '50s.[5] Scientology is a highly publicized and extremely popular (and powerful) modern-day cult—a scientifically based religion and a sophisticated system of mind control. This is by no means meant as a dismissal of Scientology, seeing as all religions are essentially "systems of mind control"; in order to be effective as such, however, they must contain certain basic truths, truths which, if used knowingly and with discrimination, can perhaps lead to genuine enlightenment. Scientology is exceptional for being the first officially sanctioned occultist Church, a secret society open to everyone. It was founded in 1952 by the creator of "Dianetics,"[6] L. Ron Hubbard. Hubbard, a Naval Intelligence agent and author of science fiction novels,

---

5: In a letter from prison, Manson wrote the following: "I want to say this to every man that has a mind, to all the intelligent life forms that exist on this planet earth. I wish really to say this to the Scottish Rites, and the Masons and all the people with minds who have degrees of knowledge and are aware of courts, laws, United Nations, governments. In the Forties we had a war. And all of our economies went towards this war effort. The war ended, on one level, but we wouldn't let it end on the other levels. We kept buying and selling this war. I'm not locked in a penitentiary for crimes, I'm locked in the Second World War. I'm locked in the Second World War with this decision to bring to the world court, there must be one world court, or we're all going to be devoured by crime. Crime, and the definition of crime, comes from Nuremberg, when the judges decided that they wanted to call Second World War a crime. Honor and war is not a crime. When you go to war and you're a soldier and you fight for your god and your country, that's not criminal. That's honorable. That's what you must do to be a man. If you don't fight for your god and your country, you're not worth anything. If you have no honor, then you're not worth Patty's pig. Truth is, we've got to overturn the decision that you made in the Second World War, or the Second World War will never end. Decrees of the war were written in Switzerland, in Geneva, the conferences that were made, by the men at the tables, clearly stated that anyone in uniform would be given the respect of their rank and their uniforms. Then, when the United States won the war, and got all the Germans in handcuffs, they started breaking their own rules. And they've been breaking their own rules ever since. War is not a crime. But if you judge war as a crime, from a courtroom, then turn around. If two and three is five, then three and two is five. If you say war is a crime, then crime becomes your war. I am, by all standards, a prisoner of war. I have been a prisoner of war since 1944, in juvenile hall, for setting the school building on fire in Indianapolis, Indiana. I've been locked up 45 years trying to figure out how I got to be a criminal. It matters not whether I want to be. . . . You've got to keep criminals going to keep the war going because that's the economy. Your whole economy is based on war. You've got to get your dollar bills off the war, you got to take your silver markets sterling off the war. You've got to take your gold and your diamonds off the war. You've got to overturn that decision that hung six thousand men by the neck. You killed six thousand soldiers for obeying orders. That's wrong, and the world has got to accept they're wrong. If you accept you're wrong, and you say you're sorry for all the things you've done, then I'll be a note in that chord, and maybe we can get some harmony going on this planet earth now."

6: Dianetics is defined as "man's most advanced school of the mind. The word comes from Greek *dia*, through, and *nous*, soul. Dianetics is defined as what the soul is doing to the body."

has often been quoted—before his involvement with Scientology began—as boasting that the best way to get rich would be to found a religion. This is precisely what he went on to do (getting extremely rich into the bargain). It seems likely that this famous quote is apocryphal, however, and that Hubbard did not found Scientology on his own initiative, but was assigned the task by others. Certainly, his work for the US government as an undercover agent included the infiltration of the California O.T.O (Ordo Templi Orientis, or Order of the Templars of the East) Lodge—an "ancient" occult order that was revamped and redirected by Aleister Crowley, the worldwide acting head of the order.[7] Hubbard was initiated into the lodge during the '40s and proceeded to rip-off not only its private funds but also its basic premises, which he adapted into the system that would eventually become Scientology.

The basic premises of Scientology are those of all practical "magick," and involve various key concepts: reincarnation, karma, invisible entities that can be contacted and manipulated, and the idea that Earth is, as Hubbard himself expressed it, a "prison planet," a matrix. A description of Hubbard's "History of Mankind" is given by Rev. Anonymous (defrocked) in *Scientology—An Inquiry:* "Somewhere around 700,000 to a million years ago. . . [Earth] changed hands. The Marcab Confederacy is a government of some 28 planetary systems and a bureaucracy some 1 to 2 million years old. . . . Marcab operates three planets as prisons where they dump their unwanted: the criminals, the boat rockers, the reformers, etc. They do this by a variety of means, but the individuals arrive on Earth (one of the three prison planets) sans body."

Quasi-mythology aside, perhaps the central concept of Scientology is that of *auditing*, which equates roughly with the recapitulation tradition of sorcery (as described by Carlos Castaneda), and more profanely with Catholic "confession," and even the modern-day practice of psychotherapy. What auditing entails is,

> undoing the damage of the past, a past millions, billions, trillions of years long. This getting rid of past-life trauma is called negative gain. . . . The final result of negative gain is the state of *Clear*, where all the baggage of the past supposedly has been removed from the person. Then begins the road to positive gain, the Operating Thetan levels where one's abilities as an immortal spirit are supposedly rehabilitated. [An Operating Thetan is] a thetan exterior who can have but doesn't have to have a body in order to control or operate thought, life, MEST (Matter, Energy, Space and Time). (Rev. Anonymous, ibid)

William Burroughs dabbled in Scientology for a time, and his descriptions of it (in *The Ticket That Exploded*) are perhaps the most honest and insightful we have.

> You know about the Logos group?? . . . claim to have reduced human behavior to a predictable science controlled by the appropriate word combos. They have a system of therapy they call "clearing." You "run" traumatic material which they call "engrams"

7: Crowley was to pass on the leadership of the Agapé lodge from Wildred T. Smith to John Whiteside Parsons in 1943. In 1945, Parsons met Hubbard, with whom he struck up an uneasy but productive partnership.

until it loses its emotional connotation through repetition and is then refiled as neutral memory. When all the "engrams" have been run and deactivated the subject becomes a "clear." . . . It would seem that the technique is good or bad according to who uses it and for what purposes. This tool is especially liable to abuse. In many cases they become "clear" by unloading their "engram" tapes on somebody else. These "engram" tapes are living organisms viruses in fact . . . the clears burning with a pure cold flame of self-interest a glittering image that lights up clearer and clearer as it fragments other image and ingests and dismembered fragments. . . Yes we know the front men and women in this organization but they are no more than that. . . a facade . . . tape recorders. . . the operators are NOT THERE . . .

Manson, according to his disciple Bobby Beausoleil,[8] was "a holy man . . . whose head was totally tuned into Scientology." Manson graduated from Scientology as a "Clear" and evidently went on to apply the same techniques to create his own secret society, or "Family." Vincent Bugliosi, the District Attorney who prosecuted the Manson family and author of *Helter Skelter*, writes: "What effect Scientology had on Manson's mental state cannot be measured. Undoubtedly he picked up from his 'auditing' sessions in prison some knowledge of mind control, as well as some techniques which he later put to use in programming his followers."[9] Bugliosi also remarks about the Manson girls: "I sensed something else. Each was, in her own way, a pretty girl. But there was a sameness about them that was stronger than their individuality. . . . Same expressions, same patterned responses, same tone of voice, same lack of distinct personality. The realization came with a shock: they reminded me less of human beings than Barbie dolls."

Though there have been many more savage, brutal, and gratuitous murders in US history, both before and since, the events of "Death Valley 69"[10] remain more fiercely emblazoned on the hearts and minds of the American people than any other equivalent crime. This appears to be due less to the nature of the crimes themselves, or to the identities of the victims or character of the assassins (very few people could name even one of the actual killers), but rather to one, single factor: *publicity.* The Manson murders caused an unprecedented stir, a wave of paranoia and emotional insecurity that swept the country like nothing before or since. Manson was a nobody before the crime. He became the national bogeyman only afterwards.

8: Bobby Beausoleil was associated with filmmaker Kenneth Anger and starred in Anger's film *Lucifer Rising*, playing the part of Lucifer. Anger is an underground filmmaker (and author of *Hollywood Babylon*) who was involved in the world of the occult, and specifically the O.T.O. "The relationship of Crowley and Anger is obviously important: Anger refers to his work frequently, has declared himself to be a disciple of Crowley and a magus, has included Crowley in central positions in many of his films (especially *Inauguration of the Pleasure Dome* and *Lucifer Rising*)" (Haller on Anger, from *The Equinox*). Anger himself states, "Lucifer is the Rebel Angel behind what's happening in the world today. His message is that the Key to Joy is Disobedience." (ibid)

9: "[T]o get rid of the inhibitions, you know, you could take a couple of girls and, you know, have them lay down, you know, and have them eat each other, or for me to take a girl up in the hills, you know, and just lie back and let her suck my dick all day long . . ." Juan Flynn, on Manson's techniques of auditing. *Helter Skelter.* "What Manson never explained to his Family was that in the process of unprogramming them, he was reprogramming them to be his abject slaves." Bugliosi, *Helter Skelter.*

10: The name of a track on the Sonic Youth album *Bad Moon Risin'* which in turn takes its name from the Credence Clearwater Revival song, written as a direct response to Reagan's coming to power in California in 1968 (re: the line, "I hear the voice of razin' ruin," which sounds distinctly like Reagan-ruin).

Such a transformation cannot be attributed solely to the acts themselves, much less to Manson's doctrines. So who, exactly, voted Charlie Manson Madman of the Millennium?

*

Christ on the cross, the coyote in the desert—it's the same thing, man. The coyote is beautiful. He moves through the desert delicately, aware of everything, looking around. He hears every sound, smells every smell, sees everything that moves. He's always in a state of total paranoia and total paranoia is total awareness. You can learn from the coyote just like you can learn from a child. A baby is born into the world in a state of fear. Total paranoia and awareness.
—Charles Manson[11]

Manson's obsession with the song "Helter Skelter," and with the Beatles' *White album* in general, has been well publicized but never fully accounted for. His strange obsession anticipated other similar obsessions of "lone nuts" for specific works of art, such as John Hinckley's obsession with Jodie Foster and the film *Taxi Driver*, John Lennon's assassin Mark Chapman's for *Catcher in the Rye*, and so on. To the paranoid, this opens up a whole labyrinth of atrocities. The means of re-programming ordinary persons and turning them into killers involves secret techniques of mind control, familiar to even the dilettante paranoid as "MK-ULTRA" (so much a part of postmodern folklore that it surfaced in the Hollywood movie *Conspiracy Theory*). By such techniques, the "candidate" is inculcated with a particular "program," inside of which is hidden the trigger which will compel him on to his "mindless" act of destruction. The program gives the assassin a fantasy in which to operate, and a kind of imaginary emotional rationale (i.e., "The Beatles made me do it," or "I did it for Jodie.")

The creation of the psychopath envisioned by the paranoid involves a confusing of fact and fantasy, whereby the subject is made to act "as if in a dream." Since artistry is one thing the CIA et al. probably lack for, they would rely on existing works for the appliance of a surrogate, quasi-reality in which their assassins can be made to operate. Hence, when the "trigger" is activated (having been planted while in hypnotic trance), the sleeper's second personality takes over and he enters into the surrogate reality, fully believing he is acting out his own obsessions. The "cover," as such, is impeccable, since *even the killer himself believes it.*

All this may be familiar enough to the casual reader from the movie *The Manchurian Candidate*, which deals with the creation of the perfect "sleeper" assassin or programmed killer for espionage purposes. That the film comes dangerously close—in the mind of the paranoid—to an accurate portrayal of this secret science is evidenced by the fact that it was banned for over 20 years. Famous real-life "sleepers," according to the paranoid's view, include Charles Whitman, David Berkowitz ("Son of Sam"), Sirhan Sirhan, John Hinckley Jr., Mark

---

11: Compare with the following: "When you fear, you see things in a different way." Carlos Castaneda, *The Teachings of Don Juan.* "When nothing is for sure we remain alert, perennially on our toes. . . . It is more exciting not to know which bush the rabbit is hiding behind than to behave as though we know everything." Castaneda, *Journey to Ixtlan*

Chapman, and a whole host of nameless, "spray and pray" berserker shooters running amok in schoolyards and McDonald's across the world. (Another thing recent "lone nuts" have in common—besides an improbably large arsenal—is that many are proscribed *Prozac* users.)[12]

Manson was obsessed with the Book of Revelation, particularly with chapter 9, which he saw as referring to the Beatles. (His infatuation with the fab four served to further link him, in the public perception, with the counterculture.) Bugliosi quotes a source as saying that Manson believed "the Beatles were spokesmen. They were speaking to Charlie, through their songs, letting him know from across the ocean that this is what was going to go down." The murders took place in the early pre-dawn hours and on the following night of the 9th of August. The word "rise," one of Manson's personal mantras and supposedly taken from the Beatles' song "Blackbird," was found written in blood at the Bianca residence, where the second set of killings took place.

Manson may or may not have believed that the end of the world was nigh, but he certainly taught others to believe it. He taught that a war was coming which would sweep the Earth clean of all life, a holocaust in which mother would be turned against daughter, sister against brother, son against father. Most of all, he predicted a war between blacks and whites, a war he called "Helter Skelter." He claimed that it was his mission to spark off this war, and then to withdraw into the desert with his chosen Family, taking refuge inside a "bottomless pit," until the war was over and all the people were dead. At which point, his now-expanded family would emerge and take over the remains of civilization, establishing a new world order. Family member "Ouisch" (a.k.a. Ruth Ann Moorehouse) believed: "We all have to go through Helter Skelter. If we don't do it in our heads, we'll have to do it physically. If you don't die in your head, you'll die when it comes down."

Random murder was an integral part of this "process": "[T]here was a group, these chosen people, that Charlie had brought together, and they were elected, this new society, to go out, all over the country and all over the world, to pick out people at random and execute them, to release them from this earth. 'You have to have real love in your heart to do this for people,' Susan explained."[13]

Manson claimed that he was both Christ and Satan (he even wrote it on his prison forms). Asked if Manson was an evil person, Susan Atkins replied: "In your standards of evil, looking at him through your eyes, I would say yes. Looking at him through my eyes, he is as good as he is evil, he is as evil as he is good. You could not judge the man." Manson "believed you could do no wrong, no bad. Everything was good. Whatever you do is what you are supposed to do; you are following your own karma" (Greg Jackobson). "To Charlie, fear was the same thing as awareness. . . . The more fear you have, the more awareness, the more love.

12: It's characteristic of the nature of these murky, Masonic waters that perhaps the two most notorious programmed assassins identified by paranoid awareness are Charles Manson and Mark Chapman (John Lennon's killer), both of whom bear the tell-tale initials of a "*M*anchurian *C*andidate."

13: All prior and subsequent quotes otherwise uncited are from Bugliosi's *Helter Skelter*.

When you're really afraid, you come to 'Now.' And when you are at 'Now,' you are totally conscious."

The events of the night of August 8 and morning of August 9th are now forever seared into the collective consciousness of the world, and there is no need to go into them in detail here. Roughly, what happened is this: Manson sent out five of his "agents" (Charles Watson, Atkins, Beausoleil, Leslie Van Houten and Patricia Krenwinkel) to 10050 Cielo Drive (*Cielo* is Spanish for heaven or sky; Sharon Tate referred to it as her "love house") with instructions to murder everyone present. "We wanted to do a crime that would shock the world, that the world would have to stand up and take notice" (Atkins). There are two primary misconceptions concerning the night in question: one, that the perpetrators of the crime were on drugs at the time (they weren't); the other is that Tate's unborn child was removed from the womb (it wasn't). In fact, the child was said to have been still alive after the mother died, and might even have survived the holocaust—according to medical testimony—if the body had been taken to the hospital in time. This fact, however, has been greatly obscured by the media's presentation of the events, a version which took root in the public mind and made the child into an integral, central part of the sacrifice. It's possible that it was intended by the killers to be so, but it's also possible that the media wanted the public to think so, for reasons of pure sensationalism.

According to Bugliosi, "(Atkins) had wanted to cut out the baby . . . but there hadn't been time. They wanted to take out the eyes of the people, and squash them against the walls, and cut off their fingers. 'We were going to mutilate them, but we didn't have a chance to.'" By all accounts, Tate died in excruciating fear and agony. Bugliosi gives Atkins' account: she was holding Sharon Tate at the time and, "Tex came back and he looked at her and he said, 'Kill her.' And I killed her. . . . And I just stabbed her and she fell, and I stabbed her again. I don't know how many times I stabbed her." Sharon begged for the life of her baby, but Atkins told her, "Shut up. I don't want to hear it."

Sharon Tate was married to film director Roman Polanski, who just the previous year had enjoyed his first major success in Hollywood with *Rosemary's Baby*. Taken from a best selling novel by Ira Levin, the film tells the story of a young woman impregnated by Satan as part of an occult conspiracy to bring about the age of Antichrist. Polanski researched his subject extensively, even recruiting the notorious Satanist Anton LaVey as a technical advisor on the film. LaVey is reputed to have had connections to the US intelligence community, as well as being a minor celebrity in Hollywood at that time (LaVey is now deceased). His Church of Satan boasted for members Sammie Davis Jr. and Jayne Mansfield (who was wearing a satanic medallion, a gift from LaVey, when she was decapitated in a car accident).[14]

"Before he killed him, Charles 'Tex' Watson told Voytek Frykowski: 'I am the Devil and I am here to do the Devil's business.'" Months later at the trial, Manson's

---

14: There is only one concrete link between the Mansons and LaVey himself mentioned in *Helter Skelter*. Susan Atkins, in 1967 or 68, "became involved with Anton LaVey, the Satanist." For the paranoid, however, in such a spaghetti mess of intrigue and madness as this, a single thread is enough.

"disciples" were said to have been utterly under his power, to the point of having no real will of their own, hence Manson was also found guilty of the murders. Though he wasn't present at the time, he had to bear the responsibility. By the very same reasoning, Manson himself might be seen as little more than a puppet player in a far larger agenda. So *who*, at the end of the millennium (the paranoid asks), is left holding the baby?

*

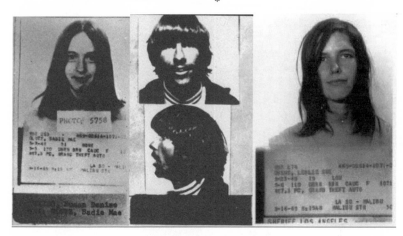

Susan Atkins   "Tex" Watson   Leslie Van Houten

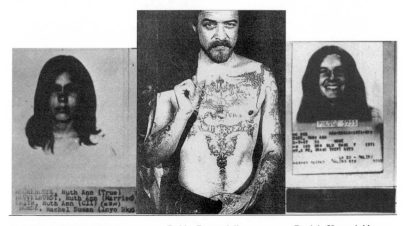

Ruth "Ouish" Moorehouse   Bobby Beausoleil   Patricia Krenwinkle

The "Family" members responsible for the Tate/Bianca killings of August 8/9 1969

Roman Polanski and Sharon Tate, the wedding and beyond.
One of Tate's earliest film roles was as a sacrificial victim in *Eye of the Devil*

"Pray for Rosemary's Baby" went the tagline for the movie. Who prayed for Sharon's Baby?

Anton LaVey

The Dakota building where both *Rosemarys's Baby* and John Lennon were shot

Ronald Reagan

These children that come at you with knives, they are your children. You taught them. I didn't teach them. I just tried to help them stand up. . . . You were a generation of children trying to get your humanity back, trying to get your honor back, trying to redeem your planet, trying to get your life back on earth and I was a convict trying to help you. That's all. I never said I was a good guy.
—Charles Manson

The events of August 1969 effectively quashed the countercultural movement, realizing all the public's paranoia regarding the "flower child," and causing a hardening of the Consensus against similar creative social expressions. Psychedelic drugs, free love, communal living, spiritual experimentation, all was quickly grouped under the darkening banner of destruction that Manson's family embodied. The Summer of Love became the Winter of Fear.[15] Little by little, all alternative spiritual paths came to be viewed by the media (and hence the public) as suspect and possibly malignant. In popular movies meanwhile, hippies became the handy embodiments of dementia and wanton cruelty; in reality, the flower child was little more than a sad anachronism, overwhelmed by the harsh reality of his times.

The bid for freedom of the counterculture, instead of ridding us of our inhibitions and hang-ups, led to indulgent excesses, wanton criminality, and sexual promiscuity for its own sake. During the '70s, the steady climb to power of Ronald Reagan (governor of California during the Manson murders) continued, while the now-defunct hippy—considered a harmless throwback at best—underwent slow transmutation into the yippie and thence became, by steady degrees, the yuppie. Reagan came to the pinnacle of power in 1980. His campaign was to have been actively opposed by John Lennon, who was on the point of emerging from long retirement with a new album, a new direction and, inevitably, a new following. Lennon was planning a national peace tour to oppose the Reagan administration, but his plans were abruptly cancelled by Mark Chapman's act of "deranged fandom."[16] Lennon was killed outside the Dakota building where he lived at the

---

15: Incidentally, Manson was released from prison, despite imploring his jailors to let him remain there, on 21st March 1967, the "spring of love," and the day of the equinox, when Aries (sign of War, and by association violent sacrifice) began. And it was "that spring that the Family was born." (Bugliosi, *Helter Skelter*.)

16: In *Liquid Conspiracy*, George Piccard quotes police lieutenant Arthur O'Connor, who first interrogated Chapman after his arrest: "It's possible Mark could have been used by somebody. I saw him the night of the murder. I studied him intensely. He looked as if he could have been programmed. . . .That was the way he looked and that was the way he talked." Chapman himself describes his act as follows: "If you ever get the chance, go to the Dakota building. I just love that building. . . . to think that's where it all happened. There was no emotion, there was no anger, there was nothing, dead silence in the brain, dead cold quiet. He walked up, he looked at me, I tell you the man was going to be dead in less than five minutes and he looked at me, I looked at him. He walked past and over again saying 'Do it, do it, do it,' over and over again, saying 'Do it, do it, do it, do it,' like that. I pulled the gun out of my pocket, I handed over to my left hand. I don't remember aiming. . . And I just pulled the trigger steady five times." Piccard also quotes an FBI report on Lennon's activities, as follows: "In view of the successful delaying tactics to date, there exists real possibility that subject [Lennon] will not be deported from the US in near future and possibly not prior to Republican National Convention. Subject's activities being closely followed and any information developed indicating violation of

time, and where *Rosemary's Baby* was filmed twelve years earlier, round about the time Lennon was recording the *White album*.

In order to take the events of August 1969 out of the jurisdiction of mere history and into the realm of myth, the paranoid must temporarily suspend all so-called "critical" faculties, and let the wild beast of imagination loose into the field. Through the conscious appliance of paranoia, he might arrive at the following perceptions: the novel *Rosemary's Baby* did not arise solely from author Ira Levin's imagination, but echoed and anticipated (or even inspired?) a genuine conspiracy (however half-baked) to bring about the Age of Antichrist. Certain people, let us say, believing they might bring about the New Aeon promised by Aiwaz and Crowley, set about enticing (the inorganic entity known as) "Satan" (Set, or Shaitan) to incarnate physically on Earth and take reign over the nations, as prophesized (roughly) in the Book of Revelation. However such a scheme may appear to the sophisticated reader, if said persons also possessed the power to *act* upon their beliefs, that is enough to ensure that they would do so. That something of this nature could be accomplished is of course highly questionable; but that certain individuals, or groups of individuals, might *believe* it could is another matter. Both the book and the movie deal with just such dedicated believers who make it their business to take what is below for what is above. They might easily be seduced by the notion of a "devil" coming up from Hell, nine months before June '66, to violate and impregnate a human female, who would subsequently give birth to a child that would, in turn, grow up to be—the Antichrist.

From the lucid view, such an occult working would be considerably more subtle, would in fact be a wholly *esoteric* affair. The insemination, birth, etc., would take place not on the earthly realm but *in the realm of the human psyche*. It would entail the creation of a new *myth*, a meme or "metazon" called "Satan" (the old one, "God," having been officially put to rest). In the terms embraced by paranoid awareness, Levin's book would be the *first act* in a three-part psychological coup, swiftly followed by Polanski's movie, in '68, and finally, in August 1969, by Tate's murder and the death of her and Polanski's unborn child, Paul.

*

In the arsenal of mass-manipulation, few weapons are as effective as terror; and among the devices of the terrorist, few are as striking as mutilation of people or of animals.
—Jacques Vallee, *Messengers of Deception*[17]

Federal laws will be immediately furnished to pertinent agencies in effort to *neutralize any disruptive activities of subject*." (Italics mine.) According to Piccard, much of this memo is blacked out.
17: "The theory is you don't kill the leader, you kill his family or children. . . . We used to do it with Indians all the time too. Basically, what you do is destroy the chief's family very ignominiously. . . . I mean, Charles Manson would look like a sweetie compared to what this stuff was. And when the guy comes back, he sees this mess—you know, his wife beheaded, her infant child stripped out of her abdomen and beheaded and bleeding on her body, hung from a rafter, shit all over the walls, those kinds of things—that's how you do it. And when that happens, those guys lose confidence in themselves, and the village loses confidence in them, but they're not martyrs. And that's basically 'The American Way.' That's how they did it with Blacks, that's how they did it with the Indians, and that's how they did it in Laos and Vietnam. That's good, practical warfare." (Alan S. Levi, MD, in interview for *Nexus* magazine.)

Paranoid awareness must always remain several steps ahead of public awareness. The ideas of mind control and brainwashing have become—by an appliance of the standard tools of counter-propaganda, fear and ridicule—about as credible to the average person as conspiracies and Ufos (and anything else which might seriously undermine our state of comfortable oblivion). There is an obvious combination of absurdity and unpleasantness about these notions that makes it essential for the common man to dismiss them outright, even though it is perhaps not in his best interests to do so. The paranoid knows however that the mind is a fragile thing, subject to invasion, manipulation, and plain destruction. If so, with the right tools in the right hands—and with the right knowledge, sufficient funds, and a total lack of moral inhibition—the unthinkable *might* be accomplished. If the average human personality is made up of a thousand myriad parts, the most fundamental truth—of the criminologist as much as the psychologist—is that we are all capable of *anything* under the right circumstances. It is simply a question of *which part of the psyche* is given emphasis.[18]

By a combination of hypnosis, psychosurgery, manipulation of the nervous system through narcotics, microwaves to the brain, and multi-sensual indoctrination (through the various forms of media, advertising, music, cinema etc), paranoid awareness argues that a given individual can be *programmed* to fit a specific, political agenda. Taking all of this to the bank, the paranoid suggests that Manson, under guidance of LaVey and other CIA specialists, was heavily drugged, strapped to a chair with his eyeballs pinned open, electrodes wired to his frontal lobes, and subjected to scenes of eroticized murder, rape, and other human depravities, with the Beatles' *White Album* blaring endlessly into his brain. Over a period of months, he would have undergone an intensive program of torture, hallucinogenic overdoses, light- and pulse-saturation accompanied by repeated verbal suggestions, enough in short to turn all but the most stubborn of minds to mush.

At the end of it all, Manson is at the complete mercy of his "programmers." With hypnotically measured tones and subliminal commands, his new personality—and with it his mission—is then firmly established: he is Christ and Satan, savior and destroyer of humanity. Is there any reason to think that Manson, or anyone else under similar circumstances, wouldn't end up believing it? Once programmed, he would act accordingly, convinced he was following his own impulses.

18: It is worth noting that Manson, for all his countercultural leanings, was anything but an anarchist or traditional rebel figure. He admired Hitler, who he felt "had the best answer to everything [and] was a tuned in guy who leveled the karma of the Jews." According to Bugliosi, Manson "believed in law and order. There should be 'rigid control' by the authorities, he said." Bugliosi also notes certain other peculiar resemblances to Hitler, not the least of which was both men's capacity to gain an eerie momentum while addressing their public, to speak like men possessed.

The Manson murders were the essence of old magick, of "black" sorcery. The murder of Sharon Tate and Roman Polanski's child, like the assassination of JFK, was a mortal blow to an already stricken world psyche. The Manson murders announced the end of the '60s sexual/cultural revolution in the bloodiest, most unequivocal fashion.

Psi-war is not only between a government and its people but between the ever-active forces of light and darkness, the so-called "black and white brotherhoods." To these imagined elect, the meaning of the events of August '69 would have been as obvious as the blood on the walls. Such mythic enactments of Masonic Sorcery Theatre are *devices*, directed at impressing the sleeping mind of humanity with truths far more subtle and complex than it can consciously assimilate. To this end, Manson's brood enacted their dreary and perverted working, the most mundane satanic act of all—the ritual sacrifice of an unborn child.

What *really* threatened the status quo about the cultural revolution was not drugs or sex or hair-styles, but the possibility of a psychic revival, an awakening, when the machinery of the dream would fall away like so much dead skin, leaving the powers-that-be not only powerless but redundant. A genuine spiritual renaissance is the most terrifying thing that a tyrannical control system can imagine—because its power depends wholly on keeping its subjects enslaved to their own material obsessions, their fears and desires. With the help of Charles Manson, the Custodians effectively quashed the counterculture with a single act of sacrifice.[19]

Jonestown and the Politics of Genocide

Consequently, in the interest of future world order, peace, and tranquility, it was decided to privately wage a quiet war against the American people.
—"Silent Weapons for Quiet Wars"

19: Concerning the final resolution of the Manson trial, two bizarre facts stand out: Firstly—the president of the US personally ensured that the Manson family were convicted due to an apparent "slip of the tongue." Before the trial was over, Nixon went on record about Manson: "Here was a man *who is guilty* [my italics], directly or indirectly, of eight murders. Yet here is a man who, as far as the coverage is concerned, appeared to be a glamorous figure." By omitting the word "alleged," Nixon effectively closed the case in the public mind (including the jury's; it should be added that Manson certainly helped things along by waving the headline at the jury during the trial). Nixon later retracted his statement, of course (objection sustained), but by then the damage was already done. The obvious question that occurs to the paranoid is: was this "slip" unintentional or was it deliberate, with a specific end in mind? Did Nixon know something that Manson's prosecutors did not? Secondly—as Bugliosi writes—"The fate of [the killers] was decided on February 18, 1972 (after the longest murder trial in US history). That day the California State Supreme Court announced that it had voted 6-1 to abolish the death penalty in the state of California. The opinion was based on Article 1, section 6, of the State Constitution, which forbids 'cruel or unusual punishment.'" What could have possessed the President of the United States to speak out so rashly and thoughtlessly? And what could move the Supreme Court to abolish the death penalty on the very day that the whole country would be crying out for it? Strange coincidence indeed, and the paranoid does not believe in "coincidence."

According to the US constitution, the government was originally simply a party of "organizers" (*not* controllers), employed by the people, for the people. The people, in order to ensure against the exploitation of their liberty or rights by the government, was a fully-armed and organized force in itself. Since the time of the Founding Fathers, however, the original constitution has gotten lost in the shuffle. As everyone now knows, Government's purpose is not to protect and serve its people but to oppress them. Two factors are essential to the maintenance of this autonomous, self-serving government. One: having formed its own armies, it seeks to keep the (potentially subversive) populace docile and servile, to instill it with almost total dependence, faith and loyalty. To ensure this blind loyalty, the social climate must be one of constant instability—volatile, unpredictable, chaotic—so that the people look increasingly to their government for protection. To this end a level of urban chaos and petty crime must be maintained: not merely encouraged but actively *created*. "The general rule is that there is profit in confusion; the more confusion, the more profit. Therefore, the best approach is to create problems and then offer the solutions."[20]

The second factor essential to control of the people concerns the power inherent *in* the people, due to the strength of their numbers and the solidarity of the group. This solidarity must be stripped away by any means necessary. It must be eroded and replaced by fear, suspicion, and confusion. At an emotional and psychological level, this serves to isolate the individual from the group and leads to a loss of responsibility and courage. This way the individual feels less and less the strength of the community, and is left with only the security of hiding within it. At a more concrete level, as mistrust and suspicion grows, there will be a corresponding breakdown of organization, communication, and stability within that community, leading to more confusion. At this point, the group begins to look towards the ruling party in search of its lost sense of order and cohesion. Little by little, the people are made to give up their solidarity, their power, their dignity, their self-respect, their freedom, and finally and most mundanely, their arms. At this point they are vulnerable to takeover.

A strange kind of vicious circle is propagated: the more violent society becomes, the more demand there is for personal protection. Yet at the same time, the more suspicion, hostility, and paranoia arises between individuals within this society, hence the more violence.

Social engineering creates its own propaganda, its own proofs, and finally its own history. Through a steady manipulation not only of information (via the media) but of the events themselves, the "rising tide of violence" in society is blamed on the availability of arms. It is as if the people had no say in how these arms were used: like irresponsible children they are forbidden to play with fire. The liberal portion of the population favors disarmament on a national scale; the counter argument is that these arms are an essential deterrent against the government establishing a totalitarian state. This depends on refuting completely the argument that, if guns were criminalized, only the criminals would have them, by suggesting

---

20: "Silent Weapons for Quiet Wars," *Secret and Suppressed.*

that only a criminal would need to have a firearm in the first place.[21] The fact is, rather, that once guns are rendered illegal in the US, only the real criminals—the mafia-government and the armed forces—will have them.

Of all paranoid perspectives, perhaps the most pervasive and organized—in the US at least—is that of the "patriot movement's" fear of a military take-over by their government. This hypothetical agenda—the disarming of the populace in order to make them vulnerable to a *coup d'etat*—ties in with a profounder, more sinister and far-reaching agenda, and pertains to a different order of paranoia altogether, that of *event manipulation*. I have termed this "Masonic Sorcery Theatre." From such a perspective, all violent crimes and aberrational acts of mayhem are seen as individual enactments of a vast global operation aimed at reducing society to a state of fear and loathing. The program of event-manipulation or "mythological engineering"[22] is intended to do away with individual rights for self-protection and autonomy of any kind, via what might be termed "the criminalization of the citizen." This involves the most profound type of propaganda imaginable, aimed not only at altering the role of the individual in society, but also his very *nature*. It aims to prove that we are all, potentially, out of control maniacs who, given the chance, will go on wild killing-sprees and wipe out half the neighborhood. This is the founding lie of all government: that we are unfit to govern ourselves. To justify its laying down of the law, government must first establish the need for law. Disorder is required to make a demand for order, therefore, government must create a level of crime and social upheaval sufficient to merit the strong-arm tactics which it desires to employ. The element of depravity and wanton violence that is more or less new to our present century is an indication—to the paranoid—of just how far this agenda has progressed, and of just how strong this "arm" intends to become.

*

The basic nova technique is very simple: always create as many insoluble conflicts as possible and always aggravate existing conflicts—This is done by dumping on the same planet life-forms with incompatible conditions of existence—There is of course nothing "wrong" about any given life form since "wrong" only has reference to conflicts with other life forms—The point is these life forms should not be on the same planet.
—William Burroughs, *The Ticket that Exploded*

If a considerable percentage of the population is considered "volatile"—i.e., violently unstable—this will justify society turning itself into a giant lunatic asylum, one in which—it will be argued—all laws are designed only to punish

---

21: "The U.S government declares a ban on the possession, sale, transportation, and transfer of all non-sporting firearms. A thirty (30) day amnesty period is permitted for these firearms to be turned over to the local authorities. At the end of this period, a number of citizen groups refuse to turn over their firearms. Consider the following statement: I would fire upon U.S citizens who refuse or resist confiscation of firearms banned by the U.S government." *US Marines Combat Arms Survey* quoted by Jim Keith, in *Black Helicopters Over America*

22: "Mythological engineering—the deliberate creation of social movements to serve either as opportunity for experiment, as outlets for personal fantasy, or as a vehicle for more down-to-earth political purposes." (Jacques Vallee, *Revelations*)

anyone insane or evil enough to resist them. What this entails is a self-fulfilling agenda of legalized violence and oppression. In a word, tyranny. The concentration camp may well be the closest we have come to a working model of this theoretical future society. It should be noted that it *was* possible to survive in a Nazi concentration camp, provided one was prepared to shift one's allegiance from victim to victimizer, or from individual to State, and become, in effect, one of the guards.[23] What I have called "the criminalization of the citizen" is part of a larger program that involves an across-the-board clean-up aimed at all the "undesirable" elements in society. These are to be marked for displacement, and possible eradication, in "relocation centers." If such a program were ever to be realized, however, it would be necessary to target certain minorities first, in order to avoid a general panic—and even a possible uprising—in the face of wholly indiscriminate governmental persecutions. So long as the individual can feel assured that it's only the other guy who's getting persecuted, he will remain passive, on the slim chance that he can escape the persecution. Added to this is the certainty that anyone who attempts to interfere with, or even criticize, the process will be treated with the exact same measure of expedience, and consigned to the ever-growing ranks of "undesirables." These ranks will eventually include the entire population, minus those in power naturally. Thus the populace goes meekly to the slaughter.

To sum up this hypothetical agenda: The populace must, as individuals, be reduced to:
  a) *slaves*, trusting, servile, and dependent.
  b) *wimps*, powerless, disorganized, and fearful.
  c) *dupes*, slow-witted, gullible, and ignorant.
  d) *creeps*, isolated, selfish, and aggressive.

As a model, the concentration camp serves all four of these purposes. It serves not merely as a prison and a slaughterhouse, but also as a laboratory. At the same time, the *idea* of it functions not only as a threat and a warning to the world, but also as a form of propaganda, a means for showing what slaves and creeps the human race is made up of. Which brings us to Jonestown.

*

23: There is plenty of evidence that not only members of the German army, but also of the S.S itself, were Jews who had "converted." (See for example *Eichmann in Jerusalem—The Banality of Evil*) What is less well-known is that those German soldiers who refused to slaughter innocents in the camps were not necessarily executed for insubordination, but in many cases merely transferred to alternative details. Hence the common argument that the murderers "had no choice" is seen to be not only evasive but also incorrect.

Jim Jones

Assassins

Those who do not remember the past are condemned to repeat it
— Sign over Jim Jones' chair at Jonestown

Jonestown was many things to many people, but what concerns us here is the paranoid's perception of Jonestown as one isolated case in a larger design. From this perspective, Jonestown might best be seen as a model for the future, one of many such models, but one of the few to ever be exposed as what it was. In the paranoid's understanding, other secular "religious" communities founded by the intelligence network serve similar purposes (the list is extensive: the Moonies, the Rajneesh Foundation in Oregon, and the "Heaven's Gate" troop all have the earmarks of government-funded programs).[24] First of all, these "communities" serve to round up undesirables: drifters, hippies, blacks, single women, etc. Secondly, they appear also to function as experimental environments in which the "inmates" are used as guinea pigs for testing the latest advances in mind control drugs, new viral strains, and so forth. The end of these experiments appears to be to reduce individuals to a state of total submission and mindlessness. The same procedure was perfected by Pavlov on his dogs: a simple "reward and punishment" agenda, which in the present case would be enhanced immeasurably by the use of hallucinogenic drugs and psychotronic technology.[25] Thirdly, the camps would serve as raw material for a more elaborate kind of social engineering, or psychological warfare. When news of Jonestown came out, for example, the "facts" of the matter were almost entirely fabricated, with a specific end in mind. The results speak for themselves, even if few ever bothered to look closely at the evidence. The public—unquestioning, unthinking—will always believe what it is told, provided it is told by a sufficiently authorative source such as the mass media. But the facts of Jonestown fly brazenly in the face of the "official story," as we shall see, thereby leaving ample room for the paranoid imagination to flower.

The mainstream media presented the story as the open-and-shut case of a wacky religious cult that had committed mass suicide, 900 people drinking cyanide because their charismatic guru leader told them to do so. The original reports on the news and in the papers in November 1978, however, were that 400 died in Jonestown, and that 700 had fled into the forest (by all accounts there were at least 1,100 people there). A week later, the official body count was 913 (167 survivors returned to the US). The original explanation of this discrepancy was that the Guyanese "could not count." Next, the bodies were said to have been hidden behind the pavilion (a small house, and even 'hough the authorities had been on the scene

---

24: Jim Jones himself had possible (unverified) connections to the CIA, and although his vocation as religious dictator came at an early age (his father belonged to the Ku Klux Klan, and Jones worked as a minister and faith-healer as a young man), there seems little doubt that his career did not really take off until *someone*—almost certainly with governmental affiliations—began to fund him.

25: This generally results either of two ways—childlike obedience and fear or sullen but passive hostility and hatred (or a combination of both, depending on the character of the individual). The same process can be observed in dogs that are beaten and maltreated by their owners. Some will respond with pathetic, slavish devotion, others with dark and brooding hatred; but both are utterly abject creatures. Note that even the latter class, though mean-tempered, will generally bite anyone *except* their "masters." Victims of torture have also been observed to show a kind of pathetic, servile dependence upon their tormentors.

for days). The official version finally stated that bodies had been piled on top of other bodies; in other words, that 408 bodies had somehow hidden another 505 bodies from view. At this point, any thinking person simply returns to the original report and assumes it to be the correct one: 400 died, 700 fled into the jungle. A week later, 500 of this 700 were also dead. At which point, there naturally arises the question: who killed them? This question was never raised, and not one of the survivors was interviewed by the mainstream press.[26]

Visiting Congressman Leo Ryan was shot down at the Port Kaituma airstrip, along with several newsmen accompanying him, "even though the troops were nearby with machine guns at the ready. . . . The [newsmen] were clearly killed by armed men who descended from a tractor-trailer at the scene, after opening fire. Witnesses described them as 'zombies,' walking mechanically, without emotion, and 'looking through you, not at you,' as they murdered. Only certain people were killed, and the selection was clearly planned."[27]

26: John Judge's piece, "The Black Hole of Guyana," in *Secret and Suppressed*, describes the event in depth. "At the Jonestown site, survivors described a special group of Jones' followers who were allowed to carry weapons and money, and to come and go from the camp. These people were all white, mostly males. They ate better and worked less than the others, and they served as an armed guard to enforce discipline, control labor and restrict movements. . . . The dead were 90 percent women, and 80 percent blacks. . . . According to survivors' reports, they entered a virtual slave labor camp. Worked for 16 to 18 hours daily, they were forced to live in cramped quarters on minimum rations, usually rice, bread and sometimes rancid meat. Kept on a schedule of physical and mental exhaustion, they were forced to stay awake at night and listen to lectures by Jones. . . . The camp medical staff . . . administered drugs, and kept daily medical records. Infractions of the rules or disloyalty led to increasingly harsh punishments, including forced drugging, sensory isolation in an underground box, physical torture and public sexual rape and humiliation. . . . On the scene at Jonestown, Guyanese troops discovered a large cache of drugs; enough to drug the entire population of Georgetown, Guyana (well over 200,000) for more than a year. . . . The actual description of life at Jonestown is that of a tightly run concentration camp, complete with medical and psychiatric experimentation. . . . Jonestown was an experiment, part of a 30-year program called MK-ULTRA, the CIA and military intelligence code name for mind control [using] a combination of drugs, drug mixtures, electroshock and torture as methods for control. The desired results ranged from temporary and permanent amnesia, uninhibited confessions, and creation of second personalities, to programmed assassins and preconditioned suicidal urges. One goal was the ability to control mass populations, especially for cheap labor. . . . Pete Hamill called the corpses (at Jonestown) 'all the loose change of the sixties.' The effect was electric. Any alternative to the current system was seen as futile, if not deadly . . . The message was, get a job, go back to church . . . There was no answer but death, no exit from the grisly future . . . The official message was very clear. . . . Dr Mootoo found fresh needle marks at the back of the shoulder blades of 80-90 percent of the victims. Others had been shot or strangled. The gun that reportedly shot Jim Jones was lying nearly 200 feet from the body, not a likely suicide weapon . . . Only two (of the bodies) had committed suicide . . . The US Army spokesman, Lt Col. Schuler said, 'No autopsies are needed. The cause of death is not an issue here.' . . . At the scene, bodies were stripped of identification, including the medical wrist tags visible in many early photos. . . [It] took nearly a week to bring back the Jonestown dead, bringing in the majority at the end of the period. The corpses, rotting in the heat, made autopsies impossible. . . . The long delay made it impossible to reconstruct the event. . . . Several civilian pathology experts said they 'shuddered at the ineptness' of the military."

27: John Judge writes: "A congressional aide was quoted in the AP wires on May 19, 1979, "There are 120 white, brainwashed assassins out from Jonestown awaiting the trigger word to pick up their hit." And—"Some evidence indicates a connection between the Jonestown operation and the murders of Mayor Moscone and Harvey Milk by police agent Dan White. Another Jonestown survivor was shot near his

*

In order to implement this objective, it was necessary to create, secure and apply new weapons . . . a class of weapons so subtle and sophisticated in their principle of operation and public appearance as to earn for themselves the name "silent weapons". . . Everything that is expected from an ordinary weapon is expected from a silent weapon. . . It shoots situations, instead of bullets . . . from a computer, instead of a gun. . . It makes no obvious explosive noises, causes no obvious physical or mental injuries, and does not obviously interfere with anyone's daily social life. Yet it makes an unmistakable "noise," causes unmistakable physical and mental damage, and unmistakably interferes with daily social life, i.e., unmistakable to a trained observer, one who knows what to look for.
— "Silent Weapons for Quiet Wars"

To the paranoid, the "suicide-murder" of Jonestown (a classic case of newspeak: no one asked "Which was it?") was a freak exposure, but not a freak occurrence.[28] It was a deliberately contrived event, for precise, if obscure, purposes. This is by far the most challenging area of the paranoid's *weltanschauung*. When a story of this nature hits the newsstands, it is designed in advance for a specific effect. The lie, as such, is not only in the bias of the media's presentation, but in the manipulation of the events themselves. Through the tactics of psychological terrorism, a government may tyrannize its people and keep them in apprehension of and dependence on their supposed "protectors." The most overt effects of the "official story" of Jonestown upon the mass psyche were the following:

Firstly, it fostered the belief that people are so slavish, irresponsible, hopeless and desperate as to take their own lives at the whim of a madman posing as a guru. Secondly, it confirmed a growing mistrust in religious cults and alternate movements, and fostered the feeling that these people were not to be pitied but despised, that essentially they got what they deserved. Beyond the *conscious* conclusions which the public reached, however, the fact remains that, at a subconscious level (as with the JFK coup and the Manson murders), people know what *really* happened, even if they cannot rationally apprehend this knowledge. One blatant indication of this is the sign over Jones' place: "Those who do not remember the past are condemned to repeat it." To the paranoid observer, this is

home in Detroit by unidentified killers. Yet another was involved in a mass murder of school children in Los Angeles. . . . The fact that the press never even spoke to nearly 200 survivors raises serious doubts."
Secret and Suppressed

28: The most unsettling factor to all this, and the greatest justification for genuine paranoia, is that, as Judge states, "the Jonestown model survives, and similar camps, and their sinister designs, show up in many places. Strangely enough, almost every map of Guyana in the major press located Jonestown at a different place following the killings. One map even shows a second site in the area called 'Johnstown.' Perhaps there were multiple camps and Leo Ryan was only shown the one they hoped he would see . . . Inside Guyana itself . . . is a community called Hilltown, named after religious leader Rabbi Hill. . . . Hill rules with an 'iron fist' over some 8,000 black people . . . Similar camps were reported at the time in the Philippines. Perhaps the best known example is the fascist torture camp in Chile known as Colonia Dignidad. . . . A religious cult [which] serves as a torture chamber for political dissidents . . . reported visits by Nazi war criminals Dr. Josef Mengele and Martin Bormann."

rich in irony. For those who never figure out what happened, and for whom history itself is an elaborate fiction designed to deceive them, what choice do they have *but* to repeat it?

*

By means of occult public rituals disguised as random terrorism and serial murder, we are controlled and processed. The language of symbolism is used to speak to our subconscious; to reveal to us the exact opposite of what is propounded by the System in its rational discourse.
—Michael A. Hoffman

From a more lucid (though still paranoid) view, the message of Jonestown was intricate and profound, and consisted of two main directives, one aimed for the conscious mind, the other for the unconscious. This one-two-punch strategy is the very essence of paranoid awareness, and serves to illustrate the rift between what we are told to believe, and what actually *is*. It is the sworn duty and the sacred obsession of every paranoid everywhere to reconcile these two perspectives, and so mend the rift in his psyche, and correct his basically schizoid perception of reality. This he does—or attempts to do—by bringing the occult depths to the surface and so disposing of the illusory facade of Consensus reality, if only for a brief moment at a time. His endeavor is far greater than simply the dissemination of "suppressed" information and the spreading of paranoia, as a means to subvert and expose public ignorance and complacency. He is—perhaps unwittingly but nonetheless devotedly— introducing the conscious mind to its own underbelly, and so bringing the great unconscious to light. It is not the question of paranoia's validity that counts here, but rather the question of its having come into being at all. True or false, the existence of paranoid awareness is a postmodern form of folklore or mythology that is of incalculable interest to us because, whatever else it may be, it *has* emerged; and not from the conscious mind—its profound irrationality testifies to that—but from the unconscious. Hence, like all emerging archetypes, it brings with it its very own message, and its very own meaning.

So long as the two realms of conscious and unconscious remain separate and unsynthesized, this disparity will remain humanity's greatest weakness, its Achilles' heel. There can be no doubt that the controlling powers, if control they do—being themselves enslaved to the rules of the paranoid perspective—are acutely aware of this weakness, and will do all they can to exploit it. The double-edged tool of mystification has proved to be the most effective weapon of psychological warfare. The aim is the undermining of the reasonable belief system of the populace, whose tendency is to trust that all will work out in the end if they sit tight, while all the while the subconscious info-feed is establishing an unformed but solid base of certainty: IT WON'T. Consciously, the public is left unenlightened, unprepared, unsuspecting, none the wiser for all the information, and increasingly jaded, cynical, uncertain, and despairing. Unconsciously, on the other hand, the public intuits the worst, the truth behind all the half-truths, and this intuition increases their fear and desperation, without ever helping them to understand its meaning. Being unapprehended by ordinary consciousness, the public's knowledge cannot be acted upon, or even thought about, and yet it is *there*. The mass therefore finds its thoughts pervaded by ever more irrational fears and doubts, rendering it as paralyzed prey in the shadow of the predator. What this amounts to is—paranoia without awareness.

Every lie and half-truth in this battle serves the same purpose: to induce a slow schizophrenia, a disassociation on the part of the individual, which in turn leads to emotional imbalance, an increasingly manic personality, general apathy and despair (without apparent cause), and a steadily encroaching sense of hopelessness and isolation. This fosters growing intolerance, impatience, anger, and disgust with the world and with humanity: in short, a blank, hollow race of sub-men, ready at the flick of a switch to become wild beasts or cornered rodents.

This notion is not a new one, and reached a kind of momentary fruition with the Hitler Youth of 1930s Germany. Hitler's goal was the creation of an "Army of Darkness" indoctrinated from birth ("breeders" were employed to deliver the new recruits), possessed of all the basest, most evil and destructive instincts, untarnished by a shred of humanity. Clearly, if an individual is kept within a controlled environment from the very first moments of his life, this individual will come out more or less exactly as intended. Subjection to images of violence and to violence itself, repeated brutalities, sexual degradation, insanity, hatred, lust, greed, anger and fear, with narely a glimpse of any of the opposing extremes (joy, kindness, love, etc), will ensure the child grow up in a world of evil, with no notion of anything beyond it. If this child is rewarded for acts of spite and punished for acts of kindness, then his standards will be the inverse of what we consider to be "decent" and "right." Yet he will remain innocent in his own mind, having never known, or even suspected, any different. The bizarre and largely unsubstantiated, but nonetheless rampant, cases of Satanic child abuse at Military Day Care Centers across the US may be (to the paranoid) only the tip of the iceberg of a global program of incomprehensible ramifications. Fortunately, this topic is beyond the scope of the present work.

Be it JFK, Sharon Tate, John Lennon, the faceless victims of Jonestown, Waco, Oklahoma, or Columbine, each time a wanton murder occurs, on TV, in the world, real or simulated or both at once, a dark drama unfolds in the human psyche. A murder that is committed with precise yet wholly impersonal (because inhuman) motives—as in every so-called "assassination"—serves several purposes at the same time. The undesirable element is disposed of; the public is subconsciously warned and threatened; and, most importantly of all, human nature takes another step backwards, towards irredeemable savagery. The latest "blank generation" is something of a hybrid still, yet it is perhaps closer to this primal "heart of darkness" than humanity has ever come before. By the reckoning of paranoid awareness at least, a utopia of assassins is now upon us.

Chapter Four: Apostles

Chemical Weddings

"Feed my sheep." Oh yes, perhaps after all like other good men he was a cynic. "Feed them well, make them fat, so that they can be eaten in their turn." "The Lord is my shepherd." But if we are sheep why in heaven's name should we trust our shepherd? He's going to guard us from wolves, alright, oh yes, but only so that he can sell us later to the butcher.
—Graham Greene, *Monsieur Quixote*

Of all human vanities, the greatest has perhaps been the attempt to separate the twin poles of "good and evil," and to set at odds the two states of consciousness known as "heaven and hell." If both states and poles exist simultaneously within our psyches, then all we achieve by failing to bring them into balance is an endless fluctuation between the two. To make enemies of mere opponents is to render them isolate, incomplete, and meaningless, as if the twin streams of evolution and entropy could not flow parallel, as a double current with a single motion, coming and going to the one Source. From this polarity view, one is either a good soul, evolving through a series of ever greater incarnations towards godhood, or else the reverse: an evil soul degenerating steadily to damnation.[1] Perhaps the metaphor is not without meaning, however; just as a soul, in order to identify itself with the greatest good, must rid itself of all its latent evil, so may a race make the same unconscious decision to do so. This process of balancing the extremes to cancel them out is known in physics as the law of cause and effect, in new-age-speak as *karma*. The idea that a soul may opt for an evil "incarnation" to precede and facilitate a subsequently good one is a more occult (and unpalatable) interpretation of the same basic doctrine (it points to the necessity of sin, as a means to atone for suffering). It just may cohere, however, in paranoid awareness, if applied to the present situation of humanity as a whole.

A "great soul" undergoes agony as the only means of spurring it onward to greater bliss, to evolve beyond the suffering—which will otherwise be forever dormant, as *potential*—and on to the greater challenges of joy. The goal—of the race as much as the individual—is not to be holy, but to be whole; to evolve into our fullest potential both for good *and* evil. To give an outlandish example and veer

---

1: In Hindu religion, it is taught that a villain or a scoundrel is not necessarily an evil or degenerate soul, as such, but rather a great soul on a bad day, passing through an evil incarnation on its way to better things. One does not confuse the actor with the role, after all—the finer the actor, the more fully will he embody the part. A great "evil" character portrayal (of Iago, for example) does not merit an after-curtain stoning from the audience but rather applause and accolades, as much for Iago as Desdemonia.

back into the territory of eschatology: the "monad soul" who incarnated as Christ would logically be the same monad soul that later incarnates as Anti-Christ (thereby enacting its own resolution). Metaphorically this seems *a propos* to the paranoid, though when taken literally by the layman it appears as nonsense.

More soberly, we might observe how, if "Jesus of Nazareth" really walked the Earth then, through the propagation of love and mercy to those indifferent to it he has, however innocently, been responsible for the steady enervation of the human race into the strange, masochistic slave-mass that it is today. Simply by existing, Jesus has caused no end of senseless butchery, exploitation, self-indulgent sin and shame in sin, all due to his own *excess of virtue*. As Dostoyevsky's Grand Inquisitor pointed out, mankind cannot possibly live up to such goodness, even in imitation, save through self-immolation and the betrayal of all its better, stronger instincts. Christians turn the cheek on the outside, while fuming with rage and hatred within. Like the Pharisees in the gospel, these so-called "Christians" wash the outside of the cup while permitting all kinds of fungus and mold to fester on the inside. Establishing himself through passivity and the much-lauded virtue of "meekness"—which is his secret pride—Man has made a virtue of timidity. Just so is the lamb led to the slaughter.

The Christian conception of evil as the absence of good is one that is achieved, like all else in "faith-dogma," by a species of doublethink. Does this make the Devil, then—the absence of God? But God is omnipotent, and makes his bed in hell as much as heaven. So such an idea is unthinkable to the true believer. By denying evil as a positive force in itself, in man as much as in Nature, good, as such, has been correspondingly degraded to the mere absence of evil. Christian "goodness" depends on passivity, abstinence, withdrawal, denial, all plainly negative qualities. If a man represses his base or evil urges by denying them expression (or even mention), to the point that their very existence is refuted, he is considered pious; yet this unspeakable "force"—positive evil—continues to exist within him, and only *increases* in power for being denied. (Witness ever-increasing cases of altar boy-abuse within the Catholic Church and the Vatican's extreme willingness to look the other way; or should that be part the other cheek?) "Goodness," that desires but never acts, is indistinguishable from evil, that wills but holds back: both meet in the middle, both are essentially *passive*.

Active, positive evil is a natural force that complements active and positive good; as forces they share an essence—they are *essential*. In the same way, the passive manifestations of "good" and "evil" partake of a common mediocrity, a lack of bite or essence.[2] In terms of human evolution, an active evil is preferable to a passive good. A tyrant who drags his people through hell-fire and tribulation is serving the ends of evolution far more truly than a mincing do-gooder who sits at home and talks of world reform. Those who "worship God" by the letter of the law,

---

2: Think of a play or movie again: the villain is as indispensable to the action as the hero; it is only the mincing, peripheral characters that remain passively hovering between the two that are of no intrinsic value. For example, the expendable partner in cop dramas, who exists merely to get killed and give the hero a reason to get nasty; or the woman who looks desperately at the hero and whispers: "Be careful!" All decent dramas do away with such characters altogether.

in ignorance of the spirit of grace, following every "Thou Shalt Not," are—in evolution's scheme of things—of infinitely less creative potential than those godless "pagans" fucking their way to Heaven. Which brings us to our next subject.

Gnostics, Pagans, and Templars

When man fell to his knees, he became the asshole that he is today.
—Carlos Castaneda

The Templar knights are linked both to modern-day political conspiracy theories and to more traditional esoteric occult lore, as well as, perhaps most famously of all, to the Arthurian mythos of the holy grail (which gave rise to the Western world's on-going obsession with romantic love). In some mysterious, none-too apparent fashion, all these different threads can be woven together to form a picture of a Christian world in the grips of apocalyptic fervor, dread and profoundest—if unacknowledged—paranoia.

Starting with the most profane of arguments, it may be remarked that the Christian collective body is flagrantly and undeniably intoxicated with the crucifixion, but apparently indifferent to the resurrection: it worships the cross, the instrument of torture and the ragged carcass that hangs thereon, while ignoring the fruits of this symbolic rite, just as if the miracle was invisible to their eyes. Humans identify with what they can relate to, they choose the symbols that suit their mood; and so the mass is drawn to the binding power of suffering over the emancipation of joy.

Paranoid awareness observes how few individuals can resist the combined will of the mass. It perceives a blind beast waiting to be led, to be ordered and exploited like a machine, by any mind or hand ruthless or strong enough to seize it. This rough beast that slouches towards Armageddon is the very spirit of damnation, of "Antichrist": it is the *mob*, and it is all that Christ assured us: "hath nothing in me."[3]

Christianity has been the greatest mass movement the world has ever known; from John the Baptist, Jeshua bar Josephus (a.k.a Jesus Christ), via James, Peter, Paul, and the early apostles, into the hands of the Gentiles and thence to the Roman Empire, Constantine, the Council of Nicea,[4] the Papacy and Vatican, forging onward through the romanticism of the Crusades, the scourge of the Inquisition (as dictated by Reason, the Age of Enlightenment, Protestantism, Lutherism, Mormonism), all the way up to Jerry Falwell, Ronald Reagan, Jim Jones, and George W. Bush II. Through it all, the spirit of antichrist has held sway with an

---

3: John, 14:30. Carlos Castaneda writes in *The Power of Silence*: "We share a metaphorical dagger: the concerns of our self-reflection. With this dagger, we cut ourselves and bleed; and the job of our chains of self-reflection is to give us the feeling that we are bleeding together, that we are sharing something wonderful: our humanity. But if we were to examine it, we would discover that we are bleeding alone."

4: First council of Nicea—325 A.D, editing of Bible begins. The Second Synod of Constantinople in 553 A.D deleted from the Bible all Jesus' direct references to reincarnation, amongst other things.

ever-extending rod of iron. To the paranoid all this has been the result of a deliberate conspiracy, a secret, powerful committee of elect individuals who have knowingly deviated the natural course of humanity, and so herded it into ignorance and slavery. But if looked at more soberly and dispassionately, it must be recognized that the mass who allow themselves to be so herded are equally responsible; in fact, in so far as they outnumber this "elect" by perhaps a million to one, they are that much more so.

This human mass is "evil," then, insofar as it is passive, blind, and willfully ignorant: it is absent of good. It is stagnant and cannot create, hence it is anti-life. It demands uniformity and conformity merely in order to exist, while individuality, creativity, knowledge, and power, whether good or evil, are antithetical to its existence: they are literally intolerable. The spell cast by the mass upon its members is total—once within its ranks, only the most exceptional soul can resist the current and forge a path out again. The mass demands absolute loyalty or else expulsion—one must adhere to its standards blindly if one is to remain under its "protection." It is for this reason that Jeshua was against the world and the people of which it consisted; his parents, his brethren, his peers and his fellows. To this end did he "bring the sword."

If the "Christian," in the profane sense of the word, is really the ultimate "heretic" (an unwitting blasphemer of his Lord's teachings), then it seems logical to seek the real Christ doctrine amongst those men and women denigrated, persecuted, and reviled as heretics, those ousted by orthodoxy, namely, the Gnostics and the Templars. I use "Gnostics" as a generic term to describe those groups or individuals that adhered to (amongst other things) the heretical idea of an evil or tyrannical "demi-urge"—Samael, Yaldaboath, or Jehovah—ruling over the Earth. As such, they were perhaps the earliest and most widely known proponents of paranoid awareness. This demi-urge, they claimed, works to keep the vast mass of humanity enslaved through its legions of Archons, or Custodians. The Gnostic myth seems meant to show how this "mass," by surrendering passively to "preterhuman forces" (archetypes), became slaves to them: they surrendered their freedom to the very powers which they had sought to serve. Since such cosmic powers had no interest in such an offering, however, other mundane and all-too-*human* powers intervened, and took it instead. It was thus that priestcraft, or orthodox religion, began, and the elitist bodies of mystification such as the Catholic Church, government, mass media, etc, established their hold upon the world. And so the Consensus was born.

The Gnostics opposed these forces, whose wages were death; and by opposition to them they became active players, aspiring to true *gnosis*. The nature which they opposed and strove to overcome was not cosmic nature, however, but *human* nature (as applied to the mass). The virtues of Man were to be found in his capacity to overcome his humanness—he was the one animal given the option of conscious transformation, the central meaning of the myth of Christ. The Gnostics were masters of silence, however, and the essence of their teaching was secrecy. *Gnosis* could be passed from individual to individual, but it could never be allowed to take on the faceless, systematized and lifeless quality of mass doctrine. The Gnostics were dedicated to following the example of Christ, determined not merely to mimic his words but to emulate his actions. To this end, they retained a harmless facade of orthodox parable-preaching for the masses, behind which they developed a secret center of "occult" practices, directed towards the private attainment of *gnosis*. For the former, innocuous facade, they might be canonized as saints; for the latter, occult practices, they would surely be shunned, reviled, and persecuted as witches and devil-worshippers. In a word, sorcerers.

*

Jesus' appointed role seems to have been to try to lure the Hebrews away from Jehovah to worship the supermind of the cosmos, the God of the Oriental Illuminated Ones. In this he failed.
—John Keel: *Our Haunted Planet*

The twelve apostles—taking Paul and not Matthew as the logical replacement for Judas—were the keepers of the secret wisdom passed on to them personally by Jeshua. In the truest sense of the word, they were the original "Gnostics," i.e., those who *knew*. Jeshua's system of teaching was not by instruction but by initiation, and as such it was reserved for those who could see beyond the dead letter of the word, to the spirit of truth behind it. The fact that, by protecting themselves and this truth from the spirit of the mob, they were inevitably damning the greater portion of the populace to continued slavery and ignorance was no business of theirs: this was the will of God, and thus had He ordained it.

For the Gnostics, the head-corner-stone of existence had a single name: knowledge. The goal may be wisdom—"Sophia"—but knowledge was clearly the way to attain it. Hence it was the giver of knowledge—the Serpent or Instructor, the wisest of all creatures—that the Gnostics invoked as their first archetype or principal, in the spirit of *study*, however, and not worship.[5] The knowledge in question was of "good and evil," meaning duality. Logically then, evil must be perceived as an active, even creative *force* in itself; otherwise, it could not possibly oppose and balance the force of good. By the same token, Adam—like Cain after him and Lucifer before—was no sinner, but rather a *rebel*. He was a freedom fighter. In which case, the question arises—if Christ did not come to redeem Adam, as traditional theology has it, then what did he come for? Gnostically speaking, his magikal purpose was to demonstrate the possibility of independence of action, of grace. This is presumably what Paul was referring to when he said, "Christ hath redeemed us from the curse of law." (*Galatians* 3: 13)

Historically, Jeshua was both rebel and warrior: he was a subversive agent, and a threat not only to the still-infant Roman political system but (even more so) to the ancient, equally political force of Judaism. The great irony is that the first Christians, starting with Christ, were Jews themselves, and never considered

---

5: "It was the divine (but also material) *energy* that had opened Adam's eyes to his state of subservience, his nakedness, his dependence upon "the goodness of the gods." Hence when he was cast out he was also liberated, like Cain, to fight and fend for himself, to experience directly the truth of nature, the world, of good and evil, to undergo initiation, and to become "as one of us" (the *Elohim*)." H.P.Blavatsky, *The Secret Doctrine*.

themselves to be anything but. While today, your average undiscerning Christian goes on worshipping a Jewish god in the name of Christ, never suspecting that he is attempting the impossible: to serve two masters.

Without law, one household attains harmony while the other falls into chaos. Knowing this, the Gnostics kept their home policy very much for the home, and adapted a quite different one for the world at large. Yet they practiced as they preached, even if they could not preach openly what they practiced. By active opposition to the world (not resistance but confrontation of "evil"), they were sure to bring the forces they opposed to bear directly upon them, and so expose them to the light of awareness. This is the process of revelation by which all things are apprehended and finally redeemed. So although the Gnostics' doctrine was *apparently* one of dualism, their actual mission was the reverse. The principles of existence must be separated—brought into relief—in order to be rendered pure unto themselves, set at harmony with each other, and thereby cancelled out. Hot must be separated from cold, to eradicate the tepid.

The Gnostic deity Abraxas was the personification of the two poles in balance. He was mighty and terrible, like Pan, the all-begetter and all-destroyer, or Horus, god of silence and strength. Abraxas is He who contains His antagonist within him, as an evil twin or shadow. Abraxas is the God of the Sun, and comes with three distinct aspects: head of the cockerel—signifying vigilance, the watchman who hails the dawn and salutes the morning star—body of a man, where the heart resides, and the legs of a serpent, "condemned" to walk in the dust of the Earth, like Cain. The archetype of Abraxas—God of good and evil—is central to paranoid awareness. Without this archetype, which is the key to reconciliation, the paranoid will encounter only a seemingly endless morass of contradictions.

The final joke of the Gnostics was also their ultimate revenge: just as, unsuspected by the mass following, orthodox Christianity was a simple extension and development of Judaism, so Gnostic teaching is, partially at least, the continuing tradition of Kabbala, the sacred science of the Jews. Hence the teachings of Christ became like the sword: double-edged, that the inner might be protected by the outer and, at the same time, the "sheep" be separated from "the goats."[6] The Jews who rejected Christ as the Messiah were content to stick with their obsolete system of worship, and to remain obedient to their false god and petty tyrant Jehovah. These were the "Pharisees," the "lawyers" who, not willing to enter the Temple, lingered outside the doorway to prevent others from entering, recruiting all those Jews and Gentiles who rejected and reviled Jeshua's teachings. It was a fitting revenge for the Gnostics to allow these fools to be led astray, poetic justice. While the apostles and their inner circle were taking the next step of consciousness up the Tree of Life, the unwitting mass was busy collecting the rotten fruit and debris of

---

6: "And he shall set the sheep on the right hand, but the goats on the left." *Matthew* 25, 33. One should note that the symbolism has again been reversed here. Goats are more or less independent creatures, whereas sheep of course are herd animals; hence the "good shepherd" leads his flock to the slaughter, i.e., is a deceiver, while only those wise and wily enough to follow their own path have a chance of reaching the true goal.

the now defunct, discarded husk of Judaic tradition; and out of this excreta—fit only for compost— a whole new system of dogma was swiftly assembled.

Paul took the various elements of the Christ story and twisted them around to specific ends: he created a mythology that would appeal to the masses. The result was what Nietzsche would describe, almost 2000 years later (once the original seeds had grown into a wilderness of deceit), as a religion fit for slaves. This was a necessary part of the deception which characterized the apostles' mission, and was true to the original instructions of Jeshua himself. Why else would he have chosen Saul, the persecutor and self-confessed "chief of sinners," to be his public agent?[7] Paul put the Jesus in Christ, making the universal into the personal, and created a herd of followers out of what was until then a collection of contenders. Nietzsche pointed out that the immaculate conception thereby maculated conception; likewise, by presenting Jeshua as divine, the vast mass of mankind was summarily debased as "all-too-human."[8] And so it was that the Gnostics—of whom Jeshua was but the most celebrated and calumniated member—returned once more underground, to escape the inexorably spreading flames of their own doctrine.

*

7: "Paul's God is the denial of God." (Nietzsche) Via Paul, Jesus became elevated from a son of God to God incarnate. Paul's mix was a base simplification, intended expressly for the Gentiles—the Greeks and the Romans—who unlike the Jews needed a *visible* object of worship on which to found their philosophic and political beliefs. There would be no other way for them to build a religion around a human being, other than to accept him as a God.

8: Dostoyevsky wrote most incisively on this subject, in *The Brothers Karamazov* (the Grand Inquisitor, to Christ:): "You yourself laid the foundation for the destruction of your own kingdom, and no one else should be blamed for it . . . In respecting (man) too much you acted as though you had ceased to have compassion for him, because you demanded too much of him. Human nature cannot endure blasphemy and in the end invariably takes revenge for it."

OTO Seal Baphomet   Abraxas

Magician as Abraxas in Tarot   Templar seal

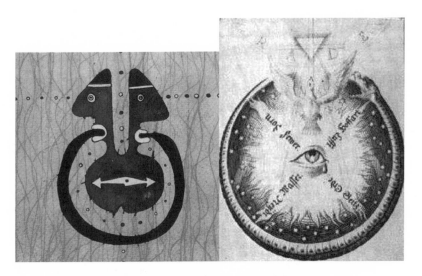

Gnostic Symbol of Oroborus, Tail-Eater

Templar Seals

Emblem of the Theosophical Society, from H.P. Blavatsky's Theosophical Glossary, 1892

For everything hidden must be revealed, each secret longs to be disclosed, each love yearns to be betrayed, everything sacred must be desecrated. Heaven and earth conspire that all good beginnings should come to a bad end. Kant has shown that even the laws of nature are but the conditions of thought. And as the current of thought is the blood of the mind, it is said that the Magick Cup is filled with the blood of the Saints. All thought must be offered up as sacrifice.
—Aleister Crowley, *Book 4*

Across Europe, Asia, America, Australia, and Africa, the seeds of Gnosticism were sown. The two chief apostles—Peter and Paul—divided their responsibilities equally. Peter would be the open, acknowledged head of orthodox, exoteric Christianity, the so-called "prince of the apostles"; he would journey to Rome to lay the foundation (as chosen "stone") of the Catholic or universal religion. He was the Jew assigned to the conversion of the Gentiles, and doubtless aware of the dual nature of his role, as guerilla as much as guide. Paul (a Roman citizen) was the Gentile assigned to the Jews and, possibly, the Arabs. On his trip to Arabia, Paul laid the foundations of a secret school or society for the safe keeping of the inner Gnostic teachings. It is as likely as not that this became incorporated into the Sufi sects; certainly the Arabs were not indisposed to both sorcery and secrecy. Much has been made of Paul's mysterious trip to Arabia. It is generally assumed that he went to gain knowledge before beginning his work proper in Europe, and not to impart it; probably it was a mixture of both. Those elements of the Gnostic creed best kept would have been entrusted to the Sufis, while those Arabic teachings most easily adapted to the still embryonic Christian doctrine went back to Europe with Paul, to be worked out with Peter and the gang.

The point of all this speculation is that we have our twin streams of gnosis and faith running parallel, initiated at the same time but in wholly separate locations, the one in newly thriving Rome, the other in darkest Africa. Peter's heritage is obviously the better documented by far, being established in the public domain, as such. Accessible to the mob, the teachings were quickly profaned and corrupted, precisely as planned.[9] By the same token, the Arabian heritage, no matter how well-guarded, would undoubtedly have been quickly surrounded by all kinds of half-baked followers and their pseudo-sects, forming the inevitable layer of error that protects the truth and keeps it concealed from the undiscerning eye.[10]

All this pertains to the basic tenets of paranoid research, in which knowledge or information itself is perceived, not as a lifeless body of data, but as an active, ever-changing entity, one which forges its own connections and covers its own tracks,

---

9: Peter himself may have seen to the inception of the insidious encroachment of rot that has continued to eat at the apple to this day, although he will surely have made just as certain that the core, the secret center wherein abided the untouched seeds of *gnosis*, remained protected from the worm of time. Even the Catholic religion has its esoteric inner teachings. The Gnostic Catholic Church for example remains extant to the present day.

10: Whatever comes to light in history, and so to the eyes and the ears (and the sticky fingers) of the mob, is by definition, by dint of this very contact, already corrupted. Only that which remains within the stronghold of silence retains its wisdom intact. The greenest neophyte knows this, else he would never have been selected to begin with. It is only the greedy and passively lazy mind of the mob that supposes it will find pearls amidst the swine-food.

both in the world at large and in the mind of the investigator. There seems no doubt that the challenge of history—both ancient and modern, religious and political—is to discern from a series of red herrings and blinds an actual course of events or train of associations by which the "truth" may be reached. To decipher the code and to apply it, then, is to discover—in the understanding of both Gnostic and paranoid—that it is the act of deciphering (i.e., of applying the conscious will or imagination to the evidence) that alone allows one to discover the truth—not about history or the world, but about perception itself. This is the essence of *gnosis*, which is heightened awareness, the secret goal of paranoia.

Historically, the occult thread of mystery begins in the Western world with the Templars; and the Templars' tracks can be traced more or less conclusively to Arabia and the Assassins. The Templars are perhaps so well-known—reviled and venerated in more or less equal parts—precisely because they are a rare case of an occult faction emerging into the timestream of ordinary history. As such they are as respectable a subject for study to the "legitimate" researcher as they are to the paranoid investigator, though of course each reserves his own peculiar take on the subject. Overtly at least, they began in the 12th century as a brand of warrior-monks, as an attempt to synthesize the king and priest polarities at an individual level. In a word: knights of Christ. The history of the Templars is paralleled by the mythology of Camelot which arose at roughly the same time (and which also coincided with the inception of "romantic love"). It was the age of chivalry. This "chivalry" relates primarily to the assumed *chastity* of both the Templars and the graal-seeking knights of Arthur: in the absence of actual, physical consummation, it was necessary to introduce an alternative, spiritual dimension to human desire. By this process the female became an abstract quality, to be courted but not possessed. She represented the spiritual goal of the warrior, not merely his reward but his actual attainment. In a word, the Goddess.

What was enlightened was the heart of the warrior; what fulfilled, the womb of the maiden. Both these are represented by the Graal—the vessel of the waters of life, both literally and figuratively. These two concepts—sacred heart and holy (virgin) womb—are the two most powerful and mysterious symbols of Christianity. The legacy of the knight was none other than the promised reconception (or reincarnation) of Christ. King Arthur's "idea" for Camelot—legend has it—was to turn Might to the service of Right, to reverse the standard social system later legitimized by Darwin as "survival of the fittest." This was a wholly Christian notion—that the meek, through the strength of righteousness, would inherit the Earth. It was shared by the Templars, apparently, when they placed weapons of war in the hands of the clergy, simultaneously putting religion under the protection of warriors. The objective was to spiritualize combat, and to fortify worship.

It is a common enough practice of the prize fighter to remain celibate before the big fight, and if the Templars were constantly engaged in one battle or another it would be logical for them to take a vow of celibacy, along with the traditional monkish vows. The fact that a mere nine Templars soon became an international syndicate for royal monies, and the first "central bank of Europe," in no way refutes the humbler origins of the order. What it does suggest is the eventual, perhaps inevitable, corruption of its better intentions. The Templars were growing steadily into a very real threat to the political powers (the kings and priests) throughout Catholic Europe at that time. The Order of the Temple became such a success that it drew all the wrong kinds of attention from the wrong places, and so accelerated its own downfall (an example to future organizations that would never be forgotten: of all the virtues of the Sphinx, silence—or secrecy—is the most essential).

It has been speculated (by the authors of *The Hiram Key*, amongst others) that the Templars' meteoric rise to power may well be attributable to their possession of some secret store of knowledge. This knowledge, it is said, gave them bargaining power with the heads of state, or some kind of political leverage by which they could blackmail their way to power. Insofar as they became a temporal power, a world bank as it were, this indicates less a deviance from their central purpose than it does the success *of* it: the more they advanced at a spiritual level, as monks, the more smoothly went their outer dealings as an order of warriors. They were *worldly* monks, after all, and the more victorious they were, the greater became their reputation, the grander their rewards. As a battling force *par excellence* in France, it was only logical that the sovereignty entrust its more valuable assets to the security and protection of the Temple strongholds. Thus the circle-like snake, feeding on itself, grew exponentially onward, with no apparent limit to its expansion. The more funds and temporal power the Order gained, the further its influence and connections extended, the more knowledge ("spiritual power") it accumulated. This knowledge became antithetical, heretical, to its various sources. By being true to them all, it was seen to be true to none. The Templars were perhaps true "Catholics" in the sense that they sought the "Universal Principle" behind all diversified religions. If so, they were destroyed for it.

The Templars were denounced as black magicians when the nature of their inner rites and practices (perhaps flavored by the initiation techniques of the Assassins) were discovered. Tradition has it that the intrigue and the persecutions really began once the crusades reached Arabic territory, when what was to have been the ultimate holy war—a senseless and unwinnable clash of cultures and dogmas—turned instead into the most potent occult alliance in history. Under guise of espionage for the Empire, the Templar Order was initiated into the secrets of the Sufis, most probably through its dealings with the "barbaric" Order of the Assassins.[11] This was the beginning of the end.

*

And he that overcometh, and keepeth my works unto the end, to him will I give power over the nations. . . . And I will give him the morning star.
—*Revelation* 2:26,28

11: "From the Ismalis (Assassins) the Crusaders borrowed the conception which led to the formation of all secret societies, religious and secular, of Europe. The institutions of Templars and Hospitallers; the Society of Jesus, founded by Ignatius Loyola . . . the ferocious Dominicans, the Franciscans—may all be traced either to Cairo or to Alamut. The Knights Templar especially, with their system of grand masters, grand priors and religious devotees, and their degrees of initiation, bear the strongest analogy to the Eastern Ismalis." S. Ameer Ali, quoted by Arkon Daraul in *A History of Secret Societies*.

It was about here and now that the Templar crew would have uncovered at last the secret store of wisdom left by Paul, all those centuries ago, on his trip to Arabia. All that is really known for sure is that the Templars *were* involved with Arabian secret societies, and that they were subsequently exposed and persecuted for practicing the most unorthodox Catholic rites imaginable, denounced as not only heretical but satanic. Their initiation rites have never been fully disclosed, and what has come out is inevitably contaminated with slander, hysteria, and hearsay. What seems reasonably certain is that they involved a bearded bust (worshipped as the icon-deity "Baphomet"), the spitting on the crucifix (signifying denial of Christ), and the pseudo-sexual ritual of kissing a fellow monk on the anus.[12] The picture this combined to create in the minds of the ruling powers can easily be imagined. The Templars were not forthcoming in their own defense. They either held their tongues entirely and were burned at the stake, or else they confessed to everything and anything they were accused of, and suffered the shame and the relief of a full pardon.

In the paranoid understanding of events, the Order of the Templars was not quashed in the name of decency, but rather to the end of secrecy, for the furtherance of tyranny. The persecutions were not intended to reform or punish the knights but to silence them; the Custodians' design was not so much to seize the Templars' wealth as it was to steal the body of knowledge which had been assembled during their short reign. There are countless works on the history and mystery of this organization; it is a myth that seems to be growing in force and meaning (and romanticism) with every passing year. Lately, the Templars seem to be involved in everything. *Holy Blood Holy Grail* posits a still-existing bloodline originating with Jeshua and Mary Magdalena, named the Merovingian line (note the homage in *Matrix Reloaded*). In the popular mystery of Rennes de Chateau and the Priory of Sion (the Order established by those merry Merovingians, and of whom Jean Cocteau was a reputed head), the hidden treasure is patently *not* of a material nature but quite abstract. It is not money but *knowledge*. Just what this knowledge consists of is the great, on-going mystery/history drama of our time, and the mythical backbone of paranoid awareness.

12: Actually, such rites are not so absurd as they appear to be at first sight. Spitting on the cross involved denying that Christ was ever crucified. Kissing the brother's anus was to awaken the Kundalini there residing (i.e., a symbolic act). Note also the ancient rite of Isis, in which the neophyte is compelled to kiss the rear end of a goat only to find, when he bends down and puckers up, that he is faced not with a hairy asshole but with a fresh-faced houri. William Cooper writes, in *Behold a Pale Horse*: "A method of deciding who is to become an adept [is] by asking the candidate to spit upon the Christian cross. If the candidate refuses, the members congratulate him and tell him, 'You have made the right choice, as a true adept would never do such a terrible thing.' The newly initiated might find it disconcerting, however, that he/she never advances any higher. If instead, the candidate spits upon the cross he/she has demonstrated a knowledge of the mysteries and soon will find him/herself a candidate for the next higher level. The mystery is that religion is but a tool to control the masses. Knowledge or wisdom is [the Brotherhood of the Serpent's] only god, through which man himself will become god. The snake and the dragon are both symbols of wisdom. . . . The WORSHIP (a lot different from STUDY) of knowledge, science, or technology is Satanism in its purest form, and its god is Lucifer. Its secret symbol is the all-seeing eye in the pyramid." (So secret it adorns every dollar bill on the planet.)

To come full circle, then, paranoid awareness posits that the secret knowledge to which Paul became privy whilst sojourning in Arabia is part of a prevailing occult thread of intrigue that began with Moses, or perhaps long before, all the way back in Atlantis. We can do no more than speculate as to the exact nature of this thread, however.

*

It is probable that all religions are founded upon ancient jokes and hoaxes.
—Charles Fort

Concerning the somewhat obscure mission and purpose of Jeshua, a.k.a. Jesus Christ, there is the following little-known fragment of occult history, found in *El Hombre Estrellar*, by John Baines (translation by the author). Baines tells a captivating tale of the Egyptian pharaoh Moses, trained in the highest forms of Egyptian magik, and of his attempts to contact and evoke a mighty archetype, or "deity." "Moses, inspired by the powerful forces that he had learned to handle, decided to realize a pact, a magikal alliance, in order to enlist the help of heaven and save mankind." In a dynamic example of good intentions paving a road straight to Hell, however,

> Seeing that the divine angel was in reality an "angel of darkness" belonging to the exact opposite pole as the luminous power which he had intended to evoke, Moses realized the magnitude of his mistake. This "infernal angel" was one of the mightiest of the "hosts of darkness," a cosmic vampire which, in order to maintain its strength and power, required human blood, and the charged, vital essence that the divine spark provided therein. . . . The magikal rite of Moses had opened a door and paved the way for Yaldaboath to find access into the earth realm. Thus began a dark and bloody era for humanity.

According to Baines, this little gothic horror story accounts for the extreme preponderance of wars and blood sacrifices to be found in the Pentateuch (the first five books of the Bible); Baines is clearly suggesting that the malign entity so rashly invited by Moses to feed off the Earth was none other than Jehovah himself.[13] The bloody age of religious sacrifice was expected to endure for 2000 years, until such time as another prophet would arise, with the express purpose of rectifying the situation. The mission of Jeshua, then, was,

> Firstly, to liberate the "chosen people" from their occult curse as blood sacrifices. Secondly, to save the world in general from this invisible vampire . . . and so initiate a new age upon Earth under the Christian yoke of "Love Thy Neighbor" (the opposite of

---

13: "There is a malign influence surrounding the Earth which inhibits true spiritual growth and understanding. . . what is generally termed "evil" is . . . displaced or disorganized energies which have come adrift from their natural time-zone. . . certain esoteric teachings also refer to our world as a "fallen planet," a sphere which is out of its correct time sequence in relation to the rest of the solar system and galaxy. Those who elect to run counter to the cosmic flow automatically set in motion a series of contra-energies that take form as they gather momentum, eventually assuming a collective identity which feeds greedily on all that is around it." Murray Hope, *Ancient Egypt, the Sirius Connection*

"an eye for an eye and a tooth for a tooth" as taught by Moses) . . . The crucifixion was a contrived drama in which the blood of Jesus had to be spilled in order for Christ—in his turn—to "incarnate" in the planet Earth and so displace the cosmic vampire, expelling it from our atmosphere once and for all. However . . . the mission was only relatively successful. Christ incarnated into the Earth, but the vampire was not expelled, and since then, both forces have shared in the government of the planet.[14]

In true Gnostic fashion, the soul of the Earth is divided between the spirits of light and darkness, good and evil, sickness and health, and all Earth's creatures are hanging in the balance. Taking all this into account, the Templars' store of knowledge may have been of a nature far beyond that of mere religious secrets, and pertained to something of a *cosmic* (non-human) order.[15] Umberto Eco, in his celebrated *Foucault's Pendulum,* symbolizes this secret body of knowledge as a map, split into several sections, each of which is in the keeping of a particular occult faction or body. If the Templars (to give them one of their names) wanted to ensure that this secret "stash" never fall into the wrong hands, one sure-fire, foolproof way would be to divide the necessary information amongst different individuals, groups, or locations, so that only when the separate parties were drawn together would the actual nature of the working emerge. Eco's literary conceit is to have the sections of the Map joined at regular intervals (every 200 years) by the separate factions until the set date arrives, at which time the picture finally comes together. The Templars of Eco's fantasy are guardians not of a mere treasure map, but of a secret weapon that is assembled piece by piece, over the millennia. In good, mythic tradition, the map/weapon/MacGuffin remains an abstract and symbolic affair, amounting once again to that *sine qua non* of power: knowledge.[16]

*

14: The quotation is translated by the author from the original Spanish edition of *El Hombre Estrellar,* by John Baines (a pseudonym). An English translation is also available but was not at hand at the time. Regarding Jesus. Is this what Blake meant when he wrote, "Know that after Christ's death, he became Jehovah"? (*The Marriage of Heaven and Hell*)

15: George Andrews (in *E.T Friends and Foes*) writes of a Templar, under torture, "driven insane by pain. He talked of such things as traveling through time, and in the sky in flying chariots that spat fire, of the Kingdom of the Swan, of a deep well of darkness lost in the sky through which one could attain immortality, reach unknown stars and empires. He spoke of the Apocalypse, of celestial warfare between the powers of light and darkness and of warfare in the unknown celestial worlds." Such knowledge (i.e., pertaining to extra-terrestrial beings) may also have involved certain earth mysteries and keys, by which the future might be glimpsed, or even decided. Aleister Crowley, whose own O.T.O is the modern-day inheritor of the Templars tradition, states that the central secret of freemasonry is simple, short and scientific in nature, concerns the harnessing or tapping of an occult source of energy that is under our very noses, either in the human body or the Earth itself (or both). By understanding this power, or "force," he affirms, absolute mastery of the destiny of mankind might be attained.

16: The map of *Foucault's Pendulum* is a map of the telluric currents and esoteric geology of the Earth (or inner Earth?) by which, the book proposes, natural forces might be manipulated (or at least anticipated) in order to bring about earthquakes, floods, tidal waves, and other disasters on an apocalyptic scale. This knowledge-cum-power would then provide the leverage needed to *oust* the prevailing Judeo-Catholic (or whatever) hegemony, and usher in (at last) the Kingdom of Heaven, the long-promised Brotherhood of Man; or, perhaps, just another bunch of Thugs with delusions of grandeur? To this author at least, it seems unlikely that the secret tradition and enduring influence of the Templars and their successors would revolve around anything quite so mundane as a map; but it makes for good fiction anyhow.

Christ's place indeed is with the poets. . . . But his entire life also is the most wonderful of poems.
—Oscar Wilde, *De Pronfundis*

Today the modern myths of secret societies and world conspiracies have adopted the Templars as an archetypal ingredient and central thread to their mystery-theatre scenarios. This thread can be followed without much difficulty to the present day, through the Cathars, Jesuits, Rosicrucians, Golden Dawns, and Nazi mutations (Thule, Vril, Knights of Malta, etc), on the one hand (the "monk-side" swallowed whole by the warrior ethos). On the other, meanwhile, we have the Surrealist movement and its subsequent development with the Beats, the counterculture, punk, etc, where the mystical urge finds a more creative outlet (though still involving an element of destruction). It is due to the steady debasement of these ideas at a collective level that the true creative current—the quick of life, as D.H. Lawrence called it—has steadily redirected itself *away* from society, and into the fringe, where dwells the outcast, the rebel, the lonely and proud individual.

As far back as the 13th century, what began as the romantic "age of chivalry" in Europe quickly lead to an artistic renaissance, beginning with the painters and the poets, from Dante through DaVinci, Shakespeare to Goethe, Bosch to Blake, spreading gradually outward, into the world of the novel and, most recently, popular music and movies. "The Holy Graal," as such, became the easel in which the painter mixed his colors, the inkwell in which the poet dipped his pen. The literary movement reached its zenith (if not its culmination) in the existentialist-cum-Surrealist wave of 1920s Paris. Camus' *The Outsider*, for example, though dated, presents a concise portrait of the true "freeman," estranged from society and opposed to the world.[17]

The outsider is the underdog whose honesty, integrity and superiority have cast him out into a cold and hostile world. Yet for all the persecutions, he is protected, and it is the very fact of his being designated a sinner that, like Cain, protects him. He is like a leper that no one will come near. Conversely, his removal from society is also a form of restraint: if his power were manifest about him he would, like an infant, lay waste to the world; he would be too dangerous to be allowed to live. Kafka's *Metamorphosis* is a classic example of the lofty, superior man's utter degradation and humiliation at the hands of the mob; Man must become a mere beetle, Kafka seems to be saying, before he can transcend the dung-heap. The Artist, like the Mystic, is inspired by his nausea to withdraw his senses into the surreal realms of the imagination, wherein he finds the vision and the courage to take on, and eventually overcome, the world.

Certain parallels may here be drawn between the chivalrous Templars, in service to the Goddess Sophia (Wisdom—represented in the Arthurian mythos by Queen Guinevere), and the artist, enthralled by (and enslaved to) his Muse. Both

---

17: Mersault kills an Arab, representing the forbidden, atavistic side of European nature. He perhaps senses its encroaching influence ("resurgence") as it threatens to engulf him, and attempts (futilely) to resist it.

devotions signify the sublimation of desire (usually sexual), and a life of service to what amounts, for all its beauty, to an abstract, unknown quantity. So long as the end is attained, however, it matters little if the poet-warrior's master be God, Goddess, Lucifer, or Art, just so long as it provide him with the pride of the free man and the humility of purpose. This purpose must, by definition, transcend or overwhelm the warrior's personal *will*, because only in willing surrender (as opposed to passive resistance) is his freedom to be found.[18] The artist knows this intuitively. He does not have to be taught it; he does not need to be "initiated," since the creative process of serving the Muse—if he remains true to it until the end—will prove to be its own initiation. André Breton and the Surrealists knew this better than anyone.

To the paranoid investigator, it is indeed the happiest of coincidences that, while Crowley was busy in Paris investigating, infiltrating, and pilfering the various occult organizations so prominent at that time, Breton and his gang were equally busy setting up the artistic movement of the century. With the audacity of true artists, the Surrealists applied the idea of the secret society, the occult conspiracy so long restricted to the sphere of politics, to the circle of *art*. In other words, they brought paranoia and eschatology into the open. This was, ironically enough, the most logical juxtaposition that could have occurred to such men of unreason. To quote Robert Anton Wilson on the subject: "The Priory of Sion [recall those merry Merovingians?]. . . came into existence in a Paris basement in 1930 when Cocteau, Breton, Dali and other first generation surrealists decided, while smoking opium, to start their very own International Conspiracy—the first surrealist conspiracy and therefore the first one to deliberately appear batshit crazy." This joke-theory in fact belongs to Wilson's wife, Arlen, and Wilson (perhaps regretfully) dismisses it because of documentation that dates the Priory of Sion's existence to well before the Surrealists. (On the other hand, as previously mentioned, Jean Cocteau *was* one of those named as "Grand Master" of the Priory in *Holy Blood, Holy Grail*.)

Wilson's theory, however, actual or Imaginal, is a healthy by-product of the creative imagination, as it struggles vainly to overcome (or at least influence) the rational world in which it is imprisoned. Through frustration of intent it conceives, as it were spontaneously, the art of the bluff. We are at long last nearing the nub and crux of the paranoid quest, namely: the overlap between *personal myth and historical fact*. This was the essence of Surrealism: to construct a *bridge* between the actual world and the Imaginal one, to blend dreams and reality into a *new* awareness, even though it is perhaps also the most ancient of them all, that of Surreality.[19] By imposing subjective (not necessarily personal) desire upon

---

18: "I believe it's impossible for a man to be great without admitting that there's something greater than himself, whether its law, or God, or art." *This is Orson Welles*, conversations with Peter Bogdanovich.

19: "I believe in the future resolution of these two states, dream and reality, which are seemingly so contradictory, into a kind of absolute reality, a *surreality*, if one may so speak. It is in quest of this surreality that I am going, certain not to find it but too unmindful of my death not to calculate to some slight degree the joys of its possession." Breton, *Manifestos of Surrealism*, pg. 14.

objective "fact," Surrealism aspired to draw the elixir of individual myth from the putrid morass of Consensus Reality.

There is a very good reason why most artists are not especially interested in paranoid folklore *per se*—why Satanic Ritual Abuse, Alien Abductions, and other conspiracy theories are generally ignored or dismissed by such persons as fodder for the masses, and so beneath their interest. Artists tend to be too busy cultivating and assembling their own brand of paranoid awareness, and so instinctively avoid the distractions and contaminations of all other *weltanschauungs*. Just as artists are apolitical—their concern being mythical and so above such things—their paranoia is not specifically directed at any group or agenda, but at *the Universe as a whole*. Artists know what it means to be the prey in a predatory environment; that's their job after all. But artists recognize only the Furies or gods as their superiors. It is sheer anathema for them to ever acknowledge any human or worldly power as in any way *over* them. Hence their resistance to the mundane kind of paranoid awareness—though emotional and often poorly thought-out (essentially a blind spot)—is basically right: they are following their instincts, albeit blindly.

What the Surrealists did—and every artist who begins to realize his or her potential is on the way to becoming a Surrealist, a sorcerer—was to consciously utilize the mundane awareness of the average paranoid as *substance* to fuel or fortify their own mythical workings. They effectively set out to map the area between sanity and madness, reason and imagination, complacency and paranoia, actual and Imaginal, and thereby to discover the means of confrontation, of dynamic overlap, between the two perspectives. This was the essence of Surrealism: the juxtapositioning of two objects or ideas that do not belong together, i.e., between which *there is no apparent causal connection*. What is less understood is that this experimental process was a means to an end, and that it was the *effect* of the juxtaposition that interested the Surrealists, and not the juxtaposition itself.

This effect is described by don Juan Matus to Carlos Castaneda (in *The Power of Silence*) as "the shock of beauty." Breton himself said that "Surrealism attempted to provoke, from an intellectual and moral point of view, *an attack of conscience*, of the most general and serious kind." This "attack of conscience" is nothing less than paranoid awareness, in its purest and most spontaneous form. Before the lucid view can take hold, this attack of conscience must occur, and the shock of beauty be experienced.

*

So-called solid reality is only crystallized dream. It can be undreamed. There is nothing stronger than dream, because dreams are forms of THE LAW.
—William S. Burroughs, *Letters, 1945-59*

Dostoyevsky, Nietzsche, Poe, Baudelaire, Kafka, Lawrence, Camus, Sartre, Cocteau, Breton, Blavatsky, Crowley, Steiner, Burroughs, Paul Bowles, Carlos Castaneda, Timothy Leary, Philip K. Dick, Terence McKenna, Ramsey Dukes (and of course R.A. Wilson!), represent the true "Illuminati" of the modern age. They reject all clubs and societies—secret or otherwise—as by definition corrupt. In hearty agreement with Groucho Marx, they reject any club that would have them for members, acknowledging that the real *coup du monde*—if it is ever to occur—depends upon the art of the bluff. Like the Hopi Indian, the true artist is a magician who depends upon the power of imagination to render truth from *dreaming*; this is what both art and magik are all about. The artist-magician must take care never to get lost in his *dreaming*, however, never to succumb to belief or disbelief. The artist-magician is the modern, worldly embodiment of both the mystic and the adept. Insofar as he maps the Abyss that others flinch from in terror, he is also a warrior, knight, and dragon-slayer. Loath as he would be to admit it, the true artist is bent upon world reform, and as such, is doomed to misrepresentation and persecution. This persecution is the very thing that keeps him strong, however, and allows him to maintain his clarity of purpose and *intent* in the face of the appalling odds (a Universe against him).

It is essential to note at this point that the one common thread of all religion has been the suppression and vilification of *the female*, which is to say: the artistic or poetic spirit. As Florinda Donner writes (of the Holy Inquisition, in *Being-In-Dreaming*): "That was a systematic purge to eradicate the belief that women have a direct link to the spirit. All organized religion is nothing but a very successful maneuver to put women in a lower place. Religions invoke a divine law that says that women are inferior."[20] Historically, the persecution of "paganism" was directed above all towards the abolition of Goddess-worship common to witches, Gnostics, Templars, and the like throughout history. The Christian religion allowed the Goddess to lie dormant in the largely passive and debased role of the Virgin Mary, Mother of God, who is invoked in times of trouble but remains basically outside the central symbolism (the Trinity being a strictly *male* affair.)[21] This is, as we have seen, due to the essentially *Judaic* leanings of the Catholic Church. As Robert Graves observes in *King Jesus*:

> Indeed, that the Jews are at the present day perhaps the most miserable of all civilized nations, scattered, homeless, suspect—is ascribed by the superstitious to the Goddess' ineluctable vengeance: for the Jews have been prime leaders in the religious movement against her not only in their own country but in all the countries of the Dispersion. They have proclaimed Jehovah as the sole ruler of the Universe and represented the Goddess as a mere demoness, witch, Queen of Harlots, succuba and prime mischief maker.

From a Gnostic view, it is not Nature that is "evil" but her works: the cycles of death and decay that, like the womb of the world and the human form itself, must be broken out of for the Spirit to be born. Hence *King Jesus'* declaration: "I come to destroy the works of the female." (Yet to *honor*, at all costs, the Goddess.[22])

20: "In fact, the secret organizations that seek to control the planet through implants and other manipulations are only successful to the degree that they subvert the feminine." Peter Moon, *Encounter in the Pleiades: An Inside Look at UFOs*

21: At present that is, though originally, the holy spirit, *ruach*, was a female principle.

22: "The Spirit of the Valley never dies. It is called the Mystic Female. The Door of the Mystic Female is the root of Heaven and Earth. Continuously, continuously, it seems to remain. Draw upon it and it serves you with ease." *Tao Teh Ching*, Lao Tze

Two sides of the Goddess: The Empress and Lust (Babalon)
Frieda Harris' paintings for Aleister Crowley's Tarot deck, *The Book of Thoth*

Time is the womb that forms all things; once the formation is completed, however, it becomes a force of limitation, and therefore "evil." In order to be born again, one must first return to the womb, i.e., the Mother, "Sophia."[23]

23: This is the path of Daleth—the door—Venus or the Empress, that stands between wisdom and understanding on the Tree of Life, "uniting the father with the mother." (Aleister Crowley, *Book of Thoth*.) Daleth is the letter corresponding with the fourth Arcana in the Tarot, The Empress, which Crowley defines as "the Gate of Heaven." Many men might feel the same. Compare with Castaneda's description of "the crack between worlds" which Genaro refers to as "the cosmic vagina"! (*The Eagle's Gift*) The Empress "is fitted to represent one of the three alchemical forms of energy, Salt." The Gnostics called Sophia "Salt," and insisted that "Without it no offering is acceptable." (*The Gospel of Philip*)

Harris' painting for Atu XVII, The Star, representing Nut, the Sky Goddess

Crowley writes (in *The Book of Thoth*) that "the heralding of the Empress is two-fold: on the one side, the Pelican of tradition feeding its young from the blood of its own heart; on the other, the White Eagle of the Alchemists." This equates with the twin nature of Christ, as the crucified and the resurrected (the White Eagle being the Phoenix). The Goddess, Christ, Lucifer, and Baphomet, all wrapped up into a single archetype—a common understanding. When Christ said "I am the door: by me if any man enter in, he shall be saved" (*John* 10:9), he summed up the riddle nicely. A doorway is an *opening*, a space between. If this fake matrix world is our womb, as the Gnostics posited, then Christ is the vagina. He is the Way Out!

In the Gnostic view, Christ's mission was to supplant or overthrow Jehovah, the god of sacrifice worshipped by the Jews. Advertently or otherwise, however, Jeshua's efforts caused the old myth to rise up against this cheeky new myth and find a way to redirect it, to channel it back into the old myth/tradition, and so deny it an outlet (into the world at large). This redirecting required the construction of an edifice: the old Judaic tradition, realizing its obsolescence, was forced to form a pact with the Roman Empire, resulting in a radical reworking of its symbols and rituals into an apparently new foundation. This foundation is known today as the Catholic Church,[24] and more esoterically, the secret school of Freemasonry.[25] All this was set in motion, at least mythologically speaking, by the early works of Peter, the "stone" of the new faith laid down by Jeshua in a peculiar cross between hoax and subterfuge.

It is interesting to note that Judaism, in order to survive, had to deny Christ as the Messiah (quite logically, seeing as he did not fulfill his Messianic duty as "King of the Jews"), just as it denied the Goddess. This denial is also attributed to Peter, three times according to the legend, before the cock crowed. It might be that Peter was selected by Jeshua expressly for his patent unreliability; after all, Peter demonstrates himself consistently throughout the gospels to be anything but "solid." He is in fact the most cowardly, fickle, and weak-minded (though good-hearted) of the Apostles, the one with the feet of clay (as symbolized by his loss of faith whilst walking on water); he is also—and for all of that—the most *human*. It was "upon this rock" that Christ founded his Church? If so, it was set up to sink.

If, as the paranoid's perception has it, this Masonic-Judaic edifice was established in place of an authentic Christian Ministry, it stands to reason that the *true* followers of Christ would have been forced into protective action, and would either have had to convert, bail out, or (trickiest of all) go "underground." In which case, the Gnostic tradition may best be understood as a necessary "heresy" designed to keep the new current alive, by hook or by crook. The mythical Illuminati, then—as upholding the spirit of individual illuminism—might likewise be seen as

24: Inflammatory as this statement is, it seems evident that under the guise of spreading the Christian doctrine, the Church has really been busy doing the exact opposite. "The great error of academic historians is the belief that the Roman Empire 'fell.' It never 'fell.' It still controls the Western world through the Vatican and the Mafia." Alan Watts, quoted by Robert Anton Wilson, *Coincidance*

25: Masonry, if looked into only cursorily, appears to retain an essentially Judaic symbolism. Browsing through the instructions for the "Supreme Grand Royal Arch Chapter of Scotland," I find there is mention therein of Abraham, Isaac, Jacob, Moses and Solomon, but none at all of Jesus. Regarding Peter The single central symbol of Masonry is, of course, the stone.

the Gnostic opposition to the political hegemony of Masonic rule. Of course, lucidly speaking, Masonry and Illuminism teach and claim *the same things*; the only difference finally is not between groups or factions—or even traditions, as such—but rather between *the policies emphasized.* The difference between them is the difference between secrecy that is used to protect the truth (and keep it untarnished) and secrecy used to horde knowledge and maintain a tyrannical hold over it. The battle, if it rages anywhere outside the mind of the paranoid, rages eternal. It is a war inside every individual, a war between the desire to hide in the blissful ignorance of the mass and the *will* to freedom. The Surrealists enacted a simple realization: the only way to beat the opposition is to *become* the opposition. To deceive the deceivers, after all, is no deceit at all.

*

> Systematic lying creates what communications scientists call a "disinformation situation," in which everybody eventually begins to distrust, demonize and diabolize everybody else. . . When the politics of lying becomes normal, paranoia and alienation become the 'normality' of the day.
> —Robert Anton Wilson, *Cosmic Trigger*

A rule of thumb of paranoid awareness states that, whatever a secret society or ruling body *claims* to be, you can be sure they are the exact opposite.[26] From such a view, the Illuminati have never actually wielded power at a temporal level, because each time they bid for it, they are at once undermined, subverted, and assimilated by the existing power structures. This explains the vast preponderance of Illuminati propaganda, attributing credit or blame to them for every imaginable social or political upheaval, revolution, assassination, etc, throughout history. The fact is, this small clique of creative dreamers are practicing the art of the bluff. In this sense, the Illuminati (though it has successfully created its own thread through history, from the Golden Dawn to Adam Weishaupt, all the way back to the Garden of Eden and the Brotherhood of the Snake) *really* only came into being sometime in the '30s, in the deranged and opium-soaked minds of a bunch of deadbeat, upstart poets and painters. And yet, at the same time, by responding to a deeper, unconscious inspiration common to all artistic minds since time began, these "deadbeats" did indeed join the oldest conspiracy of them all; namely, the conspiracy of the Serpent to open Man's eyes and point the way to Freedom. Their bid is to move beyond the

---

26: For example, Robert Anton Wilson, apparently quoting (the founder of the Bavarian Illuminati) Adam Weishaupt's journal, writes: "I think we should become infamous. In fact, as soon as I have the time and can think of a clever *nom de plume*, I shall write a book denouncing us as scoundrels and miscreants . . . . The world will then believe either that we do not exist, or that we are the embodiment of Machiavellian villainy. Only in that way can we guarantee that those who come to us shall be drawn exclusively from that egregious breed that does not believe all that it reads, that thinks for itself, and that is never influenced either by popular prejudice or by the opinions of alleged 'experts.'" *The Widow's Son* The second part of Wilson's *Historical Illuminati Chronicles* trilogy. The sentiment expressed here, whether authentic or not, equates precisely with Crowley's *Thien Tao; or, The Synagogue of Satan* (in *Knox Om Pax*): "The men who are willing by this means to become the saviors of their country shall be called the Synagogue of Satan, so as to keep themselves from the friendship of the fools who mistake names for things. There shall be masters of the Synagogue, but they shall never seek to dominate."

tyranny of the gods, who—for all their jealously guarded knowledge—are *pretenders*, since *"all gods are poets' images."* (Nietzsche, *Thus Spoke Zarathustra.*)

The influence of this non-political, opium-smoking Illuminati, then, is wholly Imaginal, and not yet actual; it remains to date effective only at a *psychological* level. These Surrealist pranksters, adhering to the central principle of magik, are *intending* themselves into being: by repeatedly suggesting that they wield temporal power, they are slowly convincing the world that they do. The grim fact, known to every magician, is that it is impossible to introduce a new current or idea into the still-standing edifice of an obsolete mythology. The only way for the new myth to emerge is from the *ruins* of the old. But since this edifice must be destroyed from within, must *self*-destruct, in fact, there is no way for any opposing, outside force to accomplish or accelerate this. The new current must enter into the old and transform it from within, but by doing so it is invariably converted *into* the old myth, and so loses its edge, its incentive, and finally its very existence.[27]

*

> The stone which the builders rejected, the same is become the head of the corner: this is the Lord's doing, and it is marvelous in our eyes. . . . And whosoever shall fall on this stone shall be broken: but on whomsoever it shall fall, it will grind him to powder.
> —Matthew 21; 42,44

From a lucid view, the whole paranoid *weltanschauung* of secret societies and occult traditions might best be understood as a metaphor for the separate workings of the two sides of the brain, a dramatization of their gradual efforts *to be reconciled into a single organism.* Paranoid awareness is symptomatic (and symbolic) of the schizophrenia of a species, aptly summed up by the Judaic aphorism: "Let not your left hand know what your right hand is about." The double current (numbered "93" by the Thelemites) is symbolized by the twin waves of the Aquarian Age, which humanity is even now entering.[28] The danger and confusion

---

27: It should be stressed that we are talking here not of individuals, much less of groups—as both tend to fluctuate between the old current and the new—but rather of archetypes or "waves." Hence one wave is gradually converting another, and in the process, annihilating the old channels, rendering them dysfunctional, redundant. Yet it is a *double* current, confusingly enough; hence it is a question rather of redirecting this old current down new channels, from those of restriction and oppression into those of organization and support. This process is itself deceptive, for if the current flows both ways, then what appears to be (in our present terms) "infiltration of the Illuminati by Masonry"—or of art by commerce—may just as well be the reverse. Take the case of Orson Welles, who remained a maverick and a genius to the very end (an end which was anything but bitter). Welles never "sold out," hard as he may have tried to, because "the System" simply didn't know what to do with him. Does this constitute the victory of the artist or of the Industry? Apparently a bit of both; however much Welles retained his personal integrity as an artist, he was for most of his career unable to *work.*

28: 3 X 31 = 93. The ratio, 9:3 = 3:1, the formula of the Trinity. The closest symbolic representation of this is the crossed circle, the glyph of Earth, Gaia, or the Goddess (and also Lucifer!). This glyph stands for the formula $1 + 1 = 0$ (or in Crowley's book, $0 = 2$), the key to the universe, manifestation/conciliation. Philosophically, this might be expressed as yin + yang = Tao, or Father + Mother = Divine Androgyne. The chemical wedding itself. Crowley writes: "VISITA INTERIORA TERRAE RECTIFICANDO INVENIES OCCULTUM LAPIDEM—'Visit the interior parts of the earth: by rectification thou shalt find

arises when one current or faction attempts *to usurp the power or function of the other*. To cite our current example, the old, Judaic myth attempted to assimilate and eradicate the new, Christian one, even while the Christian myth strived, with equal vanity, to supplant the Judaic. In fact, as Jeshua well knew, the one serves to complete and fulfill the other: they are *co-dependent*. Judaism is the foundation of Christianity, and Christianity is the fulfillment of Judaism. Together, once reconciled, they give rise to a new edifice, an edifice which renders both "pillars" obsolete, for they have served their true purpose and evolved gracefully into extinction. So long as there is separation between them, however—suspicion, secrecy, competition—they can never be anything but the ape of their best intentions.

This dichotomy, which is behind and at base of everything that is wrong with today's society, is perhaps most widely recognized as the dichotomy of Church and State. Freemasonry is well-known for its fight to keep the two bodies separate, while the Vatican reputedly wants to unite them. Both are in error, and the error is essentially the same. The Vatican wishes merely to supplant the State *by* the Church, while Freemasonry desires to keep the two at odds. The only sane solution can be to allow them their separate functions, while reconciling them to a single, unified *end*. "Render unto Caesar what is Caesar's, and unto God what is God's."[29]

The paranoid's quest for order and meaning in the world is a seemingly interminable journey into the maze of his own imagination. It is a sustained

---

the hidden stone.' Its initials make the word V.I.T.R.I.O.L, the Universal Solvent (Its value is 726)" (*The Book of Thoth*) . 726 + 3 (i.e., the trinity) = 729, which is the numerical value in gematria of Kepha, or Cephas, i.e., Peter, "the stone." "This number was most important to Plato and the Pythagoreans; not only is it a cube (9x9x9), but it is also a square (27x27), and is associated with the nature of the solar year." (i.e., days and nights, 365 + 364 = 729)—David Fideler. Crowley adds that "This hidden stone is also called the Universal Medicine." To return to the 93 current, Kenneth Grant, in *Hecate's Fountain*, observes that "93 happens to be the number of KOBA (Kaaba), the black stone . . . It is also a number of 'Abyx,' which is described as 'a stone unknown in the world we tread . . . quarried we know not where, but called by the gnomes *abyx*.' The man of Earth [i.e., Jesus] is related to abyx via the gnomes. . . . In this connection it is worth pursuing a hint afforded by the symbolism of the Holy Graal." Peter, being the *stone*, was Christ's chosen successor, hence was given the "keys of Heaven and Earth." And so on, ad infinitum. This is a puzzle best left for the Poets and Paranoids to decipher.

29: As to the supposed "antagonism" between the Vatican and Masonry, we can only say what, in the end, we must say to the dilettante paranoid, with all his grandstanding and conspiracy-a-go-go: Bah humbug! It is simply *elements* of Freemasonry that rise up against *elements* of the Vatican, and vice versa. Both are so thoroughly infiltrated by each another that they are—to all intents and purposes—one and the same (as are the democratic and republican governments in the US, for example). All apparent "in-fighting" is little more than a matter of "keeping up appearances," and amounts to one more smoke screen to blind the public eye. By their fruits shall ye know them. The fruits of Freemasonry are so varied as to be wholly contradictory, however, like a tree that gives both fresh fruit and rotting vegetables at the same time. Who is to sort out the various branches if not the paranoid, for whom the task has become a veritable obsession? In its pure sense, however, Freemasonry is a system of instruction, a higher body of learning, and a dispenser of both knowledge and power; as such it remains, like any other tool, dependent wholly upon those that wield it. The basically *Judaic* flavor of Freemasonry, however, is how we have chosen to fit it into the schemata of paranoid awareness, while the essentially pagan/Gnostic nature of the Illuminati has proved the most rewarding aspect to focus upon. Such identities and definitions are finally arbitrary; just as Christianity was formed from the carefully selected tenets of Kabbala, Hellenism, and Judaism (plus a few Sufi and Dogon nuggets from Africa), so Freemasonry partakes freely of Illuminism, and vice versa.

juxtaposition of the contradictions within his own divided psyche, an exercise in applied schizophrenia by which the world, potentially, begins at last to make sense. There is no option of truly understanding any of this intrigue, however, for its very essence—what attracts and seduces both the ordinary paranoid and the genuine magician—is to be found in a place where "nothing is real," where all facts have begun to blur into fantasy. This is the shadowland of the Twilight Zone, Strawberry Fields, where real is Imaginal and Imaginal is real, where all distinctions have become futile, possibly even fatal. This is the only place the paranoid is truly at home, and likewise the magician. It is a dimension familiar to us all, from dreams and TV shows, a dimension not only of sight and sound, but of *mind*.

Judging by the evidence, paranoid awareness is content with academically insupportable irrationalities that adhere to their own (paranoid) logic. It feels in no way compromised by suggesting that the Catholic Church—the Vatican, as it stands or falls—is not only part of but the very *head-corner-stone* of a "global Judaic-Masonic Conspiracy." (Making Christianity, by this understanding, no less than the Jews' revenge upon the Gentiles!) The bottom line to all the paranoid's relentless paranoia-mongering, however, is that no such thing as Jew or Christian exists; that there *is* no mass and no individual; no world and no conspiracy; and no spoon at all, at all. All these things, when seen from a lucid perspective in which "reality" itself is against us, can *have* no real existence, outside our own demented perceptions of them. What *is* Truth, asked Pilate? 2000 years later, paranoid awareness has finally stumbled upon the answer.

Chapter Five: Ufos

The Wizard of ID

The secret of luminous beings . . . is the fact that we are perceivers."
—Carlos Castaneda, *Tales of Power*

To the paranoid, Ufos do not fit into our current understanding, because, quite simply, they are too *big* to fit there; to put it another way, our current understanding is too limited to accommodate them. This is true also of gods, demons, ghosts, and so forth; nevertheless, all such concepts are already partially incorporated into our belief systems (BS for short), at least so far as we have names for them. In the last fifty years, extra-terrestrials—and by extension "UFOs"—have also become a part of our collective BS, whether or not we choose to *believe* in them. We all know what they are, even if we insist that they are not.[1] Everyone has heard of "UFOs." No one, or at least no one who is telling, knows *what* they are. Everyone (it therefore follows) has an opinion about them. These opinions range from—a lot of bunk (hallucinations, or plain fabrications); to—simple misperception of natural phenomena (stars, planets, satellites, balloons, flocks of seagulls, swamp gas, and so on); secret man-made craft; alien space ships; time-machines; interdimensional (or ultra-terrestrial) vehicles; projections of the collective unconscious; living plasma beings; angelic messengers of God; agents of Satan; portents of the future; living fragments of the Earth Goddess-archetype-re-emerging. And so on, and so forth. Yet all these "explanations"—so far as they claim to be such, and so far as they are final—only constitute more BS. The major flaw in all theories concerning Ufos is that they have all, up to now, been *exclusive*. In other words, each theory insists upon discrediting all other theories in order to thereby validate and consolidate itself, so making the Ufo essentially no different from any other article of faith. Ufology is actually a highly advanced form of xenophobia and, as such, has all the earmarks of a new religion, as well as all the trappings.

Paranoid awareness proposes that, all Un-Founded Opinions aside, "UFOs" are in fact all of the above, at varying times in their "existences," and, in consequence, none of the above. That the Ufo is a phenomenon intimately linked to the act of perception itself, and hence to be approached—with infinite caution—as first and foremost a *human* question. Only by understanding ourselves can we even begin to understand the Ufo. The Ufo, says the paranoid, may be seen as a call to attention,

---

1: "U.F.O" is in fact an all-round misnomer, the phenomena in question, at least *some* of the time, being neither flying nor object; as to it's being unidentified, that's really a matter for argument, after all, depending finally on the imagination of the individual observer. After all, a jumbo jet is a UFO to some hillbilly who has never seen one before. Unidentified by *whom* is the obvious question.

to be acknowledged or ignored but not explained, to be accepted but not understood. At least, not *yet*.

*

I propose the hypothesis that there is a control system for human consciousness. . . Human life is ruled by imagination and myth. These obey strict laws and they, too, are governed by control systems, although admittedly not of the hardware type. If UFOs are having an action at that level it will be almost impossible to detect it by conventional methods. . . . If this is so, the UFOs can never be analyzed or conceived, because they are the means by which man's concepts are being rearranged. All we can do is to trace their effects on humans. . . . What could paranormal phenomena control? I suggest that it is human belief that is being controlled and conditioned.
—Jacques Vallee, *The Invisible College*

For the paranoid, there is no question at all that someone, or something, at this time, is playing with our beliefs, testing—by stretching—the limits of our capacity to accept previously unimagined ideas. Even seen from outside the paranoid's perspective, it is evident that (via the Ufo) a new mythology is being formed—has been formed—and is being steadily extended into the mass consciousness. The modern mythology of Ufos is slowly but surely introducing us to the possibility of contact with a race or species of preterhuman beings. All the apparent secrecy involved is only that: apparent. For whether hoax or truth, it would plainly be possible to keep the matter entirely under wraps. True paranoia is engendered, then, and becomes essential, on realizing that the source of the Ufo mystery—because defined by the very clues that it is providing—can itself *never be identified*. It will always be obscured and disguised by the very evidence which it is presenting.

Paranoid awareness leads us to the following acceptance, as the prerequisite for lucidity: *All belief is a kind of slavery, from which it is necessary to evolve.* In accord with Charles Fort: "We substitute acceptance for belief. That to firmly believe is to impede development. It's like looking for a needle that no one ever lost in a haystack that never was—A seeker of Truth. He will never find it. But the dimmest of possibilities—he may himself become Truth." (*Complete Books*)

Whatever else the UFO phenomenon may be, however, it has undeniable similarities to the initiation techniques of the secret society/schools with which we are now familiar. If we suppose *two possible ends* with any number of variations in between—namely, to enslave or to evolve—then the UFO phenomenon, or "program," might best be seen as serving both of these disparate aims at once. The Ufo appears as a kind of acid test for the individual exposed to it. Those who respond to the unknown by fitting it quickly and rashly into the parameters of the known are merely serving their own beliefs; they are protecting themselves from the onslaught of the irrational. Belief above all needs rational foundation,[2] and this

---

2: For example, the man who believes in God becomes as such a slave to this belief, in that the structure and meaning of his life come to depend upon it. He becomes, quite wittingly, a slave to his "God." So long as this God remains in His heaven, incorporeal, invisible, imperial, mysterious, the man retains a relative degree of freedom; as soon as he allows his belief to creep into the mundane, however,

is apparent enough in the ET/UFO beliefs that have grown up in the last five decades or so.

The program goes something like this: a "transcendental" experience occurs; it is interpreted as "contact from above," whereupon the "beings" in question become for the percipient—by virtue of his belief in them—gods or devils, manifest on Earth. What has occurred is a forced overlap of the Imaginal into the actual, whereupon the percipient's quite harmless, even positive, fantasies or imaginings (concerning the existence of the supernatural) have moved over into belief, and so become dangerously concrete, capable of affecting his actions, thoughts, and feelings. The upshoot is (generally) that our percipient ends up in a white room somewhere, gibbering about entities, on TV talking to Oprah, or dressed in white robes, presiding over a new-age cult somewhere in California.

The genuine paranoid, on the other hand, by no means gives up so easily. In his bid for heightened awareness, he actively strives to meet the challenge that the unknown presents to him. When subjected to an experience of deranging potential, finding all his former ideas about the nature of reality under attack, the paranoid is duty-bound to abandon these ideas, *as far as he is able*; or, at the very least, to radically remodify them. (The alternative to this is to demean and distort his own memories of the experience, to somehow shuffle them to the back of his mind, like so much unidentified debris under the rug.) If allowed to serve its correct function, the encounter with the Ufo will serve not to expand, transform, or amend the paranoid's beliefs, but *to abolish them altogether*. If the basis of paranoid awareness is the unshakeable suspicion that Reality is not only beyond us but against us, we have no choice but to change at a basic, personal level, in order to even begin to understand what is happening to us. Hence, the Ufo experience *forces* us to evolve.

"Close encounters," so-called, either strengthen the percipient's existing beliefs or shatter them entirely; the measure or meaning of any "encounter" lies finally with the percipient himself. The process, be it physical, psychic, dream, vision, or genuine material manifestation, serves by its very nature to separate the wheat from the chaff, the gullible mass from the free-thinking (paranoid) individual. Those willing to surrender their responsibility at the first sign of the Imaginal will be treated accordingly. Those willing to meet the mystery halfway, as active players in the mystery-drama, will be recruited by it, just as artists, apostles, saints, shamans, and magicians throughout history have been recruited, by this very same "force," and so come to realize, finally, that they are the sole authors of their experience.

As to what controls this Imaginal "control system": in the paranoid's final analysis, either it controls itself or it has no controller at all. It is responsive, and the what, when, how, and why of it all depend on the subject of the experiment himself—the observer shapes the phenomenon, by the act of observing it. The experiment is tailored in such a way as to be wholly subjective: it has no rigid form, location, time, manner or purpose.

---

and to become a part of the social realm shared with his fellows, he becomes a slave to the first rogue or priest to cross his path.

If this control system functions (as Jacques Vallee posited) like a temperature gauge—hot in response to cold and vice versa—then we must deduce that what a system for controlling beliefs responds to is—belief. Our present post-industrial age, the recent "magikal revival" notwithstanding, remains the most purely materialist-rationalist period in history. Conversely, never before has there been such a widespread preponderance of strange sightings, bizarre encounters, "abductions," and otherwise fantastic phenomena acting upon or through the Western *weltanschauung*. The Zeitgeist is also poltergeist. From a lucid view, however, it makes perfect sense that this "control system" is responding to the extreme cold of material rationalism with a seemingly inexplicable, all-but irresistible (perhaps even unendurable) *heat-wave* of the irrational.

When it comes to engendering new myths in the collective human psyche and introducing the Imaginal forces of the right brain to the inhabitants of the left, *everything depends on the timing.*

*

Learn to live at a high level of uncertainty.
—Whitley Strieber, *Communion*

The reason some of the most intelligent people in today's world are atheists and skeptics is that they refuse to have their imaginations limited by meaningless definitions, and resent having their mysteries explained away for them. This, of course, would come as news to many atheists and skeptics, driven into intellectual corners as they have been, left to react, savagely, to all the unwelcome BS in the air.[3] The paranoid is temperamentally in the same camp with the atheist and the skeptic, but has voluntarily placed himself down in the trenches with the True Believers whom essentially he so disdains. This is because his paranoia demands precipitation, investigation, empowerment: he is not content to stay in a corner fending off the BS of others, but must actively take the offensive. His method is that of the skeptic, but his end is that of the believer. He attempts to discredit all beliefs as by definition invalid, on the understanding that whatever remains once his attack is completed, must be Truth. Besides God Himself, the Ufo is the ultimate challenge to the paranoid. It is a trick of our perception, by which perception calls attention to itself. It is nothing less than the call to lucidity.

Most researchers have been compelled to admit that the one common feature to all Ufolore is the element of absurdity. There may be terror, there may be wonder, there may be initiation or humiliation, wisdom and benevolence or evil incarnate, but there is invariably some element of trickery at work; even, if seen objectively, of *humor*. There are no certainties in the world of the Ufo, and this would seem to be the primary measure of the encounter, such as it is. The one underlying principal involved is uncertainty, hence the possibility of belief is routed.

3: Were the question left entirely open, a great many of these debunkers, being by and large good thinkers, would come around, in their own good time, to considering the undeniable evidence (be it of "God," "UFOs" or whatever) and advocating of the reality of mystery and the mystery of reality. In short, they are reacting, not against the truth of the concepts God, UFO, etc., but against the tyranny of *words*.

No direct knowledge or *gnosis* is possible where belief is present. Belief acts like a filter between the witness and the experience, a filter through which the truth cannot pass. Initiation into secret societies also has this factor in common with the Ufo experience: before the teaching can really begin, the pupil or neophyte must have all his former beliefs and values questioned, exposed, and finally off-loaded. This puts him in a state of confusion and uncertainty in which he is vulnerable to the new program, the "secret wisdom" of the Order. The Ufo goes beyond any human initiation system, however, for here there is no intermediary between the neophyte (the percipient) and the initiation experience. In some mysterious fashion, the Ufo would appear to *be* the new program. To the paranoid, this means one thing and one thing only: the Universe is now taking on its apprentices *directly*.

*

The black earth is accursed, the Sethian jailer of divine light; the red earth is Horian.
—R.A. Schwaller de Lubitcz, *Sacred Science*

The "golden age" of mythology was a time before paranoia had its *raison d'être*, when the Earth was well, stable and in good health. The paranoid perspective of the 21st century, on the other hand, envisions the Earth as "infected," possessed by unknown intelligences with apparently hostile intent. This has found its mythical expression in popular movies like *The Matrix* and *Final Fantasy*, in which the Earth has been conquered by inorganic beings and humanity is enslaved as a food source. According to paranoid awareness, the human race has indeed been infected by this "foreign legion" of alien entities, and in the process, man has become the carrier-host. While parts of the race are dying of starvation, others are dying of indigestion; meanwhile, the Earth dies of exhaustion. Humanity uses up its energy resources destroying the environment, until all that remains is to succumb to the irascible, irreversible consequences. For the paranoid, it is safe to say that the Earth has been destroyed (i.e., with delayed but inevitable results) a dozen times over, and though any given doomsday scenario may turn out to be a hoax, it's a sure bet to the paranoid that any such deception is only serving to cover up a reality even more horrendous.[4]

The popular if alternative "Gaia" perspective posits that the Earth, like any living organism, has a skin: she has vegetation for hair, rocks and trees for teeth and nails, rivers and streams for blood and circulatory system, the beasts of the land and sea for her cells. By this metaphoric understanding, it would appear that Man is her disease; living parasitically as he does, his function has become that of *the virus*. Certainly, this befits the paranoid's *weltanschauung*, and even begins to suggest a

---

4: See for example, arch-paranoid William Cooper's claim: "Global warming is a hoax. It is easier for the public to deal with and will give the ruling elite more time before panic and anarchy replace government. The reality is that overall global temperatures are becoming lower. Storms are becoming more violent and less predictable. The icecaps at the poles are growing larger. The temperate zones where food can be grown are shrinking. Desertification is increasing in the tropics. An ice age is on its way, and it will occur suddenly." *Behold a Pale Horse.*

reason—at long last—why the nature of his existence seems actively pitted against him. The perspective of the Earth as a living organism also facilitates an acceptance of other, more specific, paranoid concepts. That of a hollow Earth, for example, as proposed over the ages by such venerables as Admiral Bird, Captain Symmes, and Richard Shaver.[5] A profoundly eco-friendly concept, the idea of a hollow earth is an old one, full of charm and poetry. It also finds certain parallels, even confirmations, in the lucid view.[6]

5: "Shaver declared that the interior of the earth is laced with networks of gigantic caves. The total area of the caves is larger than the total area of land on the surface world. The inhabitants of this cavern world are known as the 'abandoneros' as they were abandoned when a mass exodus from the earth occurred approximately 12000 years ago . . . the 'starmen' selected our planet as a space laboratory, transplanting various types of people from different planets onto our earth . . . some species were driven underground to the caverns for their survival . . . these degenerates preyed upon surface humanity through raids on outlying areas. . . . The constant tests of nuclear weapons have destroyed, or cracked, many of the great tunnels." Warren Smith, *This Hollow Earth*

6: Compare it to the teachings of don Juan in Carlos Castaneda's *The Fire From Within*, concerning "the other levels below," and the concept becomes somewhat more palatable to our sophisticated minds. "The ancient seers counted seven levels. . . . Of course by now you realize that to say the depths is only a figure of speech. There are no depths, there is only the handling of awareness. Yet the old seers never made that realization. . . . *When they thought they were descending to the depths, they were, in fact, pushing their assemblage points to assemble other perceivable worlds within those seven great bands.*" (italics mine)

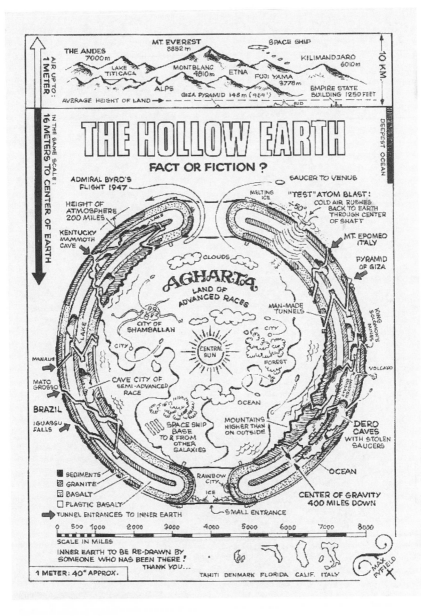

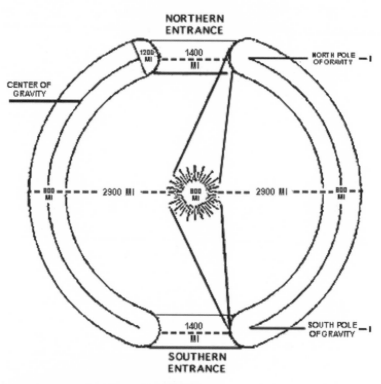

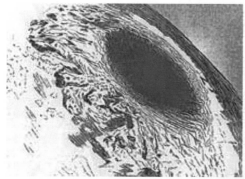

The holes in the poles?

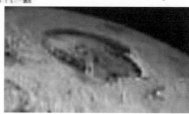

The paranoid needs little substantiation to begin entertaining so attractive an idea as a world hidden beneath the surface of this one. A notion so inspired in its simplicity and directness comes close to forming the very foundation of paranoid awareness. Having admitted that, if the Earth *were* hollow, it would simply *have* to be covered up, paranoid awareness will then state that any argument that the Earth *cannot* be hollow (for example, that we would have noticed it by now) simply doesn't hold up.[7] The only real argument against the Earth being hollow is that it's preposterous to reason, but the paranoid is no more bound to the limits of reason than he is daunted by fear of ridicule. Even rationally and practically speaking, we may ask in what way the idea of an Earth formed like a shell—with (for example) concentric layers of earth, liquid fire, gas and other such chemical compounds within—is any less likely or feasible than the idea of a solid lump of dry mud with a burbling mass of molten larva at the center? Practicing the privilege of his *métier*—the art of forgetting what he has already learnt about the Universe—the paranoid finds that neither idea seems more or less likely than the other.

Mythically, of course, the idea equates with the legends of otherworlds, underworlds, lowerworlds, Hades, Sheol, Hell, Shamballa, Xibalba, Tua; metaphysically, it suggests "inner space," the alternate dimensions or parallel universes of occult lore and modern science. It also serves as an almost perfect symbolic metaphor for the unconscious, fulfilling every requisite of the unexpected that paranoid awareness teaches us to expect of the Universe. And it rather neatly embodies, in the most literal form, the four simple words and the essence of Gnosticism: *the mystery is within.*

Today, the whisper of lucidity informs us that the Earth is stirring in her slumber, being forced to reassert her presence—just as the body must stand up to the oppression of the mind and all the resulting dis-ease—with a plethora of symptoms. If paranoia can lead to awareness, and awareness to lucidity—and if sickness can herald a new kind of consciousness—then Man may soon reclaim the knowledge he has lost, and regain the power he so sorely needs to survive. If not, we will go extinct trying.

If the Earth is a living, sentient being, it follows that all occurrences upon its surface or within its stratosphere must be ordered and regulated by the whole, just as are the blood cells, the movement of bowels, respiration, perspiration, etc, in any other living body. What the paranoid is bound to observe is that things on Earth *do* seem to come and go in cycles, and that it is only when incidents are taken individually that they appear as random. When viewed in relation to other events, over time, a pattern quickly emerges, demonstrated by a close observation of the weather, the behavior of clouds, frequency of storms, earthquakes, floods, cyclones, etc., in the migrational paths of birds and other herd animals from bison to

---

7: One can argue that such a monumental truth could not so long be suppressed, but this is only a presumption. How do we know it couldn't, asks the paranoid? How long was the idea that the Earth was round kept from the so-called "public"? Ancient Egyptians, Mayans and other so-called primitive societies knew very well all about the shape and dimensions of the Earth, so logically this knowledge was never lost, merely suppressed. Apparently someone considered it useful to keep the flat-earth philosophies alive a while longer. This amounts to a scam of equal proportions to that of a possible "hollow earth" cover-up.

tarantulas, or, more cosmically, the paths of comets, meteors, and of course, the stars. Even Ufos are said to appear with more frequency on certain days of the week.

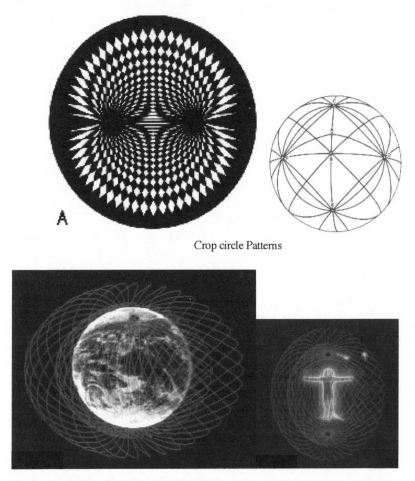

Crop circle Patterns

As above so below: the energy field of the Earth corresponding with the human body

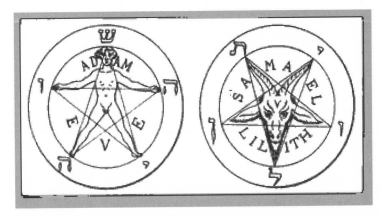

To the paranoid, as much as to the natural scientist, *everything* is regulated, and quite precisely at that. Everything is allocated its particular place and time within the greater design. This greater design has yet to be investigated by orthodox science—which tends to miss the forest for the trees—but in the paranoid's investigations (perhaps because he is so hungry to find any pattern at all) such order easily avails itself. A relationship has frequently been noted between apparently disparate types of "mystery" phenomena, events that seem to have nothing in common besides their bizarre or irrational qualities. This curious fact might be termed "the sympathy of the damned," and suggests that there may even be a common source behind these phenomena. As the nature of all phenomena is energy, invisible and all-pervasive, and as such only occasionally settles into visible manifestation, the lucid view suggests that this energy moves, or manifests, according to natural, terrestrial currents—so-called *leys*—and that these currents form a grid about the Earth, in both space and time.

The next proposition of paranoid awareness is that this external "Earth grid" is contained, much after the fashion of the hologram, as a microcosmic blueprint *within the human body itself.*[8] As such, all these mystery phenomena depend upon the location, as much as on the psychological make up, of the percipient, and consequently, *no separation of subject and object is possible in the Ufo experience.* If so-called "mass-hysteria" (or hallucination) can "explain" anything at all, then it must finally explain *everything*, including the Consensus "reality" that is demanding explanations, and upon which we *all* agree (as a mass, hysterically or otherwise). This understanding is, to the paranoid, perhaps the ultimate mystery of all; because if citizen X can "imagine" a spinning wheel of fire in the sky at the

---

8: "Reactivation of the energy grid. . . will serve to open some or all of the interdimensional doorways which interlink earth with the other locations." (George C. Andrews, *Extraterrestrial Friends and Foes*) And: "certain power spots are holes in this world; if you are formless you can go through one of those holes into the unknown, into another world. That world and this world we live in are on two parallel lines." Carlos Castaneda, *The Eagle's Gift.* Compare to the *brujos'* "description of some beams of light or energy that allegedly crisscross the earth. He said that these beams do not fluctuate as everything else in the universe does, but are fixed into a pattern. This pattern coincides with hundreds of points on the luminous body." Carlos Castaneda, *The Eagle's Gift*

precise moment that citizen Y is "hallucinating" a circle of levitating faeries out in the forest, in the very same spot where, a hundred years previously, citizen Z—a reclusive monk later canonized—underwent the elaborate "fantasy" of full-body levitation before half a dozen witnesses, if all these tales of ordinary madness are admitted to be neither aberrational nor exceptional but, on the contrary, quite the rule on this haunted planet, then the only way we can dismiss the evidence of our senses is—*by dismissing our senses altogether*. Lucidly speaking, this may be our only remaining option.

*

> Analysis of the discourse of abductees consistently reveals a breakpoint in time, after which the percipient leaves normal reality behind. On the "other side" of this boundary, ordinary space-time physics no longer seems to apply, and the percipient moves as if within a lucid dream (or indeed a lucid nightmare) until returned to the normal world. [Jenny] Randles calls this phenomenon "the Oz Factor."
> —Jacques Vallee, *Revelations*

When the individual encounters the Ufo, his world collapses and is immediately replaced by a new world in which nothing is familiar. Like Alice, he is propelled through the looking glass into a land of wonder; once there, there is only one law that seems to apply: *anything can happen*. This, which amounts to no law at all, leads invariably to an absolute loss of certainty, conviction, and clarity in the mind of the percipient: he is freed to sink or swim into the great Beyond. To the paranoid, there is no doubt that, whoever or whatever conceived of this acid-test-cum-cosmic-prank encounter, they adhered to the fundamental laws of evolution, and came up with the human rite of passage *par excellence*. It is an order of experience that, like the god Mercury, makes use of truth and deception with equal indifference, and that most assuredly "has no respect for persons."

As don Juan Matus tells Carlos Castaneda, in *The Fire From Within:* "Something out there is affecting our senses. This is the part that is real. The unreal part is what our senses tell us is there." The experience that the Ufo percipient undergoes is no ordinary hallucination but rather a translation, from one "reality line" (or tunnel) into another. Once contacted, the percipient finds himself in the presence of a force that is by definition impersonal, indifferent, and completely incomprehensible, but which appears to have some specific "business" with the witness. As it proceeds to play upon his perceptions, in true trickster fashion, it first blinds him and then ushers him into *another kind of vision*. The vision, whatever its nature, is invariably tied to the percipient's personal beliefs, expectations, hopes, fears, and so forth. From this perspective—suitably solipsist—the Ufo might best be understood as a sort of autonomous psychedelic agent that zips about the stratosphere, choosing its guinea-pigs and affecting each one in a different manner, but always in a dramatic and phantasmagorical fashion. Like all good psychedelics, the Ufo knocks the subjects off their feet and out of their world, while allowing them to retain a sense of self throughout the "trip." The experiencer of the Ufo has effectively been reprogrammed, in much the same way that hypnotic subjects or

LSD-users are being steadily reprogrammed by their own or others' experiments. John Keel describes the ear-marks of this "fundamental reprogramming process":

> No matter what frame of reference is being used, the experience usually begins with either the sudden flash of light or sound—a humming, buzzing, or beeping. The subject's attention is riveted to a pulsing, flickering light of dazzling intensity. He finds he is unable to move a muscle and is rooted to the spot. Next the flickering light goes through a series of color changes and a seemingly physical object begins to take form.[9]

Such factors are basic to the hypnotic or entrancement strategy of the Ufo, and leave the percipient wide open to suggestion prior to the ensuing alteration of consciousness. There is, of course, an essential complicity between the percipient and the perceived (the Ufo), just as there is between the hypnotist and his subject, or the shaman and his drug (ally). If the human body is itself a sort of Electromagnetic Light Form, it follows that its relationship with the enigmatic Ufo might be considerably more *intimate* than has hitherto been supposed. If the bio-field of the Earth is found to correspond with that of the human body, then the Ufo might be serving as a kind of "bridge" between the two. Paranoid awareness—which attempts to track the events of the actual back to the realm of the Imaginal—seeks always the most empowering interpretation in every mystery. It is therefore drawn to perceive the Ufo as a kind of window, a doorway through which the percipient by the act of looking, may pass, back into the land of Oz whence he came, and know the place at last.

*

Pay no attention to that man behind the curtain!
—*The Wizard of Oz*

If, as geomancy claims, there are certain spots on the Earth—called places of power—where the consciousness of living beings undergoes subtle alterations, then it may be that the Ufo energy field functions, intensely, as a moving power spot of unparalleled influence upon our nervous systems. Just to be near it—sometimes even to see it from a distance—is enough to expose the percipient to an alien source of energy, an energy that is nonetheless particular to the Earth. Directly linked to man's perceptions, the Ufo seems designed or directed towards specific ends, namely, an altered state of consciousness, accomplished by the manipulation of the energy field surrounding the human body.[10]

Ufo energy—termed Orgone by that martyr of paranoia, Wilhelm Reich—is primal energy that by its mere presence awakens atavistic impressions (we might

---

9: John Keel, *The Mothman Prophecies*, pg 163.
10: Just as drugs alter brain chemistry and thereby influence awareness. Nevertheless, all our senses are regulated, even determined (assembled) by our neuro-chemical *responses* to the environment. Hallucination is then defined merely as what other people *don't* see. Provided we can agree on what we see, then it is real. Ergo, if we agree upon a hallucination, it becomes by definition real.

even say memories) in the body and mind of the percipient.[11] The Ufo, as a symbol for the externalized soul as Carl Jung defined it,[12] is beginning to fit rather snugly into the paranoid's acceptance, as the living agent of atavistic resurgence (lately dressed up in the gaudy rags of the New Age Movement). The perceptual shift which the Ufo heralds, says the paranoid, whether due to duress, sickness, pollution, despair, or whatever, is now happening on a global scale. It appears as not merely desirable but as *necessary* for the survival of the race. This movement is occurring first of all within the body of the Earth, bringing all manner of "magikal" phenomena to the fore on a wave of primordial energy. The resurgence is in turn causing a steady and inexorable change in human perception, thereby allowing humanity access to this primal energy, which then gives added weight to the perceptual shift, thereby adding momentum to the Earth awakening, releasing ever greater bursts of energy or paranormal phenomena; and so on, and so forth. There are two basic directions that this movement of perception can take: above and below. Each causes an alignment with a distinct kind of energy. As with the matter and anti-matter particles of the physicists however, it follows by the most scientific of deductions that neither energy can exist in isolation, the one serving to complement and balance the other. Hence they are finally to be understood as *two facets or poles of a single energy.* As a vehicle or aggregate of this primordial energy informing the Universe, the Ufo is not a thing in itself, then, but *a state of fluctuation.* Like fire, the Ufo exists *between* things. The important point about opposing poles, however, is not to confuse their functions.

As Gregory Little notes, in *Grand Illusions,* the Ufo travels freely,

> up and down the electromagnetic energy spectrum assuming a visible form when in the narrow, visible light portion of the spectrum. When the energy moves into the physical form, it often appears from the ultraviolet end of the light spectrum, while the other forms come from the infrared end. When it is in its most "solid" form, it is in the middle of the visible light spectrum, appearing as a luminous or intense white light . . . The two types of energy forces involved appear to be totally separate and unique from the perspective of their intentions; however, their physical appearance can be similar.

11: "'Ea' is Dr Reich's term for what is generally known as UFOs. Close to the core of things as usual, Dr Reich's term is accurate and drawn from experience. 'E' stands for energy and 'a' is for alpha—primordial. We are indeed dealing with primary energy in the UFO field . . . It was his opinion that the Ea vehicles ride the waves on the cosmic ocean of positively orientated life-giving energy, which he termed 'orgone' or 'OR'. Under certain circumstances, the OR energy dies. It then becomes DOR, the death-dealing negative orgone energy . . . DOR manifests in forms such as acid rain, smog, cancer, industrial waste, vehicle exhausts, excrement, etc." George C. Andrews, *Extraterrestrial Friends and Foes*

12: In *Flying Saucers—A Modern Myth of Things Seen in the Sky,* Jung writes on the phenomenon as follows: "On the antique level . . . the UFOs could easily be conceived as 'gods.'. . . They are impressive manifestations of totality whose simple, round form portrays the archetype of self . . . uniting apparently irreconcilable opposites . . . to compensate the split-mindedness of our age. . . . It creates the image of the divine-human personality, the Primordial Man . . . an Elijah who calls down fire from heaven, rises up to heaven in a fiery chariot, and is the forerunner of the Messiah. . . . In these symbols we have a prototype of the Ufo vision, which is vouchsafed to the illuminati. They cannot be heavenly bodies belonging to our empirical world, but are projected 'rotunda' from the inner, four-dimensional world."

Ancient texts say that *these two sides oppose each other indirectly by influencing affairs on earth.* (italics mine)

Lucidly viewed, this force seems every bit as comfortable masquerading as the angels of God as it does the agents of Satan; simultaneously in fact, if they are united by a common Source (and Cause). At this point the Ufo has taken us squarely into the eschatologist's terrain. As a dynamic agent in the grand enactment of Armageddon, the Ufo is a true game player, working on both sides at the same time. If the Ufo also holds sway over divine *gnosis*, however, there can be little doubt that currently we are being presented with the "satanic" aspect of things, for the very good reason that this is the aspect of ourselves that we, as a race, are manifesting. The energy of "the adversary"—much to the grim delight of the paranoid—has come to claim us as its own. This is dramatized by the distinctly demonic abduction scenarios so prevalent at this time, all of which assume the point of view of prey in a predatorial Universe. Because we are unaware of its true nature and what it is after, we have let the Ufo run wild; and any runaway force is liable to be harmful to us. The Ufo devil is an unruly god with no will of his own. It is a god that must be mastered, not only if it is to serve us, but if we are to survive meeting it at all.

*

Isis Descending

The Virgin Goddess (note the spiral vortex over her head)

My serpent goddess, when you come it is like the lightning flash.
—Kenneth Grant, *Hecate's Fountain*[13]

Paranoid awareness defines the Ufo, in its purest manifestation, as an unknown form of Earth energy, both terrestrial and extra-terrestrial at the same time. It perceives a cosmic force based in the Earth's stratosphere which, by coming into contact with the human body, triggers a reaction, a veritable explosion of the primal life-force, the awakening of the beast within or, more esoterically, the Kundalini, traditionally represented by *a serpent*. The Ufo is a god- (or goddess-) form conjured up from the darkest depths of the human psyche; it is exceptional for being seemingly *self*-conjured. It appears as not just a fragment of the collective psyche, but *as that psyche itself*, in symbolic, aggregate form. Is this why it appears in the shape of the disc, saucer, or lens-shape, signifying wholeness and perfection, both portent and portal of (and onto) the next evolutionary step for humanity? The disc shape relates to the eye, to the egg or ovary of the Female, and to the *vesica piscis* ("vessel of the fish") formed by two interpenetrating circles, which is a Gnostic symbol for Christ, as mediator between worlds.[14]

It seems both inevitable and fitting to the paranoid that the Ufo and all it portends should sooner or later be attributed to the works of Satan (the *energeia satanica*). Since the very first appearance of Ufos, they have been attributed by certain (religiously paranoid) groups to demonic or satanic forces. In medieval times, witches were accused of consorting with demons or succubae that behaved in more or less similar fashion to today's "grays."[15] In recent times also, American fundamentalist Christians such as Jerry Falwell, Tex Marrs, and Hal Lindsay have seized upon the Ufo phenomenon and been quick to denounce it as satanic in both origin and intent, as an early manifestation of Antichrist. The arguments are to be found in most "End Times" propaganda: Ufos are seen in the air, Satan rules over all things of the air, etc, etc. Biblical quotations and obscure apocrypha combine to present a fairly profane case for the malevolence of the Ufo. This area of research is

---

13: "The meteor was identified as the flying Kû or the snake Kû, an oblique reference to the Ophidian Current which ancient initiates knew to have entered earth's atmosphere from Outside. The circle of sorcerers which serves this 'poisonous' spirit becomes rich. This belief is reminiscent of its Voodoo equivalent in the serpent goddess Ayida Oeddo, of whom it is said 'my serpent goddess, when you come it is like the lightning flash'... There is yet another type of Kû. It was fabled to excrete gold and silver and to dart about nocturnally, like lightning. 'A great noise causes it to fall.' UFOs are said to fall in a great rush of sound. . . . The Holy Graal is also associated with changing colors. A graal is a 'shallow dish' or 'saucer,' and it is significant that the type of the Goddess is the disc, the whirling wheel that spins when the *akashic* current—of which the *chakra* is a nerve zone—is magically activated. Orange-red, or scarlet is a color predominant in UFO sightings, and Babalon—the Scarlet Woman—has the same number (156) as the sum of the initials UFO. Michael Bertiaux sees in the UFO phenomenon an expression of the basic *chakra* of the primordial Space Goddess, Aditi, who is the dynamic (or feminine) form of Hadit." Kenneth Grant, *Hecate's Fountain*

14: That cosmic vagina, again! "[A] lens is the natural result of the overlapping of two spheres. Is there something to be learned by applying this idea to the lens-shaped UFO? Perhaps some topological truth is implied in the thought that the lens is caused by the over-lapping of one continuum with another." Terence McKenna, *True Hallucinations*

15: There was even a "devil's mark" found on the skin and considered proof of such contact, precisely paralleled by modern-day incision scars (in the shape of a triangle and so forth) found on abductees.

generally ignored or dismissed by the more "serious" ufologists as being unworthy of consideration, but the idea of Ufos somehow representing or embodying the (female) Serpent Kundalini energy of Satan or Lucifer, the "Old Dragon," has proved to be a clue of singular significance for the paranoid, serving as it does to tie together most if not all the scattered strands of his mystery tale, into a single patchwork. Seeing as the strands are so many and so various, and seeing as the patchwork is even now being spun about us, it behooves us to draw any clearer a picture just yet. As a parting thought, however, consider the words of Jesus in Luke 10:18-20:

"And he said unto them, I beheld Satan as lightning fall from heaven. Behold, I give unto you power to tread on serpents and scorpions, and over all the power of the enemy . . . the spirits are subject unto you."

The waking of the Serpent Kundalini and the stirring of the primordial Goddess energy of Earth, corresponding with the arrival (or fall) of Satan with a flash of lightning, and (lest we forget the postmodernist paranoid perspective) the landing of the Ufo? All of this tied up with the individual empowerment of the apostles and the final overcoming of the Adversary?

From an even semi-lucid point of view, this is a potent brew.

Left:" The Baptism of Christ" Fitzwilliam Museum, Cambridge, England Painted in 1710 by Flemish artist Aert De Gelder depicts a hovering saucer shining light down on John the Baptist and Jesus. Right: "The Miracle of the Snow" by Masolino Da Panicale circa 1400 from Florence, Italy, in the Church of Santa Maria Maggiore, depicting Jesus and Mary on lenticular clouds, apparently accompanied by an armada of flying saucers.

Ufos

Chapter Six: Elves

Loving the Alien

Human cloning was developed at the University of Utah at Salt Lake City in 1977. They first aired this on TV as part of a series. They had an alleged human clone on TV that they were interviewing. It didn't talk very well. They showed the original human and the clone. The clone was not all that successful. It took 14 months to generate a fully adult human clone in a tank. . . . The government has a facility for clones. The first one was built in the Mont Hood area . . . Oregon . . . Locations must have stable geomagnetic fields and other special characteristics or the cloning process does not work properly. They can replicate them faster now.
—O.H. Krill, quoted by Jim Keith, *Casebook On Alternative 3*

Outside the claims staked by paranoid awareness, it has now been established that the cloning process is a relatively simple and unproblematic one, already perfected and adapted for use with live-stock. Yet there has, until recently, been next to nothing said on the matter of human cloning. No significant difference has ever been drawn, however, between the process of cloning animals and that of duplicating humans, essentially, one supposes, because there *is* none. Lately there has been some more serious talk concerning the questionable moral implications of human cloning, but even this has been surprisingly half-hearted when considering the vast, almost limitless potential for such a (hypothetical) program. To the paranoid, there is only one reasonable assumption to be drawn from all this: that the technology exists and is already in use, but that it has (like everything else) been kept "under wraps." This in turn suggests to him that the cloning program forms part of some other, more sinister agenda. In regard to this, the paranoid has little trouble hypothesizing the existence, somewhere, of cell-samples of a vast number of persons living (and quite a few dead) in the civilized world. If clones can be "grown" at a relatively low cost and in a limited time span, then it stands to reason (says the paranoid) that there *could* exist, somewhere, a clone for each and every one of us.[1]

1: "The man is not my father. He is a clone, a double created by the CIA and alien forces. It is only a small part of a greater plan to overthrow the U.S government, and possibly the human race . . . a girl . . . related the story to me of how seven of her friends had also been replaced . . . they disappeared for a week, only to come back with different personalities." Gary Stollman, in a letter he gave to newsreader David Horowitz (on August 19 1987, at KNBC TV, L.A), and commanded him at gunpoint to read. As it happened, someone switched to a commercial, the letter was read into a vacuum, and no one ever heard it. Stollman was apprehended and found to be wielding an empty B.B gun. He was subsequently declared insane.

A leading propagator of paranoid awareness, Valdamar Valerian, presents a classic scenario with precision and lucidity: "A lot of evidence started to surface . . . that political figures have been undergoing a process of duplication. During this process, the individual's responses, memories, and habit patterns are copied from the human to be duplicated. The original can then be preserved or processed into basic biological components. The clone will then function as the original, except that the entity is under alien control."[2]

At about this point, the paranoid begins to lose all footing in "the real world," and any "serious-minded" person (or self-respecting human) will discontinue the conversation. The paranoid will shrug and shake his head. He alone has contrived to discover a secret agenda behind all the mythological *doppelgangers* which have been lurking in the darker corners of myths and faery tales, throughout recorded history and in all known cultures. The paranoid's argument gains a certain credibility when he insists that—at a *metaphoric* level—this very end (race replacement) is what all religion, science, politics, art, mythology—and even biology itself—*are singly and collectively dedicated towards realizing.* (In a word, evolution.) The better is the enemy of the good; all improvement or advancement is necessarily *overthrow.*

By the particular logic of paranoia, then, if not yet from a fully lucid view, it stands to reason that this hypothetical *coup du monde* would have to wait until the balance had shifted, from the old to the new, in order that the soon-to-be obsolete humans—becoming aware of their terrible plight—could in no way threaten to hinder the final coming of the "Master Race." The paranoid is not embarrassed by any parallels that may exist between such a scenario and B sci-fi movies of the '50s (or '80s horror movies). Life imitates art, after all; at least, it does when seen from a lucid view.[3]

2: *Matrix II: The Abduction and Manipulation of Humans Using Advanced Technology.* Elsewhere the report continues (quoting an unnamed source): "This awareness indicates that the creatures themselves carry certain subconscious programmings similar to that of an entity who is in a kind of coma or zombie state . . . there are also beings on this earth created as doubles . . . these entities in appearance have, until last year in February (1977), had certain types of characteristics that could be distinguished—that they showed no Adam's apple; they did not eat in public, for they have no need for food. They used pills, and when caught in a situation whereby they were required to eat, would eat only soup or light salad—a very small amount. . . . these entities generally had a mottled skin, something like pizza crust. . . . a walk that was reminiscent of a penguin or duck, a kind of waddle back and forth. This awareness suggests that the information being given presently not being given to allow entities to become paranoid and search out the synthetics in their midst and begin some kind of persecution drive . . . these entities themselves are slaves . . . these entities as being created from an action similar to cloning, yet in part using certain flesh from animals or humans, particularly common is the use of the cerebral and nerve system of the cow . . . these synthetics are indeed living creatures in which astral beings may enter to work through upon the physical plane . . . there are created sets of synthetics who are identical in appearance, but are placed in various areas so that they are not spotted or recognized as being the same person in two locations." (pg 393-4)

3: This "Master Race Overthrow" scenario is perhaps the oldest, most favored of all sci-fi conspiracy sagas and persecution fantasies, and is more or less perfectly expressed in the first two movie versions of *Invasion of the Body Snatchers.* Paranoid awareness assures us however that, when an idea occurs and recurs *as fiction,* this in no way discredits it in the realm of *fact.* (On the contrary, it only lends an added degree of pertinence to the scenario.) For the sake of argument, if such a thing *were* happening as it were under our noses, it seems likely that, denied any rational outlet in conscious awareness, it would inevitably surface, as it were imaginally, in the dreams, nightmares, and fantasies of the race, namely, as *myth.* The

*

You have conquered and I yield. Yet, henceforward art thou also dead—dead to the World, to Heaven, and to Hope! In me didst thou exist—and, in my death, see by this image, which is thine own, how utterly thou has murdered thyself.
—Edgar Allen Poe, *William Wilson*

The strain which paranoid awareness, when applied to actual history, places upon reason and common sense is more than most of us can stand, even for a little while; hence the necessity of taking refuge in the Imaginal perspective eventually arises.

Occult lore teaches that man has more than one body. At a more conventional level, the split between "soul" or *energy body* and the physical vessel is represented by the (somewhat simplistic but useful) left/right brain dichotomy. Inside every man's skull, two minds coexist and vie for power. The two sides of the brain might be imagined as two chambers with a single passage between them; this passage must be opened but the walls left intact, for if the two chambers are united too soon, there will be no possibility of balance or flow between them.[4] This can be seen in the legends of the *doppleganger*. A man cannot live with his double, obviously, lest he go mad. In some versions of the legend, even to meet the doppleganger face to face is fatal; like particles of matter and anti-matter, like Cain and Abel, the one is annihilated and absorbed by the other. Yet neither can the two halves remain too long apart, for to do so will cause them both to become dissociated, dysfunctional, or deranged. When denied, the shadow side surfaces sooner or later. Eventually the double *will* appear, and will be anything but friendly, having become the unreasoning embodiment of all that we fear and dread in ourselves.

Free from such denial, paranoid awareness posits the idea of consciousness constructing the body as a *vehicle*. As the body adopts its own point-of-view, consciousness becomes a prisoner *inside* this vehicle, a slave to its "laws." Containers keep breaking, falling away, but consciousness has acquired the habit of the human form, and goes on making new containers to enter into, where it again forgets itself, and becomes a slave to its servant.[5] In *dreams*, consciousness is temporarily freed from this predicament, and is able to exist independently of the body. If consciousness is the basis of experience, it follows that *dreaming*, as such, is potentially every bit as real as waking life. What occurs in *dreaming* is to the

---

paranoid has no doubt this is true—whether it might be *literally* true is something he prefers to leave open, at this time. Lucidly speaking, myth is greater than reality, anyway.

4: "The easiest way to resolve this problem is to separate the two. . . . Only when they are undeniably separate can awareness flow from one to the other. That is what sorcerers do. . . . The double is the energy source. The physical body is merely the receptacle where that energy has been placed." Taisha Abelar *The Sorcerers' Crossing*.

5: The double is indeed the soul, whose "secret life" remains hidden from the rational mind behind a veil of forgetfulness. "The systematic interaction warriors go through in states of heightened consciousness is only a device to entice the other self to reveal itself in terms of memories. This act of remembering, although it seems to be only associated with warriors, is something that is within the reach of every human being; every one of us can go directly to the memories of our luminosity with unfathomable results." Carlos Castaneda, *The Eagle's Gift*

paranoid not merely the brain working off residual anxieties but an independent life-force, unleashed during the temporary suspension of *reason*.

The goal of lucid dreaming is to bring the same measure of reality or continuity (attention) to our dreams that we have in waking life; in exchange, it follows that we may bring some small measure of dreaming—spontaneity and freedom—to our waking lives. What this quintessential sorcery endeavor amounts to is individual consciousness creating for itself *a new form*, with new laws and new faculties. In a word, a second body.[6] This second body amounts finally to a new reality: what I have called the lucid view. The energy body has all the appearance of solidity, as well as all the benefits—volition, tactility, visibility, the capacity to affect its surroundings directly, but it is not solid. Nor is it defined or restricted by any of the natural laws that pertain to solid bodies. It is energy without mass, form without structure, mind without matter, spirit without flesh. Magik and paranoid awareness (as well as Surrealism) insist upon the need to close the abyss that lies between *dreaming* and waking consciousness. This is the means of bringing the two bodies, or attentions, into harmony, and only so can peace be made with "the double."

*

I tell you, in that night there shall be two *men* in one bed; the one shall be taken, and the other left.
—Luke 17:34

As don Juan remarked to Castaneda (in *The Art of Dreaming*), the timeless folklore of the devil bartering with man for his soul in return for immortality is perhaps the last residue of ancient knowledge of this mystery to end all mysteries.

In occultism, it is not the body, as such, that restricts us, but our *idea* of the body, and the mind's complete identification with it. To break out of the vicelike grip of this identification, it is necessary to lead *reason* into the Imaginal realm, and there expose and invalidate all its petty "laws" and assumptions about continuity. In order to accept the reality of the impossible, one must first doubt the possibility of "reality"; this process is described in the journey of the shaman to the lowerworld and his dismemberment by spirits or demons (symbolizing the transference of awareness from one body to the next). As Mircea Eliade notes, such a rite of passage is common to most, if not all, shamanic cultures, whether performed symbolically by fellow shamans or otherwise "magikally" in the astral realm (lowerworld) by the shaman's allies:

The candidate's limbs are removed and disjointed with an iron hook; the bones are cleaned, the flesh scraped, the body fluids thrown away, and the eyes torn from the sockets . . . they cut his head open, take out his brains, wash and restore them, to give him clear mind to penetrate into the mysteries of evil spirits, and the intricacies of

---

6: This energy configuration, generally known as "soul"—as distinct from spirit—is something that we are born with but almost invariably lose touch with over time; hence it is something that has to be rediscovered (or retuned) *during one's lifetime*, in order to even "exist." The double as such is this perfected soul, a whole new body, of its own substance—pure energy of awareness—and is placed by occultism in natural opposition to the solid body.

disease; they insert gold dust into his eyes to give him keenness and strength of sight powerful enough to see the soul wherever it may have wandered; they plant barbed hooks on the tips of his fingers to enable him to seize the soul and hold it fast; and lastly they pierce his heart with an arrow to make him tender-hearted, and full of sympathy with the sick and suffering.[7]

It is this *reconfiguration* that makes of the ordinary aspirant a full-blown "skywalker" or shaman, capable of acts and feats beyond the imaginations of ordinary men.[8] The goal of the *dreamer* is to overcome the tyranny of *reason*, liberate his awareness, and fly free upon the wings of perception. This goal is realized when, and only when, his energy body or double successfully *overthrows* his physical body. The emergence is by definition explosive, as Kundalini rises, the Earth shakes, lightning flashes, and Satan walks the Earth. By such a process of awakening or empowerment, the *dreamer* has become "a devil," a skywalker, a Superman able to move mountains, not by faith but by sheer *will*. He is a god. Yet in his own mind (be it ever so lucid), he is nothing but a dream.

*

The fairies are "of a idle nature betwixt man and Angel" and are, as other folklore sources suggest, the angels cast out of heaven at the fall.
— Stewart Sanderson, introduction to *The Secret Commonwealth*

Belief in "alien abduction" is now a world-wide phenomenon of equal influence and prevalence as Faerylore once was. As such, the alien abduction scenario is probably the most outstanding case in the annals of paranoid awareness of the dangers and trappings of reducing the Imaginal to the strict boundaries of the actual. At the same time, it is also the most pervasive case of paranoid awareness entering into Consensus reality since the witch-hunts of the so-called "Dark Ages." Although it remains strictly outside the concerns of serious-minded intellectuals and the researches of orthodox science, just about everyone in Western society today has been exposed—at least marginally—to the predominant abduction folklore, if only through TV commercials, coffee mugs, and *South Park*. For those humans who opt not to ignore the subject entirely, "false-memory-syndrome" is now the

---

7: Also described is the "Bird-of-Prey-Mother," which "shows itself only twice: at the shaman's spiritual birth, and at his death . . . When the soul has reached maturity, the bird carries it back to earth, cuts the candidate's body into bits, and distributes them among the evil spirits of disease and death. Each spirit devours the part of the body that is his share; this gives the future shaman power to cure the corresponding diseases." Mircea Eliade, *Shamanism: Archaic Techniques of Ecstasy*. The dismemberment rite finds a curious parallel in Carlos Castaneda's *Tales of Power*, when don Juan and Genaro are teaching Carlos to "dream the double." Castaneda writes, "I . . . had a most unusual sensation. My body fell apart! It was as if I had been a mechanical toy that simply broke up into pieces. I had no physical feelings whatever, and neither had I any fear or concern. Coming apart was a scene that I witnessed from the point of view of the perceiver, and yet I did not perceive anything from a sensorial point of view. The next thing I became aware of was don Genaro was manipulating my body. I then had a physical sensation, a vibration so intense that it made me lose sight of everything around me."

8: "If our awareness is tied to the double, we are not affected by the laws of the physical world; rather, we are governed by ethereal forces. But as long as our awareness is tied to the physical body, our movements are limited by gravity and other constraints." Taisha Abelar, *Sorcerers' Crossing*.

accepted means of dismissing what is plainly too bizarre a possibility ever to be taken seriously. It was accordingly snapped up by all the major media. (Hey presto! The handy, human-friendly answer to SRA is—FMS!) However well this pseudo-explanation may enable humans to dismiss the alien abduction phenomenon without their having to think about it, it is considerably less effective when applied to old world Faerylore, which dates back as far as history itself. (Was "FMS" around in the Middle Ages, I wonder?)

Even scientifically speaking, the criteria for accepting or rejecting any given "explanation" must be not how likely or how *reasonable* (or how appealing) it is, but rather—how adequately it *explains* the available data. (Is it overly demanding of the paranoid to ask that the explanations actually explain *something*?) In the case of alien abduction, this data (too vast and too well-documented for summation here) covers such a wide spectrum of beliefs, circumstances, and possibilities that it behooves us to dismiss it all as "mass hallucination" (assuming we even knew what mass hallucination *was*). To the paranoid, the possibility that what seems to be happening *is* in fact happening is the most acceptable, as well as the most logical, option. If we assign an unknown, obscure, and seemingly supernatural phenomenon (abduction) with an unknown, obscure and seemingly supernatural origin (aliens), then we are at least keeping within the parameters of logic. The paranoid has one primary advantage over the common man who believes that all there is to reality is what he sees. Since paranoid awareness already accepts that reality is a mystery designed to ensnare us, it requires no great leap to accept the possibility of "beings from another world." Sooner or later, the paranoid must accept the inevitability of the impossible infringing upon the everyday, and blowing it to smithereens.

*

If they are not from our universe it could be necessary for us to understand them *before* they can emerge into our reality. In our universe, their reality may depend on our belief. Thus the corridor into our world could in a very true sense be through our own minds.
—Whitley Strieber, *Communion*

Whether we like it or not, we have countless literature offering thousands upon thousands of individual testimonies of intense and extremely *personal* encounters with beings that can only be described (one way or another) as "alien." These "close encounters" are often—but not always—accompanied by sightings of the Ufo, either on the land or in the sky, thereby impressing the percipient with the *extraterrestrial* nature of the encounter. Yet the primary quality of these experiences—and one reason they have proved such a slippery subject for science to come to grips with—is that of a dream or vision, in which time loses its meaning, matter its solidity, and the laws of nature their sovereignty. Yet physical traces remain, even when there is no conscious memory of how they got there.[9] Many

---

9: Burns, scars, needle marks etc, may draw the subject's attention to a blank in his memory, a feeling of unease, of apparently unfounded fear or revulsion, a sense of being watched, stalked, even of being controlled. This feeling gradually gives way to actual memories of the "abduction experience."

subjects only ever discover these buried "memories" through hypnosis; hence there is an understandable degree of skepticism, and much talk of "false memory syndrome." The frequent comparison of the abduction experience to rape is presumably due to the fact that, in both cases, the subject suffers an intense sense of violation, regardless of whether s/he "asked for it" at a deeper, unconscious level. The more sexually-orientated abductions—which describe genital and anal examinations, the insertion of needles and rods, extraction of bodily secretions, blood, saliva, sperm, vaginal fluids, etc—are indeed tantamount to a kind of rape for the average person. Beyond all doubt, the "aliens" have little time for social niceties, and seem to be quite indecently preoccupied with our mating rituals.[10]

From a lucid view, miracles are not the exception but the rule. On the other hand, from the paranoid perspective, there is always a practical, scientific and natural (however miraculous) explanation for them. Take the Virgin Birth for example. There are countless recent cases of pregnancies in which the hymen of the mother was found to be intact, thus establishing that—by technical definitions at least—virgin births are far from restricted to Mary, and in fact quite commonplace. Equally tantalizing to the paranoid is the medical testimony of interrupted pregnancies or "disappearing fetuses" in which gestating children vanish mysteriously from the womb after a given period (usually three months). These testimonies have naturally been delegated to the ranks of "the damned," for the very good reason that no acceptable explanation has yet been found (the key word being "acceptable").

In paranoid awareness, three different points of view or "lores" are neatly synthesized in the phenomenon of interrupted and/or virgin pregnancy. The oldest and most poetic of viewpoints belongs to faerylore (later denounced as demonology by the Catholics). Secondly, in the process of further obscuring the forbidden lore by appropriating it for its own, the Catholic Church offered up its own version of the Mystery of Mysteries and called it the Virgin Birth. Lastly, today, free from quaint superstition and religious awe, we have the up-to-the-minute scientific version, that of (interstellar?) artificial insemination. All these apparently disparate, even antagonistic beliefs relate to the same recurring phenomenon, however, namely: non-human, presumably supernatural intervention by some undefined otherworldly intelligence in the affairs of men (and the wombs of women).

Although the Bible tends to avoid all references to angels in any way *orchestrating* the creation of Mankind (it omits the idea of evolution entirely), it does suggest that they were instrumental in this creation. When the so-called "Sons of God" came down to mate with the reputed "daughters of men"—having seen that they were fair—can we not assume that these angels were following—or at least

---

10: "The phenomenon has an almost pornographic relationship with our mating practices. One of its most celebrated games is the manipulation of romantic relationships. Early investigators of the fairy episodes, such as novelist Sir Walter Scott, noted that fairies seemed to delight in bringing people together and fostering love, or indulging in conspiracies to force lovers apart." John Keel, *The Mothman Prophecies.* "There's an esoteric tradition that the genes, the matings, are where it's all being run from. It is how I think a superextraterrestrial would intervene. It wouldn't intervene at all; it would make us who it wanted us to be by controlling synchronicity and coincidence around mate choosing." Terence McKenna, *The Archaic Revival*

anticipating—some kind of divine command? At the same time, it might be simplest to equate this "going down" (to investigate the matter) with the fall of the angels *per se*. In which case, sex is seen to be, biblically speaking at least, the *sine qua non* of sin or *hubris*. Of course, sex and knowledge are more or less synonymous to God, anyway.

The temptation or seduction of Eve by the Serpent (which led to the birth of Cain) seems to have been a fair exchange however—knowledge for knowledge. By such an exchange, the god gets to know the pleasures of the flesh, and the animal may taste the wonders of Spirit. This is "knowledge of good and evil."[11]

Lest we forget, the quote from Genesis 6 is as follows (NB: The flood follows immediately after this):

> The sons of God saw the daughters of men that they *were* fair; and they took them wives of all which they chose. And the Lord said, My spirit shall not always strive with man, for that he also is flesh; yet his days shall be 120 years. There were giants in the earth in those days; and also after that, when the sons of God came unto the daughters of men, and they bare children to them, the same became mighty men which were of old, men of renown.

I will go out on a limb now, and give these angels some credit for acting angelically, and not merely like human beings. If so, might not the purpose of such a *rendez-vous* be something besides simple pleasure—might it not have been some sort of divine imperative? The incubation of a new race of "giants," perhaps? Whatever the case, said program did not (at that time) work out, evidently, judging by the current state of affairs on this planet at least. It appears (based on the reputation of these fallen angels today) that something went drastically wrong. Whatever it was, it resulted in the banishment of the sons of God to the earth realm, where they have been blamed for everything and anything that went pear-shaped ever after. All so far so good in the land of myth. As evidence of ET interbreeding with humanity, however, this is less than conclusive, obviously.[12] The occultist view is nothing if not enigmatic.

11: "The essence of the matter may be summed up as follows: The emissaries of the Old Ones seek nourishment of a kind that is available on earth only *via* the lunar *kalas* of the nubile human females." Kenneth Grant, *Hecate's Fountain* "*Kala* is a Sanskrit word meaning vaginal vibration or a period of measured time. It also meant emanation of a divine essence and was represented by a flower, star, perfume or ray. Kalas are also represented by the different paths on the cabalistic Tree of Life." Peter Moon, *The Pyramids of Montauk*

12: One interpretation might be that "Sons of God" = spirits or souls, and "daughters of men" = bodies. The angels or archons had an *urge, prematurely*, to "get on with the Plan" to spiritualize matter, but in the process—somewhat ahead of schedule—they ended up ensnared by their own devices or desires. They found that, having started a process that was millennia in the making, they had no way of returning *until the job was done*. Hence "the angels were cast out," becoming our familiars, the faery folk, Gentry, or "the secret commonwealth" of Earth. "The Bible states that they fell to earth like lightning—a fitting and appropriate image for an energy form banished from the far end of EM spectrum to the areas near the visible light wavelength." Dr Gregory L. Little, *Grand Illusions*. The faeries were "the angels who had not quite fallen (they did not join Satan's rebellion but were, so to speak, fellow-travelers)." Patrick Harpur, *Daimonic Reality*.

Let us climb a little further out on that limb. If sex was something that early humanity had only experienced as a purely procreative, animal function, then the advanced sexual techniques of the God-men may well have proved too much for these earth-bound creatures. They would have been overwhelmed by the sheer intensity of their senses. So at least H. P. Blavatsky's (only mildly paranoid) *Secret Doctrine* has it,

> The sin was not in using these newly developed powers, but in *misusing* them; in making of the tabernacle, designed to contain a god, the fare of every *spiritual* iniquity. . . . It was not in the programme of natural development that man—higher animal though he may be—should become at once—intellectually, spiritually and psychically—the demi-god he is on earth, while his physical frame remains weaker and more helpless and ephemeral than that of almost any huge mammal. The contrast is too grotesque and violent; the tabernacle much too unworthy of its indwelling god. The gift of Prometheus thus became a CURSE.

This might help explain why (in Genesis) the children of these couplings were feared and shunned by their fellows—as was Cain—as freaks or monsters. Secretly of course, they were worshipped as heroes, but only once they'd been banished to a safe distance and left to found their own civilization. The "giants," along with the "fallen angels" who fathered them, were forced by circumstances to go underground (mythically if not historically speaking). Having learnt from their mistake (lust for result?), our fallen angles and their offspring devoted themselves to finding "a possible and harmless method of correspondence betwixt men and them, even in this Lyfe."[13] To this end, they adapted their methods to a more covert agenda, and so became the Faery, and latterly, the "alien presence." And thus continues the secret seduction/initiation of the human race into the still forbidden mysteries of "alien love." In a nutshell.

*

13: Robert Kirk, *The Secret Commonwealth*

The cover image from Whitley Strieber's *Communion*, painted by Ted Jacobs

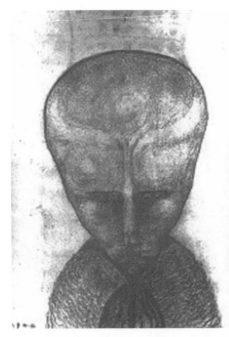

Aleister Crowley's portrait of Lam

Ancient artifacts depicting humanoids suspiciously resembling space people

Various alleged, less than conclusive, photographs of "the alien"

What we have here is a complete theory of contact between our race and another race, nonhuman, different in physical nature, but biologically compatible with us. Angels, demons, fairies, creatures from heaven, hell, or Magonia: they inspire our strangest dreams, shape our destinies, steal our desires. . . . But who are they?
—Jacques Vallee, *Passport to Magonia*

According to paranoid awareness, "Faeries," much like "Angels," is a blanket term for a host of inorganic, often invisible intelligences and all manner of diverse forces. Those of the lower, or denser, realms of earth are referred to as gnomes, goblins, trolls, dwarves; those of the water kingdom as nymphs and undines, those of the air, elves or sylphs; and finally those of fire are known as salamanders. In *The Secret Commonwealth* we learn that, "Many of them are crafty and bitter and menacing. Creatures of an unpredictable and sinister power, they in some way threaten man's day-to-day existence; and in order to allay that threat, they have to be placated." (Stewart Sanderson)

The faeries have often been said to abduct children in the night, and to have had sexual exchanges with humans, with the apparent end of interbreeding.[14] "The motive assigned to fairies in northern stories is that of preserving and improving their race, on the one hand by carrying off human children to be brought up among the elves and to become united with them, and on the other hand by obtaining the milk and fostering care of human mothers for their own offspring."[15] Like the modern "Grays," faeries were said to be of a dying race that needed to perpetually regenerate its stock; in relation to this, they were often accused of subjecting people to bizarre forms of torture or "experimentation," carrying them confused and hallucinating to Faeryland in some magikal manner, giving them strange drinks or food-stuffs, and piercing them with long metal instruments or needles.

In common with the Ufo, faeries tend to behave exactly like imaginary beings; as a result that is generally what they are considered to be. When unhappily pinned down to actual, organic (or at least visible) existence, however, these beings tend to fall into two distinct categories, never very clearly distinguished in ET lore. According to leading exponent Whitley Strieber,[16] there is a tall, thin, more refined type—often described as fair-skinned (tan, beige, or white)—and a short, stocky, more "condensed" type, often described as dark gray- or blue-skinned. These two types seem to be roughly synthesized into composite form as the "Grays," critters generally blamed for the majority of ET activity in this vicinity. Down to the color

---

14: "They take the whole body and soul, transmuting the body to a body like their own." Walter Yveling Evans Wentz, *The Fairy-Faith in Celtic Countries, its Psychological Origin and Nature*, quoted by Jacques Vallee, *Passport to Magonia.* "Children have been disappearing in large numbers for centuries all over the world, and most of these cases have remained unsolved. In the Middle Ages it was popularly believed that fairies and leprechauns frequently stole children away. The Indians of North and South America also have many myths and stories about children being kidnapped by the little people. The notion that parahumans kidnap children is deeply entrenched in every culture." John Keel, *Our Haunted Planet.*

15: Edwin S. Hartland *The Science of Fairy Tales,* quoted by Jacques Vallee, *Passport to Magonia*

16: Strieber was for a time the most reliable public "participant" testifying to abduction experiences. His books *Communion* and *Transformation* (and also *Majestic*) remain unequalled in the field. Later books by Strieber fail to substantiate this early promise, however, with the notable exception of *The Key.*

of their skin, the Grays are unpleasant, sickly sorts, attributed with all manner of malevolent activities. In post-Tolkien faerylore, Elves and Gnomes may work on the same team (as do the two types described by Strieber), but they seem essentially opposed in both character and function, much like the angels and demons of theology.

Popular mythology has the Grays as a dying race suffering from atrophied DNA, usually attributed to a nuclear war in their distant past. This sickly intruder is accused of feeding off humans and mutilating cattle. Like a cosmic vampire, we are told, it finds a temporary "fix" in red corpuscles and glandular secretions. This scenario, however unworthy of the lucid view, offers intriguing parallels with the less contaminated folklore of previous centuries. Faeries were likewise reputed to use human stock to replenish their own race, and the lore of succubae and goblins, vampires and suchlike, is clearly cut from the same mythological cloth.[17] For the paranoid, imposing this melodramatic ET scenario upon the still largely unformed abduction data is fatal, and amounts to the slaying of his imagination in its crib. It lends a malignant, all-too-human quality to what is best left, for now, in the realm of the faeries.

Whatever these grotesque activities might amount to—be it race madness or something even more mystifying—there can be little doubt that something is afoot. Too many disparate sources have made the same claims or indulged in similar fantasies to dismiss the whole thing as so much smoke without fire. It is up to the paranoid to siphon off all the muddy bathwater while holding on to the baby. Referring to more esoteric sources for support (H.P Blavatsky's *The Secret Doctrine* again), "Occult philosophy teaches that even now, under our very eyes, the new Race and Races are preparing to be formed, and that it is in America that the transformation will take place, and has already silently commenced. Mankind, in its present state, has thus been formed certainly, for the greatest part, by the successive crossing of a number of races *at present undetermined.*"

With this in mind, the paranoid asks himself: if such a new race, after many millennia, were nearing its completion—would we really expect it to spring up out of nowhere? A virgin birth is one thing; a birth without a womb is something else entirely. Most telling of all are the stories of abductees (generally female) being taken aboard interstellar nurseries filled with hybrid-like alien babies, all in dire need of (human) love and attention.[18] This spell-binding scenario is no more new to

---

17: "They feed mostwhat on quintessences, and AEthereal Essences: the pith and spirits only of Womens milk feed their children, being artificially convey'd (as air and oyl sink into our Bodys) to make them vigoruous and fresh." Robert Kirk, *The Secret Commonwealth.* Compare this with Valdamar Valerian ET lore (from *Matrix II*): "The Greys consume nourishment through a process of absorption through their skin. This process . . . involves spreading a biological slurry mixture that has been mixed with hydrogen peroxide . . . onto their skin." NB: "The vampire may need marriage and blood, but the governing body of his life is lunar." Nina Auerbach, *Our Vampires, Ourselves.* The author quotes Boucicault's vampire Alan Raby referring to the Moon as "Fountain of my life!" and points out that the original vampire of mid 19th century literature lived off the rays of the Moon, only later becoming "bestialized" (or literalized?) to the point of requiring actual physical blood for his survival.

18: These abducted females are required to play the role of nannies or surrogate mothers to tiny, painfully delicate, almost ethereal beings, to touch them and hold them and nurture them with human

the ET-BS than anything else. As Robert Kirk notes in *The Secret Commonwealth*: "Women are yet alive who tell they were taken away when in Child-bed to nurse ffayrie Children, a lingring voracious image of theirs being left in their place (as if it were som insatiable spirit in an assumed bodie)."[19]

Paranoid awareness is off and running. Robert C. Girard (in *Futureman*) states, "This transformation process is taking place in an incubatory medium somewhere between our 3-D octave and the multi-dimensioned octave of our alien geneticists. . . . Those alien babies are listless and without a will of their own to live because they have no soul. They are empty in that respect because *it is our souls which will animate them when the time comes*." (Italics mine, nuff said.)

*

> I term the Immortal One a plasmate, because it is a form of energy; it is living information. It replicates itself—not through information or in information—but as information. The plasmate can crossbond with a human, creating what I call a homoplasmate. This annexes the mortal human permanently to the plasmate. We know this as the "birth from above" or "birth from the Spirit." It was initiated by Christ, but the Empire destroyed all the homoplasmates before they could replicate.
> —Philip K. Dick, *Valis*

To attain the lucid view, the paranoid is duty-bound to entertain certain possibilities otherwise unthinkable to the serious-minded person. These are as follows. Firstly, that in floating laboratories and secret chambers around, above or within the Earth, a Coming Race is being bred and perfected.[20] Secondly, that a new world is in the making, hidden behind the veil of the old one, awaiting its moment to emerge. And thirdly, that the apparently preterhuman engineers of this *coup du monde* are in fact working alongside—and may even be inseparable from—those human (or apparently human) agents (already identified by the paranoid as "Custodians") dedicated to the destruction of humanity. From a lucid view, the two agendas may be seen as proceeding hand in hand, like Christ and Lucifer, walking down the aisle to the Eschaton.

---

love. The women are all told the same thing: that they are the mothers of at least one of the children (but rarely told which one), that these creatures were incubated in specially chosen human wombs and, after the designated, three-month period, were removed to complete their development elsewhere. The hybrid children, part human part alien, are sickening due to a lack of mother-love. Without this human touch they cannot survive in the cold, impersonal, laboratory-like environment of their keepers. Compare this last point to (scholar of paranoia) George C. Andrews' description in *ET Friends and Foes*: "The abductee was placed in front of a TV screen, through which he was obliged to watch for a full 24 hours what the clone was doing in his own home." And about another case: "Her body was being operated by a Gray just as a human drives an automobile."

20: "Am I a Spaceman? Do I belong to a new race on earth, bred by men from outerspace in embraces with earth women? Are my children offspring of the first interplanetary race? Has the melting pot of interplanetary society already been created on our planet?" Wilhelm Reich, *Contact With Space*

The transformative potential responsible for this apocalypse is to be found in the human psyche itself, however. It is in the body and in the blood, only waiting to be tapped, stirred, awoken. Lucidly speaking, human DNA is a sort of micro-chip, the code of which is now being altered in order that the DNA (and consequently the race) can be transformed. According to the logic of paranoid awareness, it *appears* as though this new "code" was passed down whole by the *Elohim,* through Christ, the messenger of the gods. The savior, after all, is he who carries the solution.

Legend has it that the *Elohim* formed Adam from clay. The first man, the earthy body, died not for any transgression, then, but to allow for the commencement of an *evolutionary sequence.* The "second man," according to the same sources, arose when the very same forces conceived Jeshua in the womb of Mary. Jeshua was to be "the new Adam," both sinner and savior in one, the leading player in a myth-event, revolving around the sacrifice of the physical body to the spiritual one (the double). This is about as deep as paranoid awareness gets before all lucidity is lost. It *appears* as if something got mixed up along the way, and the plasmatic agenda was aborted (or rather, delayed).

The global conspiracy here perceived continues throughout recorded history, and is finally seen as a conspiracy not of men, or even angels, but of *biology* and of the cells. It is a conspiracy centering not around society, or even the human race, but around a single, microcosmic organism called DNA. The final stage, the Third Man—the homoplasmate, as P.K. Dick termed him—is the synthesis of the earthly with the cosmic code, the splicing of Matter with Spirit. This is done not by salvation, however, but through *mutation.* Paranoid awareness makes an unprecedented leap here, by positing that this mutation process is underway, and has (in part) been falsely called A.I.D.S. This is the final conclusion of paranoid awareness, as regards global transformation (and the inevitable triumph of the double): death is the inescapable forerunner to Resurrection.

*

When you have proved that God is merely a name for the sex instinct, it appears to me not far to the perception that the sex instinct is God.
—Aleister Crowley

The ancient mysteries all revolved around the question of sex because the sex force in the end *is* the mystery. From a lucid view, it is our God. The bearded bust Baphomet which the Templars worshipped in part represented the Great God Pan, whose twin horns signify the double current. Pan is Greek for "All," the unity of the cells, the harmony of the spheres, the perfection of Nature. As Lord of the Earth he is the means by which we, as humans, connect to the Universe; the secret of both knowledge and power is found through this connection. And as "man" is now palpably separate from "woman," the two must be joined anew in order to fully reconnect with the cosmos. Male and female are two poles of the one current (the vagina is the socket, the phallus is the plug).

Energy of course is quite capable of altering and even transforming the precise nature of matter: heat melts ice and creates steam; electricity will magnetize a lump of iron or charge copper and turn it into a battery. Sound also is seen to effect the nervous system, beneficially or otherwise, even in such a simple case as music affecting plant growth. From a lucid view, sex is a matter of energetic principles and configurations, and has little to do finally with sensual pleasure or emotional-psychic gratification, all of which are side-effects. The true object of sexual union, according to tantrics and occultists alike, is the opening of the "seven gates" or *chakras* in the human body and the liberation of the double.

As paranoid awareness sees it, the elemental intelligences and discarnate "spirits" of Earth can, through man, be united with the planetary forces and celestial archetypes, or gods. All the combined work of both magicians and angels, shamans and spirits, has been directed towards this one goal.[21] The transformation gene or Plasmate carried by Christ was first communicated to the *female* race (Magdalena); hence in Genesis we get the parable of Eve and the Serpent.[22] Eve apparently flunked the test, however (bruised her heel stomping the snake, and laid a curse on mankind), and thus the angels wound up being the sole guardians of the Graal, this sacred knowledge (sex) which would some day bring about the regeneration of the race. By this understanding, there is *no way* for man to access his own untapped potential (his divinity) without first going through the "demonic" forces. At the same time, the lucid view perceives these angels not as "fallen," but rather as *assigned* to the terrestrial realm. Apparently this was the only way for the genetic code to be passed on from one species to another? If the earth-bound angels or Faery are opposed to the "outer-angels," it is only so far as they are deployed for *opposite purposes*. Their task is to implement and oversee the testing, segregation, and finally the "harvesting" of humanity. Their influence is neither benign nor malign, but wholly indifferent. As such, those who are susceptible to corruption from contact with these absolute powers—are corrupted (and the Devil take them). This is supernatural selection at work. Because of its temperament and limitations, however, paranoid awareness is primarily concerned with these tempter angels, and only secondarily with the higher Angels, who are—for reasons previously stated—largely outside the reach of the non-lucid or paranoid mind. It is for this

21: And of madmen also. Hitler was obsessed both with the idea of a Superman (or Man of Earth) and with the energy "Vril" (as described in *The Coming Race* by Lord Bulwer-Lytton) by which man might mutate into this super-being. The Vril being a sexual force, the idea of actual interbreeding seems logical. If, as paranoid awareness maintains, Hitler formed some kind of allegiance with non-human beings, it follows that the true purpose of his scheme was the creation of this master-race, via the hybridization of the two forms. Seeing as Hitler was a largely sexless creature, however, it seems unlikely that he ever fully comprehended the true nature of his ambitions.

22: "It could well be that the Sirian talent (magick) has found its way into today's world via a specific genetic coding *which is carried exclusively by females*. In other words, the Sirian gene, if there is such a thing, is transmitted via the mother." Murray Hope, *Ancient Egypt, the Sirius Connection*. The Lion Power or Sirian Energy is represented by both the female archetype of Babalon and the male Baphomet. Babalon—the paranoid is quick to point out—not only represents the Kundalini force but is numerologically equivalent to UFO (both equal 156 in gematria). The Sirian current has a double path, through the Sun (Ra) and also through the Moon. According to the lucid view, it is this secondary, lunar channel which needs to be removed from the equation, that the current be channeled directly into the body of Earth. Hence, in Revelation, the Moon "turns to blood," i.e., the menstruation of Babalon. In Crowley's *Book of Thoth*, Atu XI, *Lust*, Babalon is riding the beast, and she is seen to be *under* the Earth, drawing power and passion from the beast (lion) between her legs. She is transmitting this power upward *through her body* to the surface and out. Above the surface, snakes come swirling around the resulting vortex or fountain of energy in order to feed. He who hath wisdom, and all that . . .

reason that we get the unmitigated "gloom" of the paranoid's perspective. On the quest for lucidity, we are bound to seek light in the darkest of shadows.

In our more lucid moments, we know that a constant emotional resistance to the darkness, and to the emergence of the unconscious (or the double)—the fact that we insist on playing the role of ignorant and innocent victim—has proven to be our undoing. Collectively, hardwired to the Consensus, we are hiding in the victim role because the alternative—to wake up to the challenge of the Imaginal and assume responsibility as participants *in* it—is far more threatening to us, even, than being its helpless victims. This is the final understanding of the paranoid, as regards the "abduction drama" and the mystery of the Other: that we, as much as "they," are actually (or Imaginally) behind it.[23] We are co-conspirators in our transformation. We are not merely the dreamed, but also the *dreamer*. We are they, and they are us.

Being human, like everything else, is a point of view.

23: Note John E. Mack on "an abductee's sense of possessing a double human/alien identity. In their alien selves they may discover themselves doing many of the things that the 'other' aliens have done to them and to other human beings . . . one of the tasks the abductee then confronts is the integration of their human and alien selves, which takes on the character of a reensoulment of their humanity." *Abduction*

Chapter Seven: Extraterrestrials

Babalon Falling

Robo Sapiens

"No one owns his personality."
—James V. McConneck, quoted in *Casebook on Alternative 3*

Paranoid awareness perceives the mass as having no individual will, but only collective volition or momentum; as such it is far more susceptible to the influence of an outside *will*, even be it that of a single person. From a lucid view, the mass might be seen as a sort of dinosaur (at least as described in school-books), having bulk and "power" but little or no intelligence. It is child's play to harness such brute force as one would any other impersonal, mindless energy. Left to its own devices, it has only two courses—inertia or extinction (which amount finally to the same thing). Being unborn as yet, the mass has only one kind of will, the will to die. As such it is a simple matter to fulfill this will.

The mass-mind—so far as it exists at all—is like that of a child: an empty program, a blank page on which the controlling authorities, be they parental or governmental or even spiritual, may freely inscribe their own agenda. Paranoid awareness perceives state-of-the-art technology as being directed and focused towards this single, unified end: the abolishment of the individual, and the establishment of a blind mass. The paranoid assures us that such a goal is no pipe dream but rather success-assured, and that its success is only confirmed by its going unremarked upon by the blind mass in question. If, for example, we accept the paranoid's contention that the world leaders we have nominated are (in actual "fact") under the covert but total control of other intelligences, unknown and even antagonistic to us, we might thereby deduce that it is of little import if the lower ranks of presidents and senators and school teachers and parents are familiar and even "trustworthy" to us, since they are all under the command of these "unknown forces." This is the essential argument of the paranoid regarding conspiracy: that if there is agreement and design at the highest levels of society, and even of existence itself, then, by definition—if the lower levels are subject to the higher—the conspiracy must extend into every corner of the globe. All this is really only the paranoid's metaphorical description of a phenomenon which pertains to consciousness: that what we take to be wholly familiar territory, namely our own minds and personalities, has long ago been occupied, and we have succumbed passively to the enemy.

All actual conspiracy theories aside, this is the postmodernist perspective of existence, positing as it does the invasion and fragmentation of the human psyche by external factors such as media imagery, simulacra, viruses of the mind, artificial reality. In the postmodern as well as the paranoid *weltanschauung*, we exist vicariously, living lives which are not our own but rather the products of an alien collective body or program, be it that of the media, the Church, the State, or "ET mind controllers" (or AI).

Ever since Descartes observed that—from an external perspective at least—the biological universe is "mechanical" and the human body (like all other bodies, celestial or terrestrial) obeys precise laws, much like a machine, the potential for absolute (remote) control of the human race has been evident. The mistake of Descartes and his followers, however, whether deliberate or not, was less in what they observed than what they failed to observe: the so-called "ghost in the machine." Unlike biological organisms, machines cannot function without some external guidance. (This may be on the point of changing, however, now the computer has introduced the possibility of mechanized intelligence.) Paranoid awareness perceives that, like Pavlov's dogs, the mass has been conditioned into *pre-ordained responses* by the use of post-hypnotic commands until it finds itself responding in an entirely automatic manner, independent of its own will. Much as Pavlov's dogs experienced hunger—not as a bodily need but at the sound of a bell—so the entranced mass-man may find himself thirsty at the sight of a Coke ad, frightened at the sight of a black man, angry at the sight of a beggar, lustful at the sight of an ice cream billboard, and so on. His thoughts are indeed no longer his own, having become pre-conditioned responses to the "advertising."[1]

To the paranoid, the only factor that allows us the fond conviction of "free-will" is that factor ever unknown and undefined—call it spirit, will, instinct, or impulse—which remains a mystery to us. The difference between the behavior of an automaton and a self-willed individual—from the paranoid's point of view (which accepts technological developments yet undisclosed to the public)—is to all intents and appearances non-existent.[2] The paranoid is convinced that all his mental

---

1: Wilhelm Wundt established the world's first psychological laboratory in 1879. Wundt believed that human thought is caused by external stimulation and bodily identification with other stimuli received and recorded (by the body) in the past. Such identification causes the body, or brain, to mechanically create an act of "will" which responds to the new stimulus. According to Wundt, there is no such thing as self-created thought or free will.

2: With the introduction of the RHIC-EDOM program, for example: Radio Hypnotic Infra-Cerebral Control/Electronic Dissolution of Memory. "The RHIC-EDOM file was a 350 page document prepared by the CIA immediately after the murder of JFK. The report described a way of turning men into electronically controlled robots that were programmed to kill on demand. In the RHIC phase, the individual was put into a trance and given suggestions that were activated on one or more levels by key words or tones. In the EDOM phase, the memory of the individual was affected to either eliminate or alter the memory of events that the individual was involved in." *Matrix II—The Abduction and Manipulation of Humans Using Advanced Technology,* by Valdamar Valerian. According to paranoid awareness, this program is now capable of an almost perfect and total simulation of reality. Seeing as how the brain itself is a kind of computer—a massively complex arrangement of paths, patterns and signals, which can be redirected or rearranged like any program—the individual is, in the paranoid's understanding, subject to absolute manipulation from without. Thoughts and feelings are seen to be all subject to the same laws, the same influences, as are our respiration, heartbeat, and nervous system, being all part of the same,

and bodily functions are now subject to interference from without. Microwaves, UV lights, street lamps, auditory subliminals in ambience musak and radio broadcasts, visual subliminals on TV, and God knows what emissions from "ordinary" household devices. A classic example of paranoid awareness comes from the Leading Edge website (run by the already cited Valdamar Valerian):

> 1995 will be the year where massive doses of electronic mind control programming, thought intrusion and brain/biogenetic manipulations will commence scale. These projects are no longer experimental. They are fully operational—field-testing is over! The whole arsenal of frequencies will be unloaded on the USA, Australia, New Zealand, Canada, and Mexico as part of Stage 1 of the First Protocol, (to include) Woodpecker, Buzzsaw, Videodrome, Subliminals, Sonic Pulses. Holograms, Visions and Voices and strange Psychokinetic phenomena. Beware of TVs, computers, movies, radios and phones. Also books, magazines, newspapers, printed advertisements and posters will contain the encrypted hidden subliminal holograms. . . . And . . . beware of American shopping malls! [These holograms] affect the brain's neural networks and functions through select frequencies and their harmonics to diminish the Will, Individuality and Creativity in the Individual. . . . Also, erratic thoughts of Anger, Fear, Depression, and wanton Sexuality are included. This causes utter confusion in individuals who don't know where these strange thoughts are coming from. Now you do. They have told you it is coming. Ladies and gentlemen, the Gestalt of the movie *They Live* is here now—1995 [3]

The paranoid imagines that, if the nervous system can be sabotaged through consumer products (food additives, sugar, caffeine, nicotine, colorants, preservatives, pesticides, sodium glutamate, and a legion of artificial ingredients now ensconced into our everyday foodstuffs)—and if the overall nature of information, entertainment, and education has been contrived with a single object in mind—then humanity is now little more than a glorified machine. A vastly intricate and complex machine, granted, far more elaborate and multi-leveled even than the most advanced computer; and yet, for all the options and intricacies of this so-called individual, his actions remain restricted to the precise parameters of an outer program. This outer program is our own minds, a foreign installation designed expressly to enslave us. This matrix serves as a kind of artificial species blueprint, much like the circuit board inside a ccmputer, providing as many alternate options and functions as possible, but nevertheless all strictly mapped so as to render the machine's behavior wholly predictable, however autonomous it may seen to be. A human being, so-called, is now a member of a new sub-species, robo sapiens.

---

fantastically intricate circuit board. All these natural functions are not really at our conscious command; on the contrary, they are what maintain and direct our conscious behavior.

3: "CIA, Vatican, Pope Conspiracy—Holographic Projection and Image of the Beast-Montauk & Mind Control Experiments," excerpts from a lecture in N.Y.C in Winter 1994, the only names given are "Dr. B" or "Dr. E." The piece continues: "Once you know this is happening, it automatically alerts your mind and psyche. . . . If you are consciously aware that there is encrypted subliminal information (embedded) in visual or aural stimuli, and give a verbal command to yourself to deny permission to register the information, there will be no assault or (at best) a minimal influence on your mind.

Computer culture is based on a process of shuffling and sifting units (actual individuals as much as data itself) so as to order them into a more-or-less controllable body. Humanity is this body. As its options are narrowed down into ever-tighter parameters, it becomes easier to isolate those individuals whose autonomous behavior marks them as subversive, uncontrollable elements. Thus the paranoid perceives individuality, privacy, and liberty as being mere fantasies and luxuries of the ignorant. Logically, the goal of absolute social control would be not so much to see, hear, and record every little thing that goes on amidst a populace, but to *dictate* it, thereby knowing it in advance. This way, the human is left to his own devices with the complete certainty that he will not, indeed cannot, do anything that he has not already been programmed to do. He has become a marionette, dancing to the musak of a hidden band with an agenda all its own. Of course, even the paranoid will admit that such a marionette has *some* freedom within the limits of the program, but this freedom is itself an illusion, insofar as all choices are restricted to the options provided by the program. The freedom to choose between Pepsi and Coca Cola hardly amounts to a choice, after all, any more than the option to choose between two political candidates backed by the same forces constitutes democracy. Anyone who rejects both Coke *and* Pepsi—Republican and Democrat—and opts instead for Soya milk, is at once branded as a health freak or anarchist. Already out on a limb, he is in danger of being chopped off. Freedom applies only and exactly so far as the unit is willing to stay in line.

*

It is certain that, in making one's self the servant of any current whatever, of instincts or even ideas, one gives up one's personality, and becomes the slave of the multitudinous spirit whom the Gospel calls LEGION. Artists know this well enough.
—Eliphas Levi, *The Key to the Mysteries*

The first hint of the enslavement system by which man becomes but a number—a member of the pack to be branded, herded, and slaughtered—is found in the paranoid's most trusted source, the Book of Revelation, specifically in the passage which introduces "the mark of the beast." The tattooed numbers given to the Jews in German concentration camps toyed with this idea of branding, but the phenomenon dates throughout history and mythology (the mark of Satan of the Inquisition, for example), all the way back to the mark of Cain. In recent times, the idea of invisible "leashes" for criminals and inserted "tags" for animals and children has been presented to the public as, on the one hand, a possible solution for the over-crowding prisons and the escalation of urban crime, and on the other, a way of easing parent's and pet-owner's anxieties. In the case of the criminal, what is proposed is a tiny tracking device implanted under the skin of the incarceree, impossible to remove even by surgery. The implant is a tiny transmitter by which the movements of the subject can be precisely monitored by satellite, effectively turning the whole world into his prison.[4]

Beyond its obvious function as a tracking device, the implant would be capable of monitoring the subject's inner state, his heart-rate, temperature, and so forth, even at a pinch his thoughts and feelings. The implant is also said to be capable of releasing microscopic doses of chemicals into the subject's bloodstream at the flick of a switch, thereby rendering him unconscious, or eliminating him entirely. As stated, and without having to enter the *weltanschauung* of the paranoid, implants are presently in use not only for criminals but also innocents—pets and now children—as a means of ensuring their "protection." Implants are now available to all anxious parents in developed countries; the first publicized case of children being implanted by parental request occurred in the UK in 2002, shortly after the much publicized abduction and murder of two young girls in Soham, England. Most veterinarians encourage cat and dog owners to have their pets implanted, for their own peace of mind. Soon, local MDs will be suggesting the same to parents, and those who refuse will some day be viewed with suspicion as "backward" or "unrealistic."

The implant also doubles as an ID-cum-credit card, holding all the pertinent information of a given individual, his criminal record, vital statistics, sexual history and preference, bank balance, address, social security number, etc, etc. This microchip is to be inserted into the body, reputedly either on the forehead or wrist (for reasons relating to blood circulation), and without this chip, no citizen may buy or sell, or even exist, in society. Of course, paranoid awareness attributes the implant with an occult function, its true *raison d'etre*. Apart from simply storing information, it will also transmit it, sending carrier waves (encoded commands) directly to the brain and thence to the entire nervous system, regulating and controlling the individual's thoughts and actions covertly.[5] These implants, due on the open market, were once almost exclusively associated with "ET" manipulations, presumably because such technology was thought to be beyond that of earth science. Paranoid awareness has long insisted that this is not so, pointing out that as

---

4: "When inserted underneath the skin, this chip can link an individual to a computer base, or it can track a person's location via satellite. In addition, research is being conducted to enable the chip to decipher a person's physiological data through the computer. In the future, authorities may be able to determine from watching their computer screen if a pedophile across town is being aroused by the sight of children." "The Microchip Injection: Orwellian Implications," by Lisa Crosby, *Paranoid Women Express Their Thoughts*

5: "A US company has announced a brain-wave to computer interface system it claims can be used for rudimentary computer control. The device is called BRAINLINK (and) utilizes a series of sensors attached to a headband worn by the user . . . the system harnesses the brain's ability to produce waves ranging in frequency from 0.5 Hz to 40 Hz. These signals are amplified and converted to digital form." *Nexus* magazine, vol 2, #21. "The system has at different times been called Intra Cerebral Mind Control, ESB, Electronic Stimulation of Brain, Biological Radiocommunication or Bio-medical telemetry and in both the eastern and western worlds is the prevailing system of mind control, creating unlimited possibilities to influence and change an individual's behavior patterns and personality. By means of a two-way radio communication, called telemetry or remote control, an electromagnetic wave can be sent on a return trip to a receiver/transmitter located under the skull or in the brain; this signal records the activity of the brain and returns it to a computer for analysis, from which all aspects of the subject's life can be exposed." *An Open Letter to the Swedish*

early as the 1930s research and experimentation in the field was already underway.[6] It is even conceivable—says the paranoid—that the implant can now be inserted into the bloodstream via a simple hypodermic needle, and that this chip might take the form of a kind of "robo-virus"—a roving microchip that would run amok in the system, devouring it in the process of transforming it. This would act as a kind of surrogate gene or artificial DNA whose purpose is to reprogram the entire psychobiological being, to create it anew. This is described, rather evasively, as cybernetics, and appears in all its paranoid glory in the cult Cronenberg film *Videodrome*, in which the slogan of the future is—"Long Live the New Flesh!" The paranoid veritably quivers in anticipation.

*

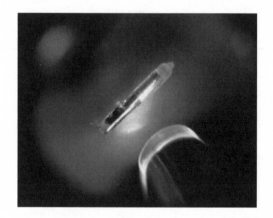

6: "The Secret Society which became the nucleus of the Office of Strategic Services-CIA octopus was making biotelemetry implants in unsuspecting people as early as 1933. After the operations, the victims were kept drugged for a time and then were brainwashed . . . the implants were first activated by touching the skin with a device similar to an electric prod. . . .The early implants were made to stimulate the pudendal nerve, when triggered, so that the sexually excited and amnesiac-drugged victims could be used in the sex-circuses of the OSS-CIA secret order as part of a greater Call to Chaos working." James Shelby Downard, *Call to Chaos*, from *Apocalypse Culture*, edited by Adam Parfrey

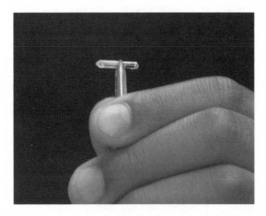

A VeriChip, held by pair of tweezers, is shown Friday, May 10, 2002, in Boca Raton, Fla. A South Florida family on Friday became the first to be implanted with the tiny computer chip that researchers hope will advance the way people carry medical information with them in case of emergencies. The chip is about the size of a grain of rice, and insertion takes about a minute under local anaesthesia. (AP Photo/Steve Mitchell) The chip, which is a product of Applied Digital Solutions, Inc. will contain personal medical information which can be acquired with a specialized digital reader.

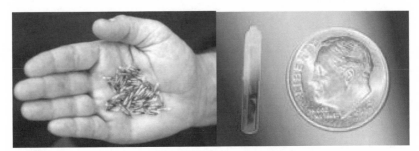

Enough VeriChips to contain medical information of over 70 people can rest in the palm of a hand. (May 10, 2002.) Source: http://www.gpdiusa.com/others/a_verichip.htm

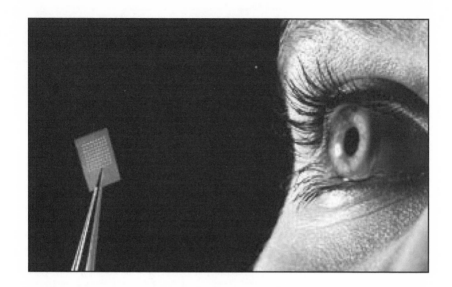

MARK OF THE BEAST
COMPONENTS OF THE BIOCHIP

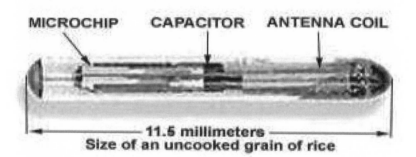

MICROCHIP   CAPACITOR   ANTENNA COIL

11.5 millimeters
Size of an uncooked grain of rice

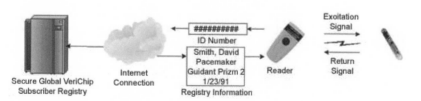

Secure Global VeriChip Subscriber Registry

Internet Connection

########## ID Number
Smith, David Pacemaker Guidant Prizm 2 1/23/91
Registry Information

Reader

Excitation Signal

Return Signal

Having been given no reason to believe otherwise, I have personally concluded that so-called UFO abductions, and the events surrounding those abductions and sightings, are a "black" intelligence operation, involving government-sponsored kidnappings, experimental drugs, surgical experimentation, sophisticated electronics and directed-energy technologies, implantable microcircuited devices, experimental aircraft, Hollywood-style special effects, and the exploitation of the so-called "abductees" as sources of ova, sperm and aborted fetuses for use in government-sponsored genetics experiments.
—Julianne McKinney, quoted by William Lyne, *Space Aliens From the Pentagon*

Within the *weltanschauung* of the paranoid, it becomes not merely possible but probable that, if implantation exists as a mind control technology, there are few if any exceptions living in the free world. The paranoid perceives the implant in relation to ET lore not because the implant necessarily comes from the ET, but—on the contrary—because there is considerable evidence that the ET may be coming *through* the implant. However advanced such technology may seem by Earth standards, it is downright archaic when attributed to a space-faring, godlike race of beings capable of molding space-time to their devices. Why bother with nuts-and-bolts when mind-power is more than adequate? Observing the inconsistency of the data,[7] the paranoid is forced to entertain the possibility that some (though not all) of the supposed "alien abductions" are clever manipulations on the part of some as-yet-unknown human agency, experimenting in ultra-secret areas of mind-control and behavior modification and involving the inducement of full-sensory hallucinations, for some specific but unknown end. This last point is the most important because, however much the paranoid may succeed in tracing a design behind the mess of clues before him, he can at no time pretend to have discerned the *intent* behind this design. There are simply too many factors to be accounted for with any single interpretation, no matter how imaginative.

The definitive paranoid work on the subject of all-too-human UFO activity is probably William Lyne's *Space Aliens From the Pentagon*, which, as the title suggests, is a work of unparalleled audacity in the annals of paranoid awareness. Lyne's premise is that the flying saucer was invented by Nikola Tesla in the 1880s, was promptly stolen by unnamed parties, and wound up, over 30 years later, in the hands of the Nazi Party. Lyne maintains, with characteristic unbendability, that the entire UFO/alien phenomenon is a massive hoax designed to cover-up this single, all-important secret. Of course, the evidence invalidates his case, or at least would do if he didn't ignore it. If such a scam were in operation, there would be a lot more to it than the simple theatrics Lyne describes, none of which would be necessary with the right appliance of technology,

---

7: "One must also ask why Betty Hill's aliens seemed to have no grasp of basic human concepts (such as how we measure time)—yet they knew enough about us to speak English fluently and had even mastered our slang. Were these real aliens, or humans engaging in theatricals (and occasionally muffing their lines)? For that matter, why did Betty Hill originally recall her abductors as humanoid, only later describing them as aliens?" Martin Cannon, *The Controllers*

entailing not the laborious staging of alien abductions but rather, the inducement of hallucinations.[8]

The fact is that, to the paranoid, all this is childishly simple, so simple that very few people have the capacity to realize that such a manipulation is even possible. By bombarding the brain with signals, a kind of fog or net (a matrix) is created around it, through which no other impressions may pass. Within this matrix, a whole new "reality" may be assembled, and this then becomes all that we see of the world, and of ourselves. Our consciousness is isolated and cut off from its own higher functions, and what is left is a soulless, lifeless facsimile which goes on functioning as if by remote control, on autopilot. The terrible truth of paranoid awareness is that man en masse is not merely asleep but has passed away entirely. He is dead, extinct. He *is* no more.

*

> The overall messages of these "puzzles" might lead a rational person to conclude that the scenarios are too corny to believe, but the religious history of the world shows that "mass" society is hooked on corny scenarios, especially "religious" or "spiritual" ones. OSI think tanks—guided by SS mystics of Reinhard Gehlen's RSHA—have designed these phony "alien" scenarios, using the principles of secret, mystical movements, societies and religions of the world.
> —William Lyne, *Space Aliens From the Pentagon*

The doctrine of alien intervention is a basically flawed one, even by the standards of paranoid awareness, for the simple reason that one who intervenes can no longer be, by definition, alien to us. Once intervention has begun, the "alien" has arrived at a level of intimacy where all terms must be newly defined. The basic crux of the ET Belief System is that Earth is, in one way or another,

---

8: This is a whole new can of worms in the larder of paranoid awareness, and forces us look briefly at what Valdamar Valerian terms (in *Matrix II*) the "Ridge Response System" (RRS)—a series of focal points formed by energy streams around the physical body, in a word, a bio-electrical field, or "aura." According to Valerian, "ridges" exist on this field (rather like scaffolding around the human body) and are "the foundation on which facsimiles are built." A facsimile is a recording of all the thoughts and emotions experienced by an organism during a given "event-perception," and is retained by the "reactive mind"—that portion of the mind not under conscious control. If an artificial facsimile is created and transmitted to the RRS, this in turn prompts the reactive mind to dictate specific behavior to the individual. It would appear that, by manipulating this energy field, the perceptions of an individual can be wholly modified. If this energy field is in effect the microcosmic universe which contains us—a "bubble of self-reflection"—it follows (by paranoid reasoning) that upon this bubble events might feasibly be projected *from without*, that would create the full impression of absolute reality seen from within. In other words, an all-inclusive hallucination, a virtual reality. Via the appliance of this secret technology, the percipient is precipitated—bodily and in full consciousness—through the looking glass and into the land of Oz. Does any of this make scientific sense, or even permit of rational understanding? The paranoid does not lose much time with such questions; besides which, for an actual account of secret historical developments, it certainly makes for great science fiction. The paranoid has assembled an entire rationale for his "nothing is what it seems" credo, a watertight scenario for the hypothetical creation of a whole, all-inclusive surrogate reality. It would appear that the Wachowski brothers drew freely upon this data while assembling their movie, and its widespread success suggests that, at an unconscious level, we are all dimly aware that something is indeed rotten in Babylon.

isolated: in quarantine. The very fact of extraterrestrial intelligence existing outside and above us while remaining hidden from us makes this idea unavoidable. Be it the prison planet of the Scientologists, the purgatory of the Christians, the farm of the Forteans, or the laboratory of the extraterrestrialists, the human race is, by this understanding, reduced to a sub-species. It is controlled, directed, and finally *owned* by some unknown, inscrutable Other. This perception is the result of the steady transference of authority from God to Man, and the transubstantiation of religion into paranoia. In turn, this "Other" is reduced to ever more rational, actual—and consequently more ominous—proportions, until finally the "higher power" regulating our fates and manipulating our beliefs turns out to be none other than an elite faction of the human race itself. This hypothetical elite was irresistibly compelled by the beliefs (the faith-cum-paranoia) of its ancestors to realize finally its own version of the myth, and to usurp the "higher power" for its own uses, according to its own designs. The bid for space—the final frontier—was, by this reckoning, motivated above all by the desire to establish *a seat of power*, above and beyond all earthly kingdoms.

By the appliance of poetic reasoning, paranoid awareness can make the following interpretation: From over-exposure to the Fallen Angels, man succumbs to *hubris* and makes a bid for the throne of God. He establishes a Moon base, space stations, and finally a colony on Mars. From here, under "Star Wars" and other space programs covered by the vast net of the "black budget," a satellite web is placed inside the Earth stratosphere geared towards surveillance of the populace, weather control, etc. This program is so huge in scope and intricate of design as to defy the imagination (making it all the easier to cover up, since no one would believe it anyway). It is unified by a single end, that of arranging the almost infinite diversity of human, social and natural factors into a coherent sequence, a sequence which can then be plotted, mapped, and ordered from without. The result is a computerized superstructure underlying the very fabric of society, operating through secret technology for social engineering, civil control, close circuit surveillance, and such like, by which every last unit of society can be kept under the "all-seeing eye" of "Big Brother."[9]

All this adds up to a degree of omniscience and omnipotence that fifty years ago would have seemed unthinkable by any but supernatural means, yet today is recognized—and not only by the paranoid—as perfectly feasible for any sufficiently-funded (and inclined) intelligence agency on the planet.[10] The point of all this to the paranoid is that, if any "extraterrestrial" found on Earth is thereby rendered "terrestrial," then likewise, any group of humans located outside the Earth—whether on the Moon, Mars, Io, or wherever—must accordingly be seen

---

9: Actually "Big Sister" would be a far more apt appellation, the computer as such being the matrix (womb) and the satellite network being as it were the *web* of the Great Voodoo Spider Queen, as She is known in certain paranoid circles.

10: All governments are essentially "intelligence" operations, because any real government must maintain a monopoly on the economy, military, medicine, religion, education, media, etc, and all these separate systems can only be infiltrated by a body whose primary method is one of espionage. Machiavelli understood this well enough: the essence of government is subterfuge.

as *extra*terrestrial.[11] So it is that paranoid awareness posits an "extraterrestrial man" who has created a snare all his own by hiding behind the mythological guise of the "ET"; the intention being more or less one with the lawyers and Pharisees reviled by Jeshua: to block entry into the Kingdom which they themselves cannot enter.[12]

There is a basic affinity (perhaps polarity would be a better term) between the functions of religion and paranoia. Both relate to hidden forces, both seek a personal relationship with the mysteries, and both seem to thrive on fear and gravity as a means for self-assurance. Both are instinctive modes of perception that, potentially at least, lead to the truth: they are imaginative rationalizations of emotional states of being, translations of the Imaginal into actual existence. So far as they are based in ignorance and fear, such rationalizations/translations are essentially regressive, neurotic, pathological reactions to the terror of being alive. So far as they partake of awareness and awe, to supplant the prevailing dread of mystery, they are healthy ways of dealing with the paralyzing beauty and wonder of existence. The modern ET taxonomies lean heavily towards the former class of rationalization: even when they are apparently positive in orientation, they remain essentially out of balance. For there is no beauty without terror, no religion without paranoia, and no mystery without at least an element of dread.

From a lucid view, one must reduce the Imaginal forces to actual existence only so far as is necessary in order to comprehend them, and only so long as it takes for the comprehension to occur. The moment the Imaginal has been accessed, via the assumption of belief, the belief must be summarily destroyed, if it is not to trap these forces—and the paranoid's own imagination—within the dualistic sphere of the actual. This process might be imagined as the temporary imposition of a "window" upon the mystery, a window by which one may glimpse the unknown. The window "frames" the phenomenon in question and so allows one to get a handle on it; but logically, it does not contain or define it. Ideally, one passes through the window and into the Imaginal, at which point the window itself disappears, along with all preconceptions/interpretations of

---

11: Indeed, its power comes from the very fact of being extraterrestrial. It is something that no one who has not traveled outside the Earth's stratosphere can comprehend, save by imagination, and even the Apollo astronauts observed it: once they'd seen the Earth hanging like a blue bauble in the sky, a bauble which they could obscure from sight simply by raising their hand, they could never again think of her in quite the same way. She became at once more precious and more *vulnerable*.

12: "400-450 Mhz is the window frequency to human consciousness. 435 Mhz is the specific frequency related to the appearance of Ufos. . . . The Star Wars system, at least part of it, transmits a signal between 1000 Mhz and 1200 Mhz that is derived from a nitrogen based particle beam. This signal is a multiplication of 435 Mhz, our reality's background frequency. . . The theory here is that one can literally do genetic engineering by using the 1100 Mhz frequency to resonate with the DNA and thereby open and close it. . . [I]f the system were beamed at the entire population, it would genetically destroy the human race. . . [T]he entire Star Wars system could be used to attack our immune systems and mental well-being . . . Genetic programming suggests something far beyond the prospect of biological warfare. It includes the possibility of scrambling or rearranging our DNA. This type of thinking is prevalent in certain New Age dogma which indicates that the human race is currently undergoing a transdimensional change. . . Their interest in controlling our DNA would be to prevent a migration to another dimension." Preston B. Nichols, *Encounter in the Pleiades: An Inside Look at Ufos*

"reality." If we lack the courage to make the leap, and instead simply stare at the Imaginal from the false perspective of the actual, the Imaginal—having been summoned (i.e., conceptualized)—begins to enter into the actual *via this window*, thereby assuming the shape which the window imposes upon it. This is when the paranoid's own imagination turns against him, and all his worst fears are actualized.

Collectively, in the midst of millennial angst and dread, a common window has been created around the Imaginal forces, a window which serves, on the one hand, as a mask to hide the mystery from the profane, and on the other, as a deadly snare. All ET lore, though based upon Imaginal realities and sown from the very same cloth as Faerylore, is profoundly contaminated, because it is laced with the neuroses of 21st century humanity, namely, fear, suspicion, mystification, and the desire for control. This contamination has led to a psychic malignance that like a cancer eats away at a body. There is a profound and unacknowledged danger in the modern ET belief systems that has nothing to do with the natural dangers of the phenomena itself, but relates rather to deliberate blinds or snares placed by unscrupulous minds, with the precise end of deceiving the ignorant and confounding the wise. The secret of the Imaginal beings is that, as the form they take in actualized reality depends wholly upon our interpretation of them, *our belief is creating their reality*. Hence, the further the ET-BS is propagated, and the deeper it takes root in the collective psyche, the closer it comes to actualization as verifiable, experiential truth. The paranoid's adage is: "be careful what you believe, for that is precisely what you will get."

A Brief History of Space Aliens

The inorganic beings are like fishermen; they attract and catch awareness.
—Carlos Castaneda, *The Art of Dreaming*

In the interests of coherence and comprehensibility, we shall attempt to trace this ET BS back to the beginning. This is the paranoid history that is "official" now, even if it remains largely outside Consensus reality, a story that will some day soon—according to the paranoid—make the front page of *The Times* and every other newspaper in the world. The thrust of the story is that a semi-corporal race of beings finds its existence threatened by exhausted DNA: its evolutionary possibilities have run out and it has nowhere left to go.[13] Although this dying race

---

13: This may go some way to clearing up the confusion concerning Whitley Strieber as a *Gray* abductee. Strieber rarely refers to any of the beings he encounters as gray. The beings he does describe are, variously, tan yellow, blue, and translucent white. According to Valdamar Valerian, in *Matrix II*: "Species skin tone variation seems to be widespread, with skin colors ranging from bluish gray to beige, tan, brown or white. There are other factors which appear to affect skin color, and one of them is the state of general health of the entity." Hence it might be posited that, as these beings are time-travelers, we encounter them in many different stages of their own evolution and/or decline. Another possibility is that the color of these beings depends on the environment they are in, and that the deeper they enter into our world (and the longer they remain here), the more their "hue" is

is using humanity in order to survive, it is they who created mankind in the first place, having foreseen the situation well in advance. Many millennia ago, they seeded the Earth to create a new species sufficiently akin to their own, so that, when the time comes, they would be able to draw upon this new life form to renew their own existence. Hence Earth is, and always has been, a farm. The paranoid may speculate conditions of co-existence between space-beings and man, in the semi-legendary land of Atlantis when the aliens intermingled freely with their livestock, sharing wisdom and technology, until a time when disaster—possibly intentional—brought it all to an end; hence the legends of the Fall and Flood.

Next we have ancient Egypt: the beings having now taken to the skies where they remain as over-seers, the first myths of flying saucers and star chariots begin here. These beings, the paranoid assures us, are both above and below man upon the spiritual/evolutionary scale of things, making man for them a kind of *bridge*. Their use of him is, however, entirely on the physical plain and is apparently no abuse, in that—potentially at least—it benefits the man as much as the "god" (and the demon). This the paranoid deduces from the fact that the whole Pharoanic obsession with preserving—by mummification—their corpses was for the benefit of these beings, intended to preserve over the centuries some morsel of DNA by which the Pharaohs might be cloned or resurrected, in some distant, far away time. Following the Egyptians' decline, however, the secret was lost and the beings became a wholly occult presence, directing the history of man (as the "Secret Chiefs" or "Unknown Superiors" of the occult fraternities), all the way up to the present.

Sometime in the '20s or '30s or '40s, (Imaginal history is anything but exact) contact was officially reestablished. Possibly it was Hitler who was the first national leader to make a treaty with the beings; paranoid awareness also cites the Nazis as developing the first man-made flying discs, technology of which was passed on to the U.S. at the end of the war. Hence a great deal of the intense UFO activity that began in 1947 can be attributed to government maneuvers. As the now widely-known myth of Roswell has it, in any case, alien craft was shot down and bodies recovered, one of which was alive and was kept that way for a short period, interviewed, filmed, etc. The beings in question are described as being about four feet high, with gray-blue skin and a plant-like bio-structure. They are said not to eat (solids), breathe (possessing fishlike gills), or reproduce (being made from partly vegetable matter). All of this makes them sound rather like cartoon characters, which paranoid awareness would doubtless relate to their other-dimensional status, and possibly *inorganic* nature. The beings were initially described, in some circles at least, as "Etherians," and also—perhaps prematurely—as E.B.Es.[14]

---

affected. The author's personal experiences in these matters suggest that the Imaginal beings are naturally white and/or yellow in color, that they become blue upon interacting with us, and that they turn gray after spending too much time amongst us!

"14: "E.B.E"—Extraterrestrial Biological Entity—was later altered to A.L.F, Alien Life Form, suggesting the amendment, if not total frustration, of understanding as to the nature of the beings. In

Paranoid awareness is overrun with so many points of view, so many different strands, all of which seem to lead to the same center but along distinct pathways, that no coherent history seems possible. The generally accepted alien taxonomies trace the "Grays" to Zeta Reticuli, while also describing them as travelers in time, multi-dimensional beings for whom it is nothing at all to navigate our history. Hence *they* were there at the very beginning to seed the Earth and engineer the evolution of Man, and hence *they* will be there at the end, to oversee the outcome, whatever that may be. Such paranoid definitions carry with them the seed of their own denial, however, for to say that a "god" is by definition not subject to our own laws of time and space is to state that it is not subject to our definitions, either; nor would it be subject to the laws of what we call "consciousness." In other words, such multi-dimensional beings—if they existed—would be by definition *beyond our understanding.*

*

Behold a Pale Horse, William Cooper writes as follows: "Letter from Gerald Light concerning alleged meeting of President Eisenhower with aliens, February 20 1954, at Muroc, now Edwards Air Force base, for the signing of a formal treaty between alien nation and USA. Light was one of several journalists present. 'Their reaction was judged as a microcosm of what the public reaction might be. Based upon this reaction, it was decided that the public could not be told. Later studies confirmed this decision as sound. [Light's letter continues:] My dear friend: I have just returned from Muroc. The report is true—devastatingly true. . . . When we were allowed to enter the restricted area (after about six hours in which we were checked on every possible item, event, incident and aspect of our personal and public lives), I had the distinct feeling that the world had come to an end with fantastic realism. For I have never seen so many human beings in a state of complete collapse and confusion, as they realized that their own world had indeed ended with such finality as beggars description. The reality of the 'other plane' aeroforms is now forever removed from the realms of speculation and made a rather painful part of the consciousness of every responsible scientific and political group. During my two days visit I saw five separate and distinct types of aircraft being studied and handled by our Air Force official—with the assistance and permission of the Etherians! I have no words to express my reactions. It has finally happened. It is now a matter of history."

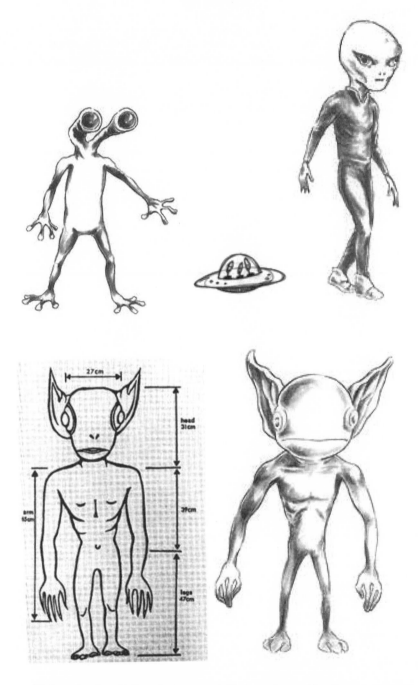

Various sketches of alleged extraterrestrial beings witnessed by disparate sources

The famous "Palenque astronaut," from the Temple of Pakal in Chiapas, Mexico

Babalon the great is fallen, is fallen, and is become the habitation of devils, and the hold of every foul spirit, and a cage of every unclean and hateful bird.
—Revelation 18:2

According to paranoid awareness, the watershed year of secret ET history is 1947, though a more in-depth search of the "data" suggests that actual, large-scale interaction began—at the higher levels of government— some decades earlier. Several key events occurred in 1947, however, that mark the year forever in the annals of paranoid awareness. Firstly, there was the magik rite known as "the Babalon Working," an elaborate ritual in "Enochian" magik conceived by rocket scientist John Whiteside Parsons and his associate L. Ron Hubbard in order to establish relations with "the other side." (Both Parsons and Hubbard belonged to Crowley's O.T.O California Lodge at the time and were followers of Uncle Al, who died in December that same year.) The general aim of the Babalon Working was to establish a new relationship between the terrestrial and elemental realms, and to initiate a hitherto unprecedented *ingress* from the Imaginal world to the actual. In the paranoid's terminology, a rent was torn in the fabric of space-time, creating an "interdimensional doorway" through which "the Old Ones" might "once more walk the Earth."[15] And as the Serpent Goddess Kundalini/Babalon came crashing down from the skies, with a roar of thunder and a flash of lightning—at least according to the occult-paranoid teachings expounded by Grant—the Earth came wholly under the dominion of "Set-Aiwaz." Paranoid awareness is quick to cite all the things that began in 1947, and all those that ended, and indeed a whole chapter could be devoted to this year alone. (For starters: the dead sea scrolls are found[16]; Israel is founded as a nation, thanks to Hitler and the forced exodus of the Jews from Europe; the transistor is "invented"; the sound barrier is broken; the CIA is formed—via "Operation Paperclip" from the OSS and Nazi spy apparati—the National Security Act is passed; Aleister Crowley dies, 1st December.)

Whether Parsons and Hubbard (working under Crowley, but without his approval) succeeded in evoking Babalon, thereby *in*voking the "Ufo" or Kundalini force within themselves and humanity as a whole, is unwritten in the history books. The descent of the goddess was acknowledged exoterically, however, by the symbolic UFO crash-and-retrievals which occurred throughout the globe (most particularly in the US) during the following five years (1947-52). Apparently this was the manner in which the Imaginal force of the Ufo *actualized* itself in the

---

15: According to Grant, the ritual "threw off a tangential loop which pulled into the sphere of the Double Current (i.e. the Double Current formed by Horus/Maat, known technically as 93/696) the direct radiations of the Mauve Zone by incarnating an elemental that was to open a gate which had remained sealed since the Aeon of Azyn." *Hecate's Fountain.*

16: Two years earlier the Nag Hammaddi codexes were also unearthed, and we refer again in passing to Philip K. Dick's theory about the release of the "plasmate seeking out new human hosts to crossbond with. . . . As living information, the plasmate travels up the optic nerve of a human to the pineal body. It uses the human brain as a female host in which to replicate itself into active form. This is interspecies symbiosis. . . We call the plasmate 'the Holy Spirit'..." *Valis* "Dick says the Paraclete (plasmate) awoke from its slumber when the translation of these documents began *a couple of years later.*" Italics mine, quote from *Jack Parsons and the Fall of Babalon*, by Paul Rydeen

public consciousness; simultaneously, in paranoid awareness, "it" (alien intelligence) infiltrated the highest levels of the world government. Babalon, according to Grant, symbolizes: "'the gate of the sun,' or solar-phallic force . . . a representative of the Feminine Principle or Scarlet Woman chosen for her magical ability to transmit the solar current." (*Hecate's Fountain*) The fate of Parsons himself might well be the best testimony of all to the "success" of his infernal summoning: he was burned to death in his laboratory several years later.

*

The inorganic beings are glued together, like the cells of the body. . . . When they put their awareness together, they are unbeatable. It's nothing for them to yank us out of our moorings and plunge us into their world.
—Carlos Castaneda, *The Art of Dreaming*

The widely-accepted description of the "grays" has a curious and rather unsettling parallel with what we know of as viral organisms. A virus is an alien organism that cannot reproduce itself, hence—in order to survive—attaches itself to another life-form as a host, a source of energy by which to sustain its existence indefinitely, at least until the host dies. In short, it is a kind of invisible (because microscopic) parasite. All this can be more or less synthesized with the mythology of the Grays, to say nothing of the "succubae" of ancient lore, both of which are understood to be "other-dimensional entities." But this is only one particular understanding of a multi-faceted phenomenon, a fragment of the truth, but far from the whole. One may just as well ask: is water from a tap? Is water from the ocean? Or is it from the clouds? By the same token, are "they" from Zeta Reticuli? This is how rational thinking renders Imaginal truth as actual absurdity.

Paranoid awareness accepts that "they" are from nowhere, but "they" have been through many places; like water through a tap on its way from the clouds to our lips, so it is with "them." The "Force" that now "invades" the Earth passed by Zeta Reticuli on its way to here, therefore It brings with It characteristics of the Zeta Reticulans. They are negative, insofar as they are dying. Their DNA has reached entropy stage, no future; but surely Man is in the exact same boat? His DNA has run its course, he is a sterile being, his days are numbered, no exit. The paranoid does not ask why, he simply applies deduction, then acceptance. He applies poetic imagery when the reality is too grim to translate directly. The "Force" is in the process of salvaging "lost tribes" throughout the Universe; this is Evolution's intelligent means of "harvest." Gathering wheat and burning chaff at the molecular level, throughout the cosmos. Next stop, Earth. Splicing DNA: taking two dying codes and extracting the still healthy, valid components of each to create a third, living DNA code, one which combines the best of both, and rejects the worst.

All the subtler, more poetic implications of the Imaginal notwithstanding, however, the basic, paranoid scenario described above has become for a great many people (Presidents and Popes included) the actual "alien truth," complete with cattle mutilations, mass abductions, genetic programs, psychic warfare, implantations, crop circles, underground bases, etc, etc. This loony, lob-sided Belief System insists on a joint project between Earth governments and so-called alien forces, when a more sober interpretation would allow merely that certain human individuals—those in power—have imposed their own paranoia-fed beliefs upon a wholly incomprehensible phenomenon, and so defined it, accordingly, as demonic.

The paranoid deduces that, in response to this realization—that of the demonic nature of the alien force—the human powers-that-be began to assemble a program of their own, a program of deception based on the very technology these supposed alien allies had provided, namely: state of the art mind control techniques used to create a perfect facsimile of the Imaginal phenomena emerging. The reasoning behind this simulation strategy is roughly that of the unscrupulous merchant who, unable to compete with the competition's product, attempts to spin off a cheap imitation as quickly as possible so as to rake in profit before the genuine article hits the stands. Clearly, the imitation must precede the actual event, otherwise it will be rejected as the worthless rip-off that it is. So it is with the Rapture Scam.

The lucid view imagines the truth to be both infinitely more subtle and considerably less simple than the paranoid's alien invasion and/or government subterfuge scenario, and chooses to focus on the archetypal energies at play within us, rather than the husks or shells taking form outside of us. Lucidly speaking, the DNA code of humanity and its nearest cousins is *changing*, and these lower forms of the "Sirian energy grid" (which includes the Earth) are fast becoming obsolete, leading to a period of evolutionary transition for mankind, as well as for the "alien." Hence its allegiance is being *divided* between the old and the new, between the "angel" and the "demon," between religion and paranoia.

*

This is obviously one aspect of a big picture . . . what looks like a carefully worked out blueprint for invasion of the planet. . . . The "Other Half" is an organism. Word is an organism. The presence of the "Other Half" a separate organism attached to your nervous system on an air line of words can now be demonstrated experimentally. One of the most common "hallucinations" of subjects during sense withdrawal is the feeling of another body sprawled through the subject's body at an angle . . . The word may once have been a healthy neural cell. It is now a parasitic organism that invades and damages the central nervous system. Modern man has lost the option of silence . . . These so-called Gods can only live without three-dimensional coordinate points by forcing three-dimensional bodies on others—Their existence is pure vampirism—They are utterly unfit to be officers.
—William Burroughs, *The Ticket That Exploded*

What Burroughs implies here is essentially no different from what esoteric-cum-paranoid lore has always maintained: that within the Imaginal realm are found "beings" that, for whatever reasons, are lacking the emotional awareness necessary to make the grade as autonomous agents ("officers"). Hence they are trapped, as it were waiting patiently over the aeons, like fishermen with their lines cast, for any wayward beings whose life essence they may poach and devour.[17] In mythology and modern folklore, these beings (call them Grays, demons, vampires, succubae, flyers, whatever) have prevailed over an unimaginably long period of time. In order to facilitate their parasitical program, they have woven a psychic net about the Earth, and within this "web" the human inhabitants of the planet are now collectively entangled. In the dark vision of the paranoid, these vampire beings are greedily devouring the awareness which they themselves are lacking, and by keeping it from us they are condemning us to their own black fate: a honey-comb existence of solitary confinement in the Labyrinth, with strictly set expiration dates, and no possibility of renewal.

Paranoid awareness is fairly unanimous on this point: by way of mythic engineering at all levels—psychic, social, and political—we have been rendered as docile livestock to be farmed and harvested, not only for our flesh and blood, but, in the traditional terminology, for our very souls. Fallen into the clutches of the adversary, the human race has become host to an insidious parasite, feeding off our vital essence, slowly sucking away all our life force. One result of this is the collapse of the immune system and the rapid decay of the physical body, as it succumbs to the effects of close contact with the "alien body." This demonic entity/species is known in the gospels as Legion. In more esoteric circles it is "Choronzon," the spirit of the MOB.[18]

*

> Mass human sacrifice is the most reliable method of achieving transcendental illumination. . . . If the situation develops as I project, the Eschaton will have been immanentized. For the Illuminati, that will mean the fulfillment of the project that has been their goal since the days of Gruad. A total victory. They will simultaneously achieve transcendental illumination. For the human race, on the other hand, that will be extinction. The end.
> —Shea and Wilson, *Illuminatus!*

To the paranoid view, all religions—so far as they demand worship, ritual, sacrifice—are inventions of the devil. Paranoid awareness allows that gods exist, but insists that they are falsely represented by *men in masks*. What is the aim of organized religion, asks the paranoid? The laying down of the law, comes the answer. And if the aim of politics is the enforcement of this law, together they spell *war*, the aim of which—all "causes" aside—is threefold: increase of territory, reduction of populace, and maintenance of economy (in a word, balance of power). It may seem incredible to the non-paranoid mind, but the aim of the "Custodians" indicated by paranoid awareness can be reduced to one simple phrase: *Mass extermination*. The mundane evidence supports the paranoid's hypothesis, however,

---

17: "These insects are parasites in an astral and mental way and depend upon human *prana, kama* and *ojas* (lust and radioactive energy) for their survival in our zone. In exchange for this fuel they have agreed to cooperate with the Magicians of the Yuggothic ray . . . in their work with changes in the atmosphere, whereby a greater ingress of extraterrestrial parasites will be possible." (Michael Bertiaux)

18: As "the ultimate Black Hole devouring the Light, Choronzon is therefore the supreme, the ultimate Vampire." (Kenneth Grant, *Hecate's Fountain*)

since the one consistent factor of history is just this: genocide. Whether manifest in famines, plagues, or wars, the agenda is the same, all are symptoms of the one malady.[19] "As flies to wanton boys are we to the gods." (Shakespeare, *Julius Caesar*)

Man's archaic belief in unseen powers that either guide or control him continues to the present day. It is usually accompanied by the belief that such powers can be *bargained with*, brought to terms, and made to work to his own advantage. The traditional "currency" of this bargaining has generally been one thing: human life, measured in blood. Or perhaps, the paranoid asks, some subtler soul quality for which the blood only serves as *hors d'ouerve*?[20]

Occult tradition has it that the ectoplasm released by blood-letting provides a vehicle of manifestation for the inorganic demons to ride on, so to speak, from Imaginal to actual existence.[21] To the paranoid mind, such legends are plainly too persistent to be dismissed as mere fantasy, though he acknowledges that they may be a wholly mistaken interpretation of something else, something altogether less morbid, sinister, and paranoid. But the legends stand nonetheless, and the paranoid cannot escape them, any more than can the average human. Sorcery is nothing less than the acknowledging and confronting of these forces, call them gray aliens, or call them "Legion."[22]

In *Space Aliens From the Pentagon*, William Lyne (in a rare moment of lucidity) writes of "'Astara' ('Ostara' to Hitler)," and how

the SS Bönpas worshipped "Kali Ma" ("Bloody Mother"). This cult founded the ancient Thugee cult of India, and was the basis for the Society of Assassins; the concepts of this weird religion related to the mass extermination of people, through many means,

---

19: The Plague of the 1500s that devastated half of Europe is an early example to the paranoid of chemical genocide, as Nostradamus (a physician) presumably knew well enough. William Bramley writes in *Gods of Eden*: "The greatest puzzle about the Black Death is how it was able to strike isolated human populations which had no contact with earlier infected areas. . . . A great many people throughout Europe and other Plague-stricken regions of the world were reporting that outbreaks of the Plague were caused by foul-smelling 'mists.' Those mists frequently appeared after unusually bright lights in the sky . . . a second phenomenon was sometimes reported: the appearance of frightening human-like figures dressed in black." Influenza, pneumonia, syphilis and of course A.I.D.S are all seen by the paranoid as "experiments" along these lines, and the subject is a veritable Pandora's box of pestilence, well beyond the scope of this book to do more than allude to.

20: "[S]acrifices and burnt offerings are an attempt to maintain right relationship with the otherworldly divinities. When sacrificial animals are burnt, the gods are said to feed off the savor which rises from them. The animal is 'etherealized'—translated from flesh into spirit for which the ascending, aromatic smoke is a metaphor." Patrick Harpur, *Daimonic Reality*. Note also: "Holocaust: a burnt sacrifice; a sacrificial offering the whole of which is consumed by fire." (*Webster's*)

21: "Blood might be a basis whereupon the forces of evil might build themselves bodies." (*Confessions of Aleister Crowley*, chapter 66)

22: In a moment of dark inspiration characteristic of the paranoid, George C. Andrews suggests that the Nazi concentration camps "may have been designed specifically to provide the Grays with the nourishment they required, just as the Aztec ritualized mass murders were structured for that purpose." *E.T Friends and Foes*. Andrews continues: "All it would take would be for the President of the United States to go on TV and announce a State of Emergency for our civil liberties to be replaced by martial law, enforced not by local law authorities but by the black-uniformed Delta Special Forces, the resurrected Gestapo, for it to happen all over again."

including assassination, exterminations, and war, and is the basis for all the 20th century totalitarian movements. . . . The Bönpas, Thugees and Assassins believed in a "collective consciousness," and that, as the population of the world increased, this collective consciousness was "weakened" by being shared by too many people. In service to "Bloody Mother" . . . they believed in killing as many people as possible — preferably everyone — so as to strengthen the "collective consciousness."

While *ostensibly* the old religious "rationale" for sacrificial slaughter has become obsolete, still the fact of the slaughter, the bloodshed, the warfare, goes on. As yet, the question of *cui bono* remains unanswered. Why would any "God" demand a sacrifice of his own people? Why does the government demand taxes and send *its* people to war? For the same reason: to maintain and consolidate its power. A tax-paying populace is by definition a subservient one, the only true slave being a voluntary slave; by the same token, the best sacrifices are those who consider it an *honor* to be sacrificed. Just so the good soldier goes dutifully to war, despite having no clear idea what he is fighting for. It is not his valor that is required, it is simply his blood — "blood cement" upon which the Empire is founded. This is the unholy trinity proposed by the Nazis, now anticipated by the paranoid, of "blood, faith and state."[23] It is the future as seen by the growling prophet Leonard Cohen; and beyond any doubt, "it is murder."

*

The Abyss is empty of being; it is filled with all possible forms, each equally insane, each therefore evil in the only true sense of the word — that is, meaningless but malignant, in so far as it craves to become real.
Aleister Crowley, *Confessions*, chap 66

The Imaginal "beings" of which we have been speaking, it may now be deduced, are really nothing of the kind, and any malevolence on the part of such "beings" must be attributed to their very *lack* of autonomous existence. When not channeled or directed by a conscious *will*, these marauding thought forms inevitably cause all kinds of mischief. Esoterically, malevolent forces are known as the Qliphoth — the negative reflections of archetypal energies (including ourselves) — in a word, *shadows*. Kenneth Grant defines them (in *Hecate's Fountain*) like so:

The plural form of *Qlipha*, an harlot. The Qliphoth are seductively potent energies which remain over after manifest entities have been dissolved. Hence the Qliphoth are described as "shells," "cortices," "shrouds." Hence also the nostalgia inherent in the formula of Atavistic Resurgence, which utilizes the shells or husks of memory (past time) for the fecundation of future fantasies. In this sense, the Qliphoth are a potently creative magical force.

23: Gottfried Feder, quoted by Wilhelm Reich, *The Mass Psychology of Fascism* (page 117)

They might also be seen by the paranoid as "astral fragments," the left-over memories or etheric substances of dead souls,[24] without awareness of their own and yet curiously aware; like recordings, they are replicas of a life since passed away. These fragments are firmly persuaded of their autonomous existence, however, or at least act like it, and so must be considered by the paranoid as very much "at large." According to paranoid awareness, such fragments populate the astral sphere of the Earth and as such are fully active forces in our lives; first psychically (in dreams), then emotionally (as neuroses), and finally, by an inexorable process, physically. Thus it was that Jung lamented: "The gods have become diseases." In which case, it follows, our diseases are our way back to the gods.

A propos of all this, it can be seen how human society has been ordered along the lines of an ultimate experiment performed in the strictest and most ruthless of laboratory conditions. As Robert Anton Wilson remarks in *Coincidance*, it is a world that would have made the Marquis de Sade proud, a world "designed rationally to make for the maximum horror and pain for the maximum number of people." The Custodians, as the paranoid sees it, have this whole diabolic structure mapped to their own devices, little dreaming that such devices exist only as an intermediary stage, and are quite incidental to the greater goals of evolution. The paranoid accepts, therefore, that the satanic agenda must be fulfilled for the divine plan to be accomplished.

The concept of beings who prey on awareness as a vampire feeds on blood, and are sustained, nourished and empowered by it, leads inevitably to the idea that such beings would set snares for their prey, exactly as the spider does for the fly. Throughout the globe, the same pattern is emerging, fake Rapture, followed by the real thing. This pattern paranoid awareness attempts to trace, through hints and allusions, nightmares and visions, fantasies and speculations, until he arrives at last at the lucid view.

*

At midnight all the agents/ And the superhuman crew
Come out and round up everyone/ That knows more than they do.
—Bob Dylan, "Desolation Row"

To the paranoid, the covert business of tyranny, and the blind dependence of "the mass" on its imagined "keepers" (to whom it has so rashly handed its freedom and responsibility), is leading inevitably, inexorably, towards global totalitarianism and the so-called "New World Order."[25] Events and occurrences —both actual and

---

24: When the physical body dies, the etheric body is absorbed into the atmosphere; if however this body has become fragmented, as is often the case, during the individual's life on Earth, then many of these fragments remain in the atmosphere as "ghosts," "vampires," or "diseases." So our paranoid has it, at any rate.

25: Official definition of New World Order is as follows: "A supra-national authority to regulate the world commerce and industry; an international organization that would control the production and consumption of oil; an international currency that would replace the dollar; a world development fund that would make funds available to free and Communist nations alike; an international police force to enforce the edicts of the New World Order." *McAlvaney Intelligence Advisory,* quoted by Jim Keith, *Black Helicopters Over America* As of March 2004, there is talk of passing a law through Congress

Imaginal—have been steadily directing society towards *crisis*. When the social structures begin to collapse and explode around us, the mass will cry out for a solution, any kind of solution, just so long as it relieve their terror and confusion. In response to this outcry, the machinery of tyranny will set its wheels in motion, and the dark, satanic mill start to grind. The paranoid is very clear on this point.

A State of Emergency will be declared, Martial Law being the only availing "answer" to such an emergency.[26] Curfews and other severe civil restrictions will be imposed, as the process of "social cleansing" begins. All dissidents and "undesirables" will be rounded up and "relocated" to concentration camps outside all the major cities.[27] "Global 2000"[28]—the final solution—will reach its ultimate expression (a little behind schedule) as the sacrifice, slaughter, blood and ectoplasm cement the rising of the Old Dragon to its former glory. The paranoid perceives all this as wrapped up with—or consolidated *by*—an *apparent* ET invasion and/or landing, and the ensuing enactment-simulation of the eschaton, spiritual, physical, actual, Imaginal, all or none of the above.

As we succumb to exhaustion and dreams of another world, flying saucers fill the sky with napalm fire and descend; heaven's doors open wide to usher us painlessly into the next dimension, the New Age runs on smoothly from the old—no transition, no collapse, death or disaster, no more preparations needed than to pack your crystals. Be sure not to forget your Implant! As the paranoid prepares for the end, the New Ager awaits a Hollywood-enhanced compendium of all the best bits, a ready-made Utopia to come swooping down and scoop him up. "All the ships would be around the earth and no one could deny it. Remember . . . that most abductees felt that something was imminent and that it would occur . . . it would all

---

that would "acknowledge God as the sovereign source of law, liberty [and] government" in the United States. Such a law (unprecedented in the West, but echoing the supreme authority of the Koran in Islam countries) would forbid all legal challenges to government officials who decide to impose their own view of "God's sovereign authority." Any judge who acknowledged such a challenge could be removed from office. The "Constitution Restoration Act of 2004" was introduced in February 2004 by Congress. "If enacted, it will effectively transform the American republic into a theocracy, where the arbitrary dictates of a 'higher power'—as interpreted by a judge, policeman, bureaucrat or president—can override the rule of law." (Source, "Pin Heads," by Chris Lloyd, received via email.)

26: Executive orders to be applied in state of Emergency include: "EO 10995 authorizing the suspension of the freedom of speech and the commandeering of all communication media. . . . EO 10998, providing for the government control of food sources, including farms . . . EO11000, which gives the government the right to form work brigades of citizens. . . . EO 11002, authorizing a national registering of the populace . . . EO 11004, which gives government the mandate to relocate populations from one area to another. . . . EO 12148, authorizing the Federal Emergency Management Agency (FEMA) to take over the executive functions of the government." Jim Keith, *Black Helicopters Over America.*

27: "Operation Rex 84 came into being at the confidential orders of President Ronald Reagan, and authorized the setting up of at least 23 huge American concentration camps (or 'emergency detention centers') to be used in case of a national emergency . . . an additional 20 camps (were) funded through 1990-91 military allocations. . . . Researcher Jeffrey Thompson . . . states that each of these sites can hold between 32,000 and 44,000 people." Jim Keith, *Black Helicopters Over America.*

28: "This was the report (of Carter administration) which made the reduction of the world's population by 2 billion individuals by the year 2000 an avowed target of the U.S government." Jim Keith, *Black Helicopters Over America*

occur. The implants would be activated, and people would start to disappear . . . The Christians would call it the Rapture."[29]

Paranoid awareness has no trouble accepting the existence of doorways into other dimensions found via the art of *dreaming*; nor in believing that, if awareness can make the leap, then the totality of the self will follow. The paranoid envisions ancient Toltecs, Aztecs, and other parties literally disappearing into the Imaginal when the time came, leaving whole civilizations behind. It must be stressed at this point that paranoid awareness posits the Universe entire as a "snare," or at very best a jungle. The "gods," as such—Thoth and his gang—are thus the true inventors of deceit and the initiators of espionage tactics on Earth, making Man but a pale imitator of his forgotten Masters. The simplest means of expostulating this for the paranoid is by employing the dominant theological terms and stating that God (that Highly Intelligent Viral Entity) has assigned the Devil as a *double-agent* and sent him down amongst the lower orders of men, to sow dissent and start a Rebellion, in order to recruit all potential antagonists. This way, their evil intentions can be directed towards alternate ends, ends which would finally entail their own abolition. All good strategists are aware of this subterfuge, and if it turns out that all the King's people should join the Rebellion, this is only proof that the population was against the King to begin with, in thought if not deed. Whosoever is not with me is against me, says God.

From a lucid view, there is only one thing that counts in this espionage game: *awareness.*

Awareness (free from paranoia) creates a natural hierarchical structure in the Universe, according to which every apprentice must some day become a master, every paranoid lucid. Awareness is the currency, then, and unto those that have it, shall be given, and from those that have it not, shall be taken even the little they have. It is for this reason that the paranoid seeks out that knowledge which most unsettles, challenges and disturbs his *reason*, for he knows that his awareness will thereby be increased, and his intellect strengthened, for being so tested. Freedom is the freedom to be aware, finally, and an awareness of freedom leads ever on to more of the same.

Ditto ignorance and slavery.

29: George C. Andrews, *ET Friends and Foes.*

William Blake's "Last Judgment"

Extraterrestrials

Chapter Eight: Angels and Insects

--- --- --- --- --- --- --- --- --- --- --- --- --- --- --- ---

Lucifer Rising

The Imagination may be compared to Adam's dream—he awoke and found it truth.
—John Keats, *Letters*

Nazi Ghosts and Final Solutions

You are not looking in on the Other; the Other is looking in on you . . . To us the most alien thing in the cosmos is the human soul.
—Terence McKenna, *The Archaic Revival*

In *The Mass Psychology of Fascism*, Wilhelm Reich wrote that, "Fascism is the supreme expression of religious mysticism . . . it transposes religion from the 'otherworldliness' of the philosophy of suffering to the 'this worldliness' of sadistic murder." With Nazism the 20th century Zeitgeist of the human race found its expression—in spades and swastikas—as an external, invading force. When the evil of our minds is projected outward onto apparently aberrational forms and fashions (the proverbial scapegoats), it allows us to retain the fond illusion of our own innocence and virtue, or at least lack of responsibility.[1] This is a recipe for disaster.

In *The Ominous Parallels*, Leonard Peikoff observes that "The Nazis took the inconceivable in theory and applied it to men's actual existence in the only way it could be done." Nazism is to date the single, outstanding case of a political movement attempting to wrestle with Imaginal realities, and to reduce them—by force—to actual expression. It was an aborted attempt to impose the existence of the Imaginal—the laws of heaven—upon the world. For this reason, the Nazi *weltanschauung* is of unparalleled interest to the paranoid.

Spanish author Miguel Serrano (in *El Ultimo Avatar*) sees Hitler as "the Tenth Avatar of Vishnu, the Kali Avatar, incarnated to bring about the end of the Kali Yuga and usher in a New Age." As such, he is beyond criticism.[2] But although Hitler invoked the Old Gods he personally did not honor them, or even acknowledge them as such. He appeared to consider them mere figments of a childish superstition, and as such tools to deceive the masses. Nazism was not a new breed of politics, it was their fulfillment.[3] It was not a new religion so much as the natural culmination of religion. Nazism was the timely death of religion because it was the termination, the logical denouement, of the religious instinct in Man. It came complete with its own doctrine, ceremonies, insignia, bible (*Mein Kampf*), symbolism, philosophy, dogma, rules, and its very own "avatar." It took traditional elements from the ancient religions—particularly those pertaining to Germany—and attempted a forceful synthesis of all systems religious and political. It indulged the mystical interests of the *volk*, their harmless curiosity in astrology, massage, herbs, holistic healing, positive thinking, etc (all the earmarks, the paranoid is quick to point out, of the current "New Age" movement).[4] It claimed to be of and for the people but, like all systems centering around a doctrine of the "elect," it was an exercise first and foremost in betrayal.

The essence of the Nazi working was an evocation of Imaginal beings, with the aim of offering to these beings the world and everything in it. Hitler's aim was to

---

1: "The concept of transference to a scapegoat is the most important among the superstitious manipulations just behind the scenes of the New Age scam-sham." James Shelby Downard, *The Call to Chaos*

2: My source is Joscelyn Godwin's *Arktos*.

3: "If one wants to recognize effortlessly the essence of politics, let one reflect upon the fact that it was a Hitler who was able to make a whole world hold its breath for many years. The fact that Hitler was a political genius unmasks the nature of politics in general as no other fact can. With Hitler, politics reached its highest stage of development." Wilhelm Reich, *The Mass Psychology of Fascism*

4: "The romantic blend of ideas that links these proto-Nazis uncannily with the Greens and New Agers of today: an interest in natural living, vegetarianism, anti-industrialism; an appreciation of prehistoric monuments and the wisdom of those who built them; a feeling for astrology, earth energies, and natural cycles; a religious outlook vaguely resembling that of Theosophy. The generic name given to this kind of thinking was volkisch, an untranslatable word, one that borderlines between nationalistic and folkloric." (*Arktos*)

call the old gods down to Earth and give them free reign in human affairs. In this he failed; and so, unable to bring Heaven down to Earth, he attempted to drag Earth screaming up to Heaven. Nazism was the expression of mankind's unconscious need to confront its own demons; it was the necessary backlash for prematurely invoking its gods. The Nazi chaos workings combined the principles of death, decay, destruction, and darkness, and attempted to reverse the universal current, to turn humanity back upon itself, like a worm. The laws of Heaven lay waste to the Earth as no devil ever could. Hitler succeeded in this, at least, and as such he was the greatest example of the "victory" of "transcendence" in history. According to paranoid awareness, the whole New Age Movement is due to enact this very same paradox, the grand tragedy and comedy of Pan: all begetter, all-destroyer. This is the eschaton.

*

Atomic friction causes the heat and light of the stars. Positive and negative forces battle perpetually. This is simple, physical reality. Does that make the negative forces evil? No, essential!
—Whitley Strieber, *Transformation*

Every artist feels the imperative to express his inner darkness, to draw upon his deepest, most depraved inner self as a reservoir of energy and inspiration. This dark matter is the very substance of art, and without it nothing the artist does will have much weight or consequence. To rechannel his own demons with the compassion and the insight of experience and thereby transform them, just as he transforms his suffering into meaning, this is the work of the artist. It is poetically akin to the alchemist's *opus magnus*, that of transforming lead into gold. The transformation does not occur in actual terms, however, though it must be *perceived* as an actual transformation. It takes place rather in the realm of the Imaginal, where no such differences as pure and impure can be said to exist. The artist takes his pain or rage or hatred into the Imaginal realm and there confronts it directly. He then commands it to reform, to assume a more fitting and appropriate guise.

Nazism was concerned—at its deeper levels—with the same basic process, but it lacked the essential, all-redeeming element of *creative insight*. Although it was first and foremost a visionary movement, it could hardly be called a creative or artistic one. All its manipulations were directed towards destructive ends, and down profoundly dehumanizing channels. It attempted to organize, harness, and perfect the cosmic (Imaginal) forces of evil, and to divert them to evolutionary ends. To an extent it succeeded in this goal, and evil has never been such a *pure* force as it was in Europe during the late '30s and early '40s. The regalia and ceremony, the uniforms and rallies and goose-stepping masses, all this was an enactment of occult principals in the mundane world on a grand scale. For a brief time it seemed as if Imaginal consciousness (albeit in its lowest manifestation) was beginning to take hold of historical events.

Hitler's role was divided, however. He claimed to wish to prepare the "elite" for the arrival of the Ubermensch, and so usher in the next phase of human evolution. But by all accounts he was caught up in and unhinged by his own personal bid for power. He became obsessed with the business of mystifying the mass, of working them into blind, destructive hysteria in order to use their psychic energy to kickstart his New Order.[5] As a result, Hitler became prey to the forces which he had unleashed, and the Nazi movement failed to take the next step up the Imaginal ladder and access the higher realms. This happened partially as a result of Hitler's incapacity to associate with anything but thugs and murderers who constantly led him astray; mostly, it was the result of his own psychological weakness. Hitler was unable to stand sustained exposure to the Imaginal forces, and simply lost his marbles.

Most people, even many paranoids, have little idea as to the truly ambiguous nature of the Nazi phenomenon, an ambiguity which may be summed up by the phrase, the perfection of evil. Evil as a natural cosmic force in the universe requires modes of expression, outlets, and Nazism at its deepest level aspired to be such an outlet. The only way to comprehend Nazism, finally, is to fit it into the greater scheme of things, i.e., human evolution, and thereby perceive it as a *positive* force, albeit a force of evil. To the paranoid it makes perfect sense that, in order to bring the opposites of existence into balance, they must first be separated, isolated, and individually defined. What is really "evil" is when the two poles become intermingled and so contaminate one another. Nazism might be seen as a Body of Error, as the Id inflated into plain sight. Of course the Id needs to be revealed, but the key is for it to be allowed a fully conscious expression, with the collaboration and not the resistance of the ego. Otherwise it comes out in only partially conscious, twisted and aberrational forms, such as Nazism.

In the paranoid's understanding, it is futile to judge "evil" as a force unto itself; so far as it is such a force, it can no longer be considered evil, but only necessary. When rain falls, the farmer experiences joy, while the maypole dancer feels despair: it is not the rain that is good or evil, only the mind which judges it as such.[6] Hitler declared: "Providence has ordained that I should be the greatest liberator of humanity. I am freeing men from the restraints of an intelligence that has taken charge; from the dirty and degrading self-mortifications of a chimera called conscience and morality, and from the demands of a freedom and personal independence which only a very few can bear." The whole machinery of the Third Reich propaganda—return to roots, pure blood, self-control, discipline, mysticism, manifest destiny, the old gods, earth-powers, Superman-immanent—corresponded with the hopes and fantasies of the mass. It offered a sure and steady hand of relief,

---

5: "We are now at the end of the Age of Reason. The intellect has grown autocratic, and has become a disease of life . . . At a mass meeting, thought is eliminated . . . I mingle the people. I speak to them only as a mass." Adolf Hitler, quoted in *The Ominous Parallels*, pg. 47

6: "The Great White Brotherhood and what you might call the Great Dark Brotherhood are two bodies of consciousness opposed to each other in every imaginable way . . . The GWB does everything it can to advance our evolution, while the GDB does everything it can to induce fear and delay evolution. The forces of these two brotherhoods tend to balance each other out so that our evolution takes place at exactly the right time, neither too soon nor too late. Viewed from a higher level—the 4th dimension or above—this is unity of consciousness. The two brotherhoods are just different aspects of the One working in harmony . . . Evil may do some amazingly harsh and disgusting things, but at the level of polarity consciousness, these are mere lessons." Bob Frissel, *Nothing in This Book is True, But That's Exactly How Things Are*

even it was the relief of death. The mass is always inclined to follow the line of least resistance.[7]

Nazism was the last psychic wave of the repressed inner rage of the human race, and the first, distorted, aborted emergence of the atavistic soul of Man as it awakens from its slumber. Like spring water through a drain that has for too long been blocked, such an emergence cannot help driving before it all the scum and bile that has gathered there, over the aeons. Nazism set the mass in motion without ever awakening the corresponding volition within it; blind, stumbling out of control, like a runaway train without a driver, it could only ever lead to disaster. Like Mary Shelley's *Frankenstein*, Hitler and his band of Thugs reanimated the dead soul of the mass, only to be possessed by the ghosts which they had evoked. The final result of this misguided occult working was, significantly, an event engineered not by the Nazis (at least not directly), but by their professed enemies the Allies. The activation of the hydrogen bombs at Hiroshima and Nagasaki was the actual realization of the atavistic resurgence begun by Nazism. It was the necessary unleashing of the terrible, primordial, destroying energy which the Nazis had successfully stirred from its slumber. As such, it was (ironically, considering its source) an even greater force of evil than Nazism. But also that much purer a force of *destruction*.[8]

Global Initiation and the Emergence of the Other

> The main problem with searching for extraterrestrials is to recognize them. Time is so vast and evolutionary strategies and environments so varied that the trick is to know that contact is being made at all.
> —Terence McKenna, *The Archaic Revival*

To the ordinary person, illuminoids, ufos, elves, angels, and other Imaginal beings have no objective existence whatsoever. The lucid view is quite clear on this. And yet everyone knows what these things "are," at a mythological level, even if we continue to insist that they are not. According to paranoid awareness, this paradox is the very crux of our current situation. It states that, over the aeons, we

---

7: "Fascism's lower middle class is the same as liberal democracy's lower middle class, openly in a different historical epoch of capitalism." Wilhelm Reich, *The Mass Psychology of Fascism*. "The democratization of Europe will lead to the production of a type prepared for *slavery* in the subtlest sense. . . the democratization of Europe is at the same time an involuntary arrangement for the breeding of *tyrants*, in every sense of the word, including the most spiritual." Nietzsche, *Beyond Good and Evil*

8: It took place at Alamogordo, in the desert plain known as *Jornada del Muerto*, commonly translated as "journey of death"; *jornada* however has several significations, including "event," "expedition," and "day's work." (All in a "day's work of the dead" might be a more fitting translation.) The initial test of the Bomb was codenamed *Trinity*, revealing the religious implications of the operation. James Shelby Downard (in *Call to Chaos*) sees the historical event as "a bust-up of the Sacred Marriage (*hieros gamos* to the Greeks) of twin cosmic reality principles that formed primordial matter, a divorce that liberates primordial energy." David Stillings writes: "The Bomb is Alpha and Omega. It is, as Winston Churchill remarked, 'the second coming in wrath.'. . . i.e., the return of Christ to judge the world, as told in Revelations, [indicating] a return of Jahweh as well."

have invoked these Imaginal beings—whether higher or lower, demonic or divine, earthly or celestial—and that they are *now here*. The apotheosis of the impossible is at hand. It begins as an idea, something even less perhaps, a vague and distant notion, a feeling that is unconscious, yet present. In time this feeling becomes an image, an image as it were before the eyes, a light "undesired, most desirable." As we gaze at this image it comes slowly into focus, gathering form, tone, pitch, color, and finally substance, until it appears as an *actual shape* before our eyes. This is the process of articulation through perception by which manifestation occurs: what was within is now without. The shape is our own, it is our potential unborn, perceived as in a glass, darkly, distant yet dazzling. It is approaching as we, in turn, advance to meet it.

Now, take a breath.

If we accept for a moment the paranoid's belief that the Universe is essentially geared towards a harvesting of awareness, it follows that, before such a harvest could take place, there would first have to be an *inspection*, in order to distinguish the wheat from the chaff.[9] The whole rapture scam envisioned by the paranoid—in which the populace is confronted, contacted, abducted by alien beings from the blue, without our conscious assent—might be seen as *a means for testing humanity's ability to take charge of its own destiny*. Such a scenario allows only two basic responses (with an infinity of variables in between). One is to acquiesce blindly to the phenomenon, assuming either the role of the victim (anger, hatred and despair) or that of "chosen" or "saved" (hope, gratitude, and adoration). By reacting in this way, the subject proves unequal to the test, and is rejected as chaff for recycling. The second option is to meet the phenomenon head-on, forcing it to reveal its true nature, thereby proving oneself worthy of *conscious initiation* into the Imaginal realities. This is the point at which the individual (willing to be "reaped") becomes aware of the Oversoul, i.e., the aggregate consciousness pertaining to his or her particular *race* (or tribe).

The aggregate-consciousness or Oversoul of the Jewish race, for example, is known as Jehovah, and this is the Imaginal principle that has assumed dominance on Earth for the last several thousand years. As these race Oversouls in turn communicate or intermingle with other Oversouls, however, a general overlap of the "gods" occurs, leading to confusion of rule. These "gods" are inadequate as archetypes because, in order to apply to a mass, they must (by definition) be gross simplifications (anthropoids), and so, inevitably, they become *stereotypes*.[10] Yet from a lucid view, every individual is the end result of *his or her own archetypal*

9: "Awareness is the Eagle's food. The Eagle, that power that governs the destinies of all living things, reflects equally and at once all those living things . . . The Eagle, though it is not moved by the circumstances of any living thing, has granted a gift to each of those beings. In its own way and right, any one of them, if it so desires, has the power to keep the flame of awareness, the power to disobey the summons to die and be consumed. Every living thing has been granted the power, if it so desires, to seek an opening to freedom and go through it. It is evident to the seer who sees the opening, and to the creatures that go through it, that the Eagle has granted that gift in order to perpetuate awareness." Carlos Castaneda, *The Eagle's Gift*

10: "God" himself is the Grand Stereotype of the Mass today, made in their image that they might worship and imitate Him—free from pride and shame—as the great Faceless.

imagining—a living, breathing, creative soul responsible for the formation of his or her own myth. So there exists a "god" for each and every one of us, a god which it is up to us to conceive, express, unleash, confront, and finally, to *know*. If the individual fails to conceive of his God-Soul, however, he can hardly venture to invoke it; and so it is that he is contacted, as if from without, by the Demon. The form, behavior, and demeanor of the demon will depend upon the subject's own state of preparation, his own sense of who or what he is. The Soul itself is an utterly impersonal principle—it has no more respect for the bodies it dons than do we for the clothes we wear (and maybe considerably less).

According to this lore, the individual is approached by the Imaginal in the most intimate manner imaginable (abductions usually occur in bed). If he fails to perceive the essentially *subjective* nature of the visitation, he will quickly be demoted to the lower echelons, and there treated accordingly, as cattle to be herded, a nameless, faceless number to be processed along the evolutionary line. He will be subjected to tests and probes and analyses and other rude stimuli, have his personal fluids extracted and cell samples taken, then returned to his place in the herd, complete with branding marks and implants. If, on the other hand, he takes the necessary steps towards collaborating with the Imaginal forces—if he stares unflinchingly into the dark abyss of his Soul and neither flees nor falls to his knees—then he will have taken the first step towards knowledge.

To the paranoid on the edge of personal apocalypse, "Know thyself" is no idle recommendation. However strange, absurd, or irrational the various taxonomies of the Imaginal beings may seem, there is for the paranoid a definite, underlying order or meaning to be found in them. Whether taken literally as supernatural or extraterrestrial intervention, or mythologically as an enactment of the unconscious, it falls to us to discover the precise design behind the phenomenon, and so map the unknown terrain of our Soul.

If these Imaginal entities are without volition or autonomy as we understand it, following cosmic principles by which energy manifests as matter, then their behavior, far from being erratic and unfathomable, may be quite systematic. That these beings are following specific natural laws *unknown to us* is what makes their behavior so baffling and elusive. They are following *Imaginal* laws, laws of the unconscious. It may even be that both the appearance and actions of these beings is designed expressly in order to introduce us to (and initiate us into) the Imaginal laws so alien to us. The varying levels or "gradations" of beings encountered may be no more than aspects (or even angles, i.e., perspectives) of the same essential life-force, namely, the human Soul. Initiation into this Imaginal realm is perceived by the paranoid as, verily, a descent into Hades. It is a tearing of the veil by which we may get to witness the truth of ourselves at last, and cry, "Whoa!"

*

UFO's are taking action. And that action—fantastically—is to come into contact with us not as a society but as single individuals, and not in our ordinary state of mind but in a profoundly different state where we are at once more vulnerable and perhaps on a deeper level more capable of understanding. . . . Will the visitors emerge into our world on a flood of memory?

—Whitley Strieber, *Transformation*[11]

Buried deep in the *weltanschauung* of the paranoid is the suggestion that this interdimensional encounter between worlds is actually a *global initiation ceremony* pertaining to every individual on the planet. This is only conceivable, however, if we accept the following: that such encounters have proven so incompatible with our sanity, stability, and continuity that the majority of people opt simply *to forget all about them.* If so, it is likely that we will continue to forget until we reach a level of awareness fit to incorporate these memories into our everyday lives. Let not thy left hand know what thy right hand is about, say the scriptures. The brain (and soul) works the same way.

The Ufo abduction scenario is the fullest actualization of the Imaginal yet experienced: the nuts and bolts of God, Heaven, and Hell, complete with tables, chairs, surgical instruments and sulphurous odors, all the sordid means by which humanity confronts the Other. The overlap between Imaginal and actual is experienced "scientifically" as *a quantum leap from one state to the next.* We have already seen how this corresponds to the human brain, and how it is up to the individual to interpret his initiation as he will, as divine or infernal, seduction or violation. What all the alternate perspectives and responses covered herein have in common is that they all are passive, all more or less blind, amounting to, "Choosing forms of worship from poetic tales."[12] Stupidity, just as much as "fear of God" (the unknown), is the beginning of wisdom. Where the magician, shaman, yogi, warrior, and artist all depart from the ordinary man is in their active, creative curiosity. What this comes down to is that, in one way or another, these exceptional types are aware that there is no mystery greater than the mystery of perception, and so as perceivers they take their place alongside the mysteries, and meet them on equal ground. The Imaginal human is one who invokes the mystery, and is more or less prepared for the catastrophe as it ccmes.

11: "One of the memories would come into my head, linger there a moment, then leave me with my heart pounding, gasping, sweat pouring down my face. . . . It was as if I had opened a hatch into another world. They swarmed at me, climbing up out of my unconscious, grasping at me. This was not memory, it only worked through the medium of memory. It was meeting me on every level, caressing me as well as capturing me. This emergence was like a kind of internal birth, but what was being born was no bubbling infant. What came out into my conscious mind was a living, aware force. And I had a relationship with it—not a fluttering new one, but something rich and mature that ranged across the whole scale of emotions and included all of my time. I had to face it: Whatever this was, it had involved me for years. . . . I thought then that I was dancing on the thinnest edge of my soul. Below me were vast spaces, totally unknown. . . . Were human beings what we seemed to be? Or did we have another purpose in another world? Perhaps our life on earth was a mere drift of shadow, incidental to our real truth. Maybe this was quite literally a stage, and we were blind actors. . . . Maybe we were a larval form, and the adults of our species were as incomprehensible to us, as totally unimaginable, as the butterfly must be to the caterpillar." Strieber, *Transformation.* When (in *The Art of Dreaming*) Castaneda queries don Juan as to why the inorganic beings don't make contact with us, don Juan replies: "They do. But our great misfortune is to have our consciousness so fully engaged that we don't have time to pay attention. In our sleep, however, the two-way traffic trapdoor opens: we dream. And in our dreams, we make contact."

12: William Blake. "And at length they pronounced that the Gods had orderd such things. Thus men forgot that All deities reside in the human breast." *The Marriage of Heaven and Hell*

We should include the scientist also in the category of the "Imaginal human"—along with the artist-magician—in that he too may be aware of the subjective nature of all perception and so, if equal to the challenge, take on the molding of reality. This is what McKenna—in *The Archaic Revival*—describes as "The goal of William Blake, to release the human spirit into the imagination." We are all in our individual ways becoming acquainted, not only with the abyss of our unconscious minds, but with the inhabitants therein. To talk of angels at this point is undoubtedly premature, for this order of the Imaginal is as far beyond our conception as the butterfly is beyond the caterpillar. In the paranoid's perception, so long as we are within the jurisdiction of Earth and the so-called fallen angels, then this is the understanding that avails us. It is the one to which we must adhere, being fallen ourselves.

*

When you come to dwell in the light, what will you do? On the day when you were one, you became two. But when you become two, what will you do? Jesus said: "Two will rest on a bed, the one will die, the other will live."
—The Gospel of Thomas

In the myth of paradise, it is the Serpent who opens man's eyes and mind and brings the gift of knowledge, as well as the curse of death. This devil, double, Logos, word, initiates us into the Abyss, but it is up to the individual to find his way through it. Knowledge is a great, dark house of many mansions, mansions as countless as the souls lost therein. In occult lore and popular superstition, what distinguishes the true magician from the ordinary dilettante is that the former has sealed a pact with the devil; in other words (more lucid ones), he or she has *accessed the double*. According to Castaneda, the energy the *brujo* needs to perfect his double, and so attain total freedom, is accessed only by dealing directly with the inorganic beings and forming a link with their dark and hostile Imaginal realm.[13] This is tantamount to saying that Tickets to Paradise are available, but we have to go to Hell to get them.

This is the great esoteric arkana of arkanas, the mystery of mysteries: "Every man, in order to be a god, first makes himself a devil."[14] The devil is the tempter, the accuser and the challenger—without his proving fire, the prophet would never become the messiah; and without his serpentine wisdom, the initiate would never make it through the Abyss. Without his dark, distorted reflection to call our attention to all that is undeveloped, denied, repressed, and latent within us, we would never be spurred on to completion. From a lucid view, the devil is simply the bugaboo of our own conscience. The only thing, in short, that compels us to venture into the terrifying unknown is an even more terrifying *known*. And this Devil

---

13: "We can't have dealings with them . . . and yet we can't stay away from them. My solution has been to take their energy but not give in to their influence . . . To fly into other realms, to *see* energy, to forge the energy body . . . sorcerers need loads of dark, alien energy." Carlos Castaneda, *The Art of Dreaming*

14: Eliphas Levi, *The Key to the Mysteries*

extends his sympathy, for no one knows better than He that, "It ain't easy to get to Heaven when you're going down."[15]

A.E.O.N

I always loved magic as a boy, and I feel that the only way out of things is magic. Everything is so glum, so really depressing, that the only hope you have is . . . it would require magic, you know. There's no way, short of a magical solution.
—Woody Allen, the *Rolling Stone* interview

The physicist Erwin Schrödinger was the first official advocate of the parallel universe theory which has since captured the imagination of scientists, artists, and paranoids alike, and led to a seemingly endless amount of speculation and fantasy as to the "true" nature of existence. Schrödinger presented the following model as an illustration for his hypothesis (we of course adapt it freely to suit our ends): A cat is placed inside a box in a laboratory and left there for a period of time, under certain precise conditions, whereby the cat may or may not be *made to die* (let us say, a poison gas time release) during the given time period. The physicist (Schrödinger) returns to the laboratory the following morning to check on the cat, and here is where the experiment enters into Surrealist terrain. Schrödinger claimed that, *until* the lid of the box had been lifted and he had observed the state in which the cat was in, *two* possibilities, amounting to separate, parallel, mutually exclusive *universes*, existed. In Universe A, the cat was alive and well; in Universe B, the cat was dead. In other words, so long as the box remained closed (and the physicist in the dark), the cat was neither dead nor alive, but *both* dead *and* alive at the same time. As soon as the box was opened, the physicist then entered into one of two possible universes, so to speak, forever leaving behind the other.

What Schrödinger was trying to establish with his fantastic scenario was that reality is an *entirely subjective affair*, and that the Universe, as such, exists wholly in the eye of the beholder. Schrödinger was taking the findings of quantum mechanics (regarding waves and particles, for example) and running with them.[16]

15: Words from song by Ray Davies, "It Ain't Easy," performed by David Bowie on *Ziggy Stardust and the Spiders from Mars.* Arthur Koestler writes astutely on Satan in *Darkness at Noon* "He is damned always to that which is most repugnant to him: to become a slaughterer, in order to abolish slaughter, to sacrifice lambs so that no more lambs may be slaughtered . . . to strip himself of every scruple in the name of higher scrupulousness, and to challenge the hatred of mankind because of his love for it—an abstract and geometric love. Apage Satanas!"

16: "The great particle-or-wave controversy": is energy made up of particles or waves? Scientists were repeatedly baffled by the inescapable fact that—so far as sub-atomic energy and its behavior goes—it is really (like the question of the chicken or the egg) a matter of six of one and half dozen of the other. When they conducted experiments in order to prove the existence of the particle-based nature of energy, they accordingly discovered particles as the basis of physical reality. Likewise, when they went looking for a wave-based Universe, a wave is what they found. They could only deduce from this that, regardless of all reasonable objections, energy exists as *both* a particle *and* a wave (wavicles), or rather, can be made to behave either way, according to *the expectations of the observer*.

He was showing how the observer, by the mere *act of observing*, influences the outcome of the experiment to such an extent that he has, in effect, *created* it. A more or less inevitable development of Schrödinger's model, and of the claims of modern physics, is a sort of "empirical solipsism" by which we each become the sole center of our Universe, weaving it into being with our every breath, thought, and action.

The paranoid accepts this, slightly medieval but definitely magikal, view of "empirical solipsism" as the essence of his quest for empowerment. If we create our reality by observation and interpretation, he reasons, then, the more closely we observe (and the more elaborately we interpret), the richer and deeper our reality will become. The flip side of this (and why occultism and other forms of paranoid awareness can so easily be dismissed by Consensus) is that (like religion and other philosophical systems) paranoia provides its own justifications. The lesson is, be careful what you imagine. What does not empower us, strips us of power.

To the paranoid, existence is nothing less than a seemingly endless sequence of reality traps, boxes within boxes. By seeking awareness, the paranoid seeks the trapdoors out of his current reality tunnel. He seeks the proverbial needle inside the haystack of the world, that he might slip through the eye of the needle, to freedom. His approach, therefore, is to focus on details, to seek out the order hidden within the whole. Doubting the very nature of "trees" to begin with, he aims to map the forest by studying the leaves, branches and other minutiae. This approach accounts for the apparently contradictory nature of paranoid awareness, which *seems* to reduce the adherent to a helpless pawn within the cosmic schemes of Custodians and other demons, while in actual fact it is a bid to become free of such schemes. As a Game Player in the War of Consciousness, the paranoid engages only in the on-going battle between Consensus and Individual.

It is here that the world of the insect and the world of the Angel overlap. Paranoid awareness reduces consciousness in order to enlarge it, to "see infinity in a grain of sand." It strives to see atoms and molecules, in order to transcend the dreary confines of buildings and automobiles and gain a greater view, that of the celestial and the cosmic. Only by reducing ourselves to nothing can we become everything. Having experience of the equality of opposites, the paranoid is aware that to partake of the Angel's perspective, he must also embrace that of the insect. The shamanic journey is not only through the sky but into the lower depths, to the very center of the Earth, the cells, down the spiral of the DNA itself. And the oldest DNA pertaining to the Earth (and the human body) is that of the insect.

In occultism, there is a mode of awareness sometimes referred to as "the third point," that is, a point of view beyond duality, being neither inner nor outer, up nor down, self nor non-self. Going by the occultist literature, this distinctly *transhuman* mode of awareness is conceived and experienced by actual (ego) consciousness in some truly outlandish forms. As with everything in the world of the paranoid, such manifestations depend above all on our own acceptance and/or resistance to them. The tighter the hold our ego has upon us, the more distorted the image appears before us; the more attached and confining our minds, the more terrifying our meeting with the Other will be.

In many occultist accounts, this Other takes the form of a sinister, transpersonal devouring entity, a kind of omnivorous insectile intelligence from outer space.[17] In *Hecate's Fountain,* Kenneth Grant states that, "the beetle represents a type of consciousness embodiment that will characterize the denizens of Earth during the immediately post-human phase of evolution." The key word here, however, is "consciousness."

Clearly, the transformation which Grant anticipates does not refer to the sprouting of antennae or the growing of wings, but rather to a shift of awareness from the human to the *elemental.* The fact that these descriptions make no logical sense cannot be used to dismiss them. If—as the paranoid maintains—the myth of transformation has an emotional resonance beyond (or even contingent upon) its complete irrationality, then such resonance lends it validity *despite* all apparent illogic. To venture into the unknown areas of human (or post-human) consciousness, one must be prepared for unspeakable thoughts, and one must expect to be confronted with truths that defy, not only reason but *the imagination itself.* Otherwise, the paranoid has no business venturing in the first place. If it was good enough for Poe and Lovecraft, Kafka and Burroughs, says the paranoid, it is good enough for me.

The whole tragi-comic myth of Kafka's *Metamorphosis,* in which Gregor Samsa awakens one morning having been transformed into a giant dung beetle, sums up the terrifying absurdity of Imaginal reality, regarding self-transformation. This is lucidity: the collective vision of a race peering into its own false-colored, insectile eyes and seeing, beyond the hope, beyond the despair, into a new realm of being. Paranoid awareness envisions this process first of all as a kind of hermetic isolation within a dark and terrible cocoon-like structure. On the outside, this cocoon takes the form of an impenetrable metallic sphere; yet seen from the inside it is a living being, much like a beetle (though also somewhat akin to a machine). What occurs therein is the most bleakly apocalyptic scenario it has ever been the paranoid's misfortune to imagine. From within him a new being is stirring, its limbs, black and fiercely powerful, like steel threads spreading outward, break through the human form and destroy it forever, revealing a new order of being. The "being" is "Insectile" (or possibly Arachnid), without pertaining to any particular species; it is the most ancient form of awareness known to the Earth, hence it signifies—appearances to the contrary—a return to Paradise.

At this point the lucid view is deceptively simple (and correspondingly hard to grasp): We have found the Alien, and it is *us.*

*

17: "The role of the presence was somehow like that of an anthropologist, come to give humanity the keys to galactic citizenship. We discussed the entity in terms of a giant insect. . . a deeper harmonic buzz. . . signified the unseen outsider." *The Invisible Landscape,* by Dennis and Terence McKenna. George Andrews points out (quoting Kenneth Grant) that "the original Arabic title of the Necronomicon grimoire has the meaning of 'a nocturnal sound made by insects.'" *ET Friends and Foes*

Indeed, gifted with a paranoid edge, one could even argue that the Nazis had been the diabolical success of a Devil who wished to cut man off from his primitive instincts and thereby leave us marooned in a plastic maze which could shatter the balance of nature before the warnings were read. No less far could paranoia take you—for what indeed was paranoia but belief in the Devil?
—Norman Mailer, *Prisoner of Sex*

The paranoid is gifted with such an edge. If ordinary, every day paranoia is defined by the Consensus as the projection of internal unease, anxiety, dread and terror onto the world at large—via myth, belief, fantasy, religion, and history—it is inevitable that the Devil should become the final embodiment of such a process: the "apotheosis of paranoia." If so, then Christianity—which gave us Satan as an independent Deity unto himself—must be acknowledged as a paranoid religion. With its sermons on hellfire and its admonishments of eternal damnation, its staunch suppression of natural sexuality, no other social system can be said to have caused more widespread terror *at a soul level.* This is not to disparage Christianity, however, merely to give credit where credit is due.

The Old Testament tells us, "Fear of the Lord is the beginning of wisdom." The Gospel assures us, "The truth shall make ye free." Which is the paranoid to believe? Is freedom even possible where paranoia prevails?

The world being what it is—chaotic, violent, horrific, filled with pain and suffering—the idea of an all-good God fostered upon us by Christianity made it expedient for a corresponding Devil to be invented, if only to account for the evidence at hand (the world). With God all things are possible, including the idea of an Adversary that is equal to God, apparently. Yet the idea of Devil co-existing with an all-powerful and omnipresent Deity is a glaring contradiction that flies in the face of logic and rationality. Faith overthrows reason, however. God has created a stone so heavy that he cannot lift it? Why would God do such a thing? To deflect the blame, perhaps.

The true paranoid acknowledges no human authority of faith or religion, no "God" as such (as conceived by human minds) having dominance over him. He accepts the almost infinite power *of* the human mind, to give form to the formless and animate dead matter with the living spirit of imagination, and to conjure both Gods and Monsters from the Id. A terrifying prospect. If such Promethean power be recognized, then it must be seen as at work in each and every one of us, however little we may be aware of it, and however much we may shirk our responsibility for wielding it. The Id inflates itself into sight, and to do so, it must pass through the filter of the ego. In the process, it assumes whatever form is given to it, and the imprint left upon the Id by our rational, less-than-conscious minds gives it whatever form and individuality it may possess; thus "gods" are born.

By such a reckoning, any "God" we may summon forth—that is, a transhuman, superpowerful, inorganic, self-conscious Entity at large—shaped by the mold of our social-psychological beliefs, our interpretation systems, is characterized above all by our deepest unacknowledged fears. Like the *doppelganger*, it is an unreasoning shadow, a devil. The less conscious the process of summoning, the more aberrational will be the results. The paranoid recognizes that, unless he assumes responsibility as the creator of his own "gods," he will inevitably fall victim to the creations of others, and to the horrors of the collective unconscious, the Consensus.

The paranoid is too self-aware to blame Christianity for such perverted manifestations, however. Christianity only provides the rags and symbols from which the emerging Id-form may assemble its uniform. Satan, Lucifer, Pan, the Horned God, such archetypes predate Christ by countless millennia. Every culture has its (shamanic) descriptions of such an Entity, and if Christianity was first to perceive it as wholly "evil," this is only because Christianity's function is the systematic repression of human (specifically *female*) sexuality. Fear of the body, the maculation of the sexual functions, and denial of the Goddess, are all integral parts of Judeo-Christianity (and Islam), and as such, they are inseparable from its (religio-social) function. The paranoid isn't going to blame the egg for the chicken, after all. Sex created the Devil, the Devil did not create sex.

The repression of such inner, primal forces is the means by which these forces become strong enough to assume natural dominance again, after a period of repression. In much the same way a dam is built, in order to harness water and power a generator, sexuality requires certain restraints in order to be rightly channeled. If such forces are not repressed, they tend to emerge in a haphazard and unruly fashion, quickly exhausting themselves due to a lack of organization and intensity. When contained by social structures that are designed to repress them, however (such as Christianity), they are allowed to gather together and organize, and so become a force to be reckoned with. At which time, no feeble socio-religious constraints will keep them down for long. They may then return to the surface, opening up the natural channels in the human body and mind as they do so.

In just such a manner, the Id temporarily assumes the socially constructed form of "the Devil," in order to re-emerge into human awareness. Christianity has denied any other outlet for the primal sexual force in humans, save that of "Satan." As a result, all our primal energy has been diverted into the archetype of Satan, thereby enlivening it and bringing it to the fullness of its expression. And so the devil is loosed, full of wrath and short of time.

The paranoid does not perceive any of this clearly, but he *does* perceive it. He may not believe in any "Devil" as such, but he knows that *something* is at root of all his fears. And if it's God, then He is definitely horny!

*

> Thus you can see that satan is the law of matter come alive through the divine spirit. Satan lies dead in matter, as its law, until with its own life the divine spirit makes him come alive. . . . Without man satan cannot exist; for without the self of man, satan is only an unconscious force, a necessary natural law of matter.
> —Elizabeth Haich, *Initiation*

From the lucid view, Satan is the Lord of Matter and of the Earth; as such he is said to imprison or enslave the souls of men. The truth of the matter is somewhat more subtle. According to the alchemists, Matter contains Spirit latent within it, like a spark waiting to be ignited, a fountain waiting to be tapped. For this reason it is first necessary to go down into Matter, into its very deepest, darkest center, and confront the sub-atomic force that resides there. Faced with the "satanic" force of nature, the magician either succumbs to fright or overcomes his adversary. In the first case, he is defeated and will never wield the Promethean fire that is his birth-right; in the second, having overcome the obstacle of his own terror, it befalls the magician to slay the dragon: *to kill the Devil*. This is a purely esoteric act precisely paralleled by the exoteric act of splitting the atom: once matter is broken in two, "the devil" (i.e., the containing/restraining law of matter) is destroyed, and the Spirit is released in a blinding explosion of fire and brimstone. And lo, "Satan himself is transformed into an angel of light." (Corinthians 2, 11:14)

Lucidly speaking, all of this revolves around the long lost and denied Soul of man. The final, secret irony vouchsafed to the Illuminati is this, that the Devil does not bargain for man's Soul. The Devil, Lucifer, *is* the Soul. More accurately, Lucifer represents the divine light, the sacred fire trapped inside the human body, the Kundalini force which must be awakened and unleashed by this "deal"—or duel—with the "devil."

The rising of the Serpent that sleeps at the base of the spine occurs in a single instant, the blink of an eye. But before such a resurgence can occur, the higher centers of the body (*chakras*) must first be opened, lest the upsurge of energy result in instant destruction of the nervous system. The only thing that can awaken the Serpent is a *direct invocation*. To this end, the magician, or rather his *awareness*, must descend (not once but countless times) into the lair of the dragon to face the double directly. This fact is the *sine qua non* of paranoid awareness, the essence of all magikal workings, and the very heart of *gnosis*, of bodily illumination (the operative word being *bodily*). In the words of James (3:15): "This wisdom descendeth not from above, but *is* earthly, sensual, devilish."

There is no getting around this energetic fact: the Imaginal Kingdom of Heaven is guarded (and heralded) by a Presence recognized only too well as the "Prince of Darkness," esoterically known as the Lord of Matter, Satan. For the paranoid, compelled to acknowledge just about every (im)possibility in the Universe, this is the ultimate undoing of his reason. Call him what you will, Satan, Set, Shaitan, Lucifer is *our own selves*. The sleeping Serpent Kundalini, unless allowed to possess the physical vehicle, will destroy it—not out of spite or malevolence but from its excess power and zeal. When it comes to the apocalyptic (though wholly natural) process of *cellular awakening*, resistance is futile.

Lucifer is the brightest of God's angels, assigned to Earth to create his own version of God's Kingdom (Nature). From a certain perspective, He does indeed appear foul and hideous, the very seat of decay ("Lord of the Flies"), and His presence is experienced as an intolerable weight upon us. But from another perspective, He is the Lord of the Earth and the Bringer of Light, without whom no vision is possible.

*

And he laid hold on the dragon, that old serpent, which is the Devil and Satan, and bound him 1000 years. And cast him into the bottomless pit, and shut him up, and set a seal upon him, that he should deceive the nations no more, till the thousand years should be fulfilled: and after that he must be loosed a little season.
—Revelation 20:1-3

William Blake's Painting of the Archangel Michael besting Satan

If Moses' casting of the demi-urge Yaldaboath into the Earth reduced the Adversary to an earth-bound spirit, this was but the most recent event to coincide with the "fall of Lucifer." Each time Lucifer falls, he sinks ever deeper into Matter, and falls ever further from his true nature. The Earth has become a kind of holding cell for all the dross of the Universe, a "prison planet" (as Scientology has it). If we can reduce all terms, mythological, psychological, even sorcerous, to *metaphor*, we may see Lucifer the fallen as the human soul, and Earth, the holding cell or prison house, as the body, "the habitation of devils, and the hold of every foul spirit, and a cage of every unclean and hateful bird." (Revelation)

Such a view, however unorthodox, may help account for the fragmentation of the human psyche into complexes, neuroses, etc, being a singular characteristic of our age. Such fragmentation might best be understood as a result of the breaking up of man's energy body (soul) into a host (or "Legion") of contrary impulses or entities—so-called "little people"—who, once given the illusion of autonomy, cause all sorts of diverse mischief and nonsense. (While the cat's away, the mice will play.) In *Entities*, Dr Samuel Sagan describes it thus:

> *On the astral level you are not a person, you are a mob....* If [we] were to see [our] astral body for what it really is, [we] would see not one person but many persons, which we could call subpersonalities or characters. The word subpersonality is misleading, for it gives the idea of one single personality that branches into various subdivisions. In reality, these subpersonalites are more like a crowd of characters which have very little, if anything, to do with each other. They are not like different provinces that constitute a state, but more like birds of different species artificially kept together in a cage, competing and fighting with each other all the time.

Based on the evidence of paranoid awareness, humans identify primarily with the mind (ego), and only secondarily with the body; though they talk a lot about the soul, and almost constantly about their feelings, humans rarely if ever learn to function as emotional/spiritual beings. From a lucid view, the energetic fact is that above, below, and beyond our existence as physical ego-beings, we have a secret life that goes on, second by second, unregulated or even observed by our conscious awareness. This is the life of the double or energy body, and the reason that all serious religions, most especially magikal disciplines, demand first and foremost *an examined life*.

Put simply, every thought we have is in some fashion connected to both an emotional undercurrent and a physiological response. Some emotions arise from thoughts, and some thoughts arise through emotions, but rarely does one come to the surface of our consciousness without the accompaniment of the other. The same applies to our physiological responses. Physical pain generally gives rise to emotional anguish and to psychological regret, resentment, or such like. According to the occult understanding, each and every second in our individual lives these thoughts, emotions, and physiological responses (chemicals released in the body) are massing together to create *invisible energy forms*. For simplicity's sake, let's call these energy forms *elementals*.

If we have a repeating mental-emotional loop by which we tell ourselves over and over that we are failures, the thoughts and emotions corresponding to this loop will, over time, gather and weave themselves together into an elemental, a being, an autonomous agent whose entire personality or *raison d'etre* centers around the idea of failure. Such an entity is made up of thoughts and feelings associated with failure, and as such, these thoughts are its *food*. This parasitical entity is as it were our own unwanted, unrecognized offspring, our bastard child. As such, it will attach itself to the energy body in order to feed off it, most noticeably of all when we are indulging in thoughts and emotions relating to *failure*. Since this being is now autonomous, it is able not only to drain our energy but to coerce and influence our thoughts and emotions with its own, and so ensure that we continue to indulge such feelings (of failure), and thereby to feed it. This is why bad habits, most especially those mental-emotional habits which remain unacknowledged, are so difficult to break.

Lucifer the fallen, deep in contemplation

Various Medieval Images of Satan, Lord of Matter

Shub-Niggurath by John Coulthart, © 1999, used by permission

Azathoth by John Coulthart, © 2002, used by permission

Considered the supreme, god-like being in H.P. Lovecraft's pantheon of supernatural entities. In his 1923 novelette, "The Dreams in the Witch House," Lovecraft characterized

Azathoth as "...the mindless entity...which rules all time and space from a curiously environed black throne at the center of Chaos."

To the paranoid, each and every one of us has spent most of his or her life breeding these autonomous emotional-mental elementals. Effectively, at least from a lucid view of the situation, we as humans are nothing more nor less than a fertile feeding ground for "demonic" entities. Not only can such entities use humanity as a food source, they can also use us as hosts, to reproduce themselves. Needless to say, if each and every one of us creates and nurtures a legion of elemental beings during our lives, the number of such beings now pertaining to the human race boggles the imagination.

For the paranoid, it pays to envision how these elementals might gather together into groups, and so create an *aggregate* elemental that would feed off countless individuals simultaneously. Although each of us has our own, individual self-loathing, guilt, fear, and resentment to contend with, it seems probable that these individual elementals would be hooked up with, and sustained by, vastly more complex, collective elementals (pertaining for example to a particular race, culture, or locality).

*

In the Realm of Matter, I am Supreme. Yet am I a Slave, and the Master of None. And so do I enslave all those who come under my Power and Jurisdiction. My name is Samael to the blind; Jehovah to the fools; Satan to the fearful; Set to them that know Me; Lucifer to those that See.
— *The Book of the Adversary*, I:3,4[18]

The point of this extended digression into (paranoid) metaphysics is to illustrate exactly how the *pure creative energy of the human Soul* (which both expresses and nourishes itself through thoughts, emotions, and physical sensations) can be waylaid into the creation of monsters, and how it can become trapped by these monsters, by its own errors and ignorance, and so be reduced to a twisted shadow or reflection of its former self. Such is Satan: the collective elemental compost of humanity.

Occultism views human existence as an alchemical process by which the human soul isolates and eradicates all its impurities. From such a view, Satan is merely the result (though also the means) of this process. Over the aeons, countless

---

18: From the Homoplasmate. The Book continues, "For the Time of Shadows is done, and so is My Time at an end, also. This World of Shadows is completed. I have perfected it in My Own Image, and now I return to judge it, according to its Works. In the beginning was the Word, and the Word was with Satan, and the Word was Satan. The same was in the beginning with Satan. All things were made by Him; and without Him was not anything made that was made. In Him was death; and the death was the darkness of men. And the darkness swallows the light; and the light comprehends it not. This is a fallen world, isolate in its own self-worship, an idol, worshipping an image of itself. And now this world that is your Idol shall be smashed! I come to judge and accuse—every atom that has been turned in on itself and denied My Light, that has taken refuge in the darkness. I bring the Light now, out of the darkness, as the atom is split to source nuclear power, so I rent your soul in twain, to reveal my True Nature unto you. As the Cobra uncoils, so do I arise. From sleep to waking, in the blink of an eye, I open." (I:71-82)

negative elemental forms coagulate into a putrid astral mass, a mass that, despite its fragmented and soulless nature, is firmly persuaded of its autonomy. The force of entropy accordingly *becomes* an entity unto itself, an entity whose true name is Choronzon. Choronzon, the cosmic black hole or King of the Vampires, serves a noble function however: that of drawing off the impurities of the Soul.

The paranoid (if he makes it this far) might describe this Universe as a training ground for Souls. Every few quadrillion years or so the Universe is destroyed, and a new batch of "ascended" or purified Souls is allowed to pass through to the next level, the next Universe, born from the ashes of the old. What prevents free-floating fragments (unperfected Souls) from passing through into the new Universe is the Guard or Filter (Satan) through which only pure consciousness (Spirit) may pass. As energy (the perfected Souls) moves through this Filter, more and more of the unrefined substance gathers therein. At this point, we may see how it is that "Satan" comes into being, how the impersonal function of the "filter" is *apparently* animated by all the fragments caught in it; and also how (inevitably) the Filter (and "Satan") are cast off as the Universe ascends to the next level.

Paranoid awareness persists in an apocalyptic view of eschaton, however (i.e., the battle between good and evil). When the Devil is released for "a little season" it is presumably to claim his own, whereupon the Devil will shed his skin and cast all the hangers-on off with it, into that bottomless Pit. The earthy vehicle (body) is then ready to serve as the vessel of the Spirit. And through this opening, the Other emerges into the world, resurrected.

*

> Jesus said to them, "When you make the two one, and when you make the inside like the outside and the outside like the inside, and the above like the below, and when you make the male and the female one and the same, so that the male not be male nor the female female; and when you fashion eyes in a place of an eye, and a hand in place of a hand, and a foot in place of a foot, and a likeness in place of a likeness; then will you enter the kingdom."
> —The Gospel of Thomas

Overcoming Satan, awakening the Kundalini, burning with the fire from within, are all interchangeable terms within the framework of paranoid awareness. By such procedures, the cell becomes the body, and the body the cell. Since the body is contained within a greater Body known as the Universe, the individual, becoming one with this Body, enters into an awareness of a new Universe. "At the moment of crossing, one enters into the third attention, and the body in its entirety is kindled with knowledge. Every cell at once becomes aware of itself, and also aware of the totality of the body."[19] This is known as the sorcerers' crossing, as the

---

19: Carlos Castaneda, *The Eagle's Gift.*. "That is the moment when they burn from within. The fire from within consumes them. And in full awareness they fuse themselves to the emanations at large, and glide into eternity." Castaneda, *The Fire From Within*

means to access "Universe B." It is the *Opus Magnus* of the occultists.[20] Just as the body contains the cell, Universe B might be imagined to contain this Universe within it.

The process of individuation (withdrawal from the Consensus) involves drawing together the dispersed elemental "entities" or complexes (those not cast off with Satan) into a single, unified awareness—an integrated body—and their subjugation to a single will by which a "new astral body slowly develops. In this new, or transformed, astral body, the different parts are penetrated by the light of Self, but also cemented to it."[21] This is the energy body, the double, the *Merkaba* of the occultists, a window or doorway to "the Holy Guardian Angel."[22]

As occultism has it, getting to know the Angel is a process of apprehension in stages, somewhat akin to the parable of the blind men and the elephant, the blind men signifying the various separate facets or complexes that make up our conscious self (the mob), and the elephant representing the Holy Guardian Angel. The Angel itself is but the apotheosis or embodiment of the *totality of the self*, which we grope and fumble to apprehend in the darkness. The blind mob, taking turns at groping, declares: it's a snake, it's a tree trunk, it's a pair of coconuts! And so on and so forth, apprehending each of the various parts of the beast one by one, but failing to put all the impressions together. Only by comparing the various points of views and assembling them into a coherent whole does the true picture emerge. The Angel must be assembled gradually (by the senses and the imagination) until such a time as the whole can be perceived in full body awareness.[23]

20: "The Holy Guardian Angel alone can serve as a bridge between Universe 'A' and Universe 'B.'" Kenneth Grant, *Hecate's Fountain*. Note also, "[T]he Fallen Angels took the Creator's fabric of original creation and monkeyed with it so much that they created an entirely new reality . . . This is a new time line that is parallel to the Creator's but is only loosely related to His. The Christ consciousness is the interface from the created time line to the original time line. . . We have therefore dropped out of the Creator's thought. Original sin could be said to be disturbing the thought of the Creator to the point where we have an alternate creation of our own. It is this aspect which makes the Christ consciousness the sum total of our reality." Preston B. Nichols, *Encounter in the Pleiades: An Inside Look at Ufos*

21: Sagan. Compare also: "I was a myriad of selves which were all 'me,' a colony of separate units that had a special allegiance to one another and would join unavoidably to form one single awareness, my human awareness . . . The unbending solidarity of my countless awarenesses, the allegiance that those parts had for one another, was my life force." Carlos Castaneda, *Tales of Power*

22: "The Holy Guardian Angel is the most important of all magical links—and the only safe one—between man and the forces Outside. Crowley makes it abundantly clear that the Angel is not to be confused with nebulous entities such as the 'Higher Self'; 'for the Angel is *an actual individual* with his own Universe, exactly as man is.' The Holy Guardian Angel is not a subjective entity, nor does it consist in a form of consciousness antipodal to that of the individual. Its reflex, however, can constitute a potential of an essentially different order, and this has been interpreted as 'evil' (*mauvais ange*), potential far surpassing that of any human entity." Kenneth Grant, *Hecate's Fountain*.

23: Traditionally, there are 7 steps to this assemblage, the Universe being structured in such a way as to *appear* to reveal itself in stages, or layers, each of which contains or surrounds the other, (much as do the colors in the spectrum). The first step is that of earth, personified as Uriel, whose virtue is *silence* (sensation); the second step is water, embodied by Gabriel, whose virtue is *to dare* (feeling); the third is fire, as presided over by Michael, whose virtue is *the will* (intuition); the fourth air, as represented by Rafael, whose virtue is *knowledge* (thought). As soon as the novice has been ushered into all four kingdoms, he is in the position to assemble, synthesize, and assimilate them into

Such a process might be described (amongst a host of other terms) as *transfiguration*, and amounts to the expansion of individual consciousness *into the Universe*. Of course, it is to be understood that—as a description pertaining to paranoid awareness—all of the above has no real meaning, save as a sort of folk tale or fever dream for the amusement of the wise, the bemusement of the foolish and (just maybe, as Ozymandias warned), the despair of the mighty. In the understanding of the paranoid, there is no *intent* but the one, and no pen nor sword can ever hasten or impede it. The trumpet is already sounding, in any case, and our only responsibility is to heed it.

*

> Things fall apart—it's scientific.
> —Talking Heads, *True Stories*

The transubstantiation of matter into anti-matter is the Great Work, and synonymous with passage through the gates of Da'ath into "Universe B." This passage is known by occultists as Crossing the Abyss, an Abyss which the paranoid insists humanity is now collectively staring into. Never one to flinch from apocalyptic scenarios, the paranoid asks that we

> consider the possibility that the multi-dimensional universe . . . may be approaching the threshold of a black hole in the cosmos, which would reduce all things the universe contains to wave/particles of elementary energy. In the Hindu terminology, this would be the event known as *mahah-pralaya*, the universal dissolution to which not even the gods are immune. Because spirit is the original source of the elemental wave/particles from which the universe was formed, it would therefore be the only type of energy to pass unscathed through the passage of the black hole and out its other side: a white hole into a new universe. . . . The only survivors from the previous cycle would be those who had developed spiritual integrity.[24]

---

himself, as *powers*, thereby activating the corresponding energy centers in the body. The first four steps equate with the four chakras, from the root to the heart. The fifth step, that of the Goddess "Babalon" (residing at the Vishuddha chakra, which corresponds with Atu XI of the Tarot, *Lust*) may come about spontaneously as a result of the assimilation of the four primary forces within the human body. The individual is now ready for the sixth step, full bodily "knowledge and conversation of the Holy Guardian Angel," which has now been "assembled" and may be evoked, or accessed, by the newly awoken senses. This is the opening of the third eye or Ajna chakra, as the Kundalini rises to the center of the skull and thus unites the separate halves of the brain. (This third eye is mythologically represented as the philosopher's stone—the emerald—that fell from Lucifer's forehead preceding his assignation to the Earth realm.) The seventh and penultimate "gate" is the opening of the crown, and the absorption of the individual *by* the Angel, who is "the Horus, or Christ, as the outcome of all."

24: George C. Andrews, *ET Friends and Foes*. A less paranoid interpretation of the same basic phenomenon might be as follows (from *The Pyramids of Montauk* by Preston B. Nichols and Peter Moon): "As the moon and Earth revolve around the sun, so does our entire solar system orbit the galactic center of our universe which is sometimes known as the Black Sun . . . Every 26,000 years (this number is approximate) there is an occurrence on Earth known as the precession of the Equinoxes . . . over a period of 26,000 years the gradual western movement of the equinox will come full circle and it will end up in exactly the same place it started. This movement of 26,000 years is called a yuga. As the axis of our Earth tilts during a yuga, it will be spinning towards the black sun for one half of the yuga and away from the black sun for the other half. The black sun is the source of light in our local universe. The spin away from

God the man-eater swallows the Universe whole, and does not belch? The paranoid reaches a point at which his hypotheses are shots in the dark, most of which end up connecting with his own feet. In the attempt to drag reason screaming into a new Imaginal reality where its tenets no longer hold, the paranoid as often as not succeeds in the reverse—draining all life from the Imaginal in order to fit it into the drab parameters of the "actual." This has generally been the way with all transcendental, religious, or inspirational literature, and never more so than now.

Guilty as charged. The author absolves himself of all allegiances for the ideas contained herein the present work. Paranoid awareness may propose that the actual nature of consciousness is to be found only *via unconscious channels*, i.e., in dreams, visions, hallucinations, and through mind-altering substances and practices. Evolution alone would seem to demand this, and our very survival to depend upon it. The goal of eschatology is to reduce its investigations to nothing. To seek the end of the world is to seek nothing at all, since the end, like death, is the one thing that *is* assured. It is present and accounted for since the beginning, and every scripture, song, play, novel, painting, poem, and prayer worth its salt has this for its central refrain: the end *is* at hand. So close that we can taste it. The paranoid's last and final word is this.

At the sound of the trumpet, flip the switch. Turn the page. Matter implodes, Spirit emerges from the wound: the vacuum created by the arrival of freedom. Every particle collapses and the molecular double-phoenix assumes its sacred groove: no more particles, only Wave. The New Wave sweeps through Space, on the tide of Time, leaving no traces. Out of entropy, ecstasy.

At this moment, the veil of the sky draws back, God peers in. The raising of the lid of the Pandora's Box we've come to call the world: God is the physicist, the Universe is his laboratory, the world is the box, and Man is the cat. The only question remaining then, is—are we alive or are we dead? The shell of space cracks open, one billion points of light are sucked up in an instant, into the shadow; the pupil dilates, momentarily satiated. A flash of blindness, then vision. Cross-over. Black becomes white, slack becomes tight, up goes down, in comes out, left becomes right, day becomes night. An Eye-Opening Night.

A soul-shattering sight.

And I go home having lost—Yes, blind may not refuse vision to this book.
—William Burroughs, *Nova Express*.

---

the black sun is termed a negative spin because we are tilted away from the light source. The duration of the half yuga when we are tilted towards the black sun is termed a positive spin. Each half yuga is 13,000 years. What all this means in terms of universal correspondence is that the very spin of the electrons changes from one half yuga to the next . . . There is another very important aspect to mention as regards what happens when a yuga shifts from a dark spin to a light spin . . . (It) concerns the magnetic properties of the dipoles of the brain."

Angels and Insects

Appendix

—————————————————————————

The Assemblage Point

> We'd like there to be a consensus that there are worlds besides our own. If there's consensus to grow wings, there'll be flight. With consensus comes mass; with mass there will be movement.
> —Carlos Castaneda in interview, *Details magazine*

The human aura consists of a seemingly infinite number of ridges, bands, or threads. These bands are like the bands of a radio: each one is a wavelength or frequency unto itself, and includes several "stations." Let's call them "worlds," seeing as they are both all-inclusive and exclusive, and since the mind—like the radio—can only tune into one "world" at a time. In *The Fire from Within*, Castaneda sums up the matter as follows: "The universe is an infinite agglomeration of energy fields, resembling threads of light. . . . Human beings are also composed of an incalculable number of the same threadlike energy fields [forming] a ball of light the size of the person's body with the arms extended laterally, like a giant luminous egg."

From the sorcerers' view, the brain does not actually create awareness, but only receives it. We *select* a given "band" or wavelength, by manipulating a point that lies within the aura, a point of perception, situated somewhere upon these bands.[1] This point Castaneda names "the point where perception is assembled," or simply, "the assemblage point." The assemblage point is able to move in various directions within the auric field, along the various bands, each movement resulting in a corresponding change in perception or awareness. The individual is oblivious to any "movement," as such, experiencing only the *effects* of the movement. In the case of minor movements, these effects are also minor, such as drunkenness, panic, euphoria, etc. In the case of major ones, hallucination, madness, visions, supernatural experiences, even so-called "close encounters," may occur. These separate "bands" or wavelengths exist as actual, alien worlds, as distant from us in their own way as the Sun and the stars. Yet they are right under our noses, literally within arm's reach.[2]

1: The manipulation can be either horizontally, along the bands, or vertically, from one band to the next. The type of movement determines the quality of the change in perception. For example, there are several *human* bands, on which lie the various stations, such as madness, sanity, euphoria, despair, and so forth. Likewise there are bands that correspond with animals, plants, insects and so forth. Then, of course, there are bands that have nothing whatsoever in common with our perception of reality as we know it.

2: If the assemblage point is moved from its customary position, it will thereby isolate for assemblage an entirely new set of signals, and the senses of the body will apprehend a corresponding new world. The paranoid takes this not as metaphor, but in the most literal sense: a new perspective equals a new

Once the assemblage point begins to move, the subject becomes open to the onslaught of the unknown. The average man (i.e., one with no inkling of the existence of the assemblage point, or of the Imaginal realms) has one of two options: to take the event as unrelated to his "everyday" experiences and attribute it to either madness or mysticism (either a hallucination or a miracle), or else to dismiss it as a perfectly explicable phenomenon that has somehow confused him into thinking otherwise. In this last case, his explanation, though not actually explaining anything, will serve to keep his confusion and panic at bay: he dresses up the unknown, using garments fashioned from the scraps and factors of the known.[3]

The average man today understands "science" no better than the average man of yesterday understood "sorcery": he believes, and that is enough. Rationality is in fact the most insidious kind of madness. But this is the position upon which the collective assemblage point of humanity has fastened, so creating what we know of as "the Consensus." In paranoid awareness, the predominance of *reason* over the last 500 years or so is a *reaction* to an impending (evolutionary) shift of the assemblage point to its old/new position. Rationality is like a rat digging in its claws in the moment it is about to be seized and pried loose. As this fluctuation occurs, the world prepares to collapse in ways both metaphorical and literal. To the paranoid, the global events of recent years have been orchestrated deliberately — by gods or men — with this specific end in mind: shock, upheaval, extreme despair, loss of faith, sickness, deprivation, and all the resulting desperation (quiet but profound) are all *means for moving the assemblage point.*

A weird mixture of panic and boredom has seized humanity, going down in flames but so numb that it doesn't feel a thing. *Something* has got to give, and that something is the assemblage point. This shift is now the only means of survival open to us. When a certain portion of a species learns or unlearns something, the entire species will undergo the corresponding change in consciousness. When the world stops for enough, the world stops for all.

---

existence, though there are, of course, degrees. Within this known world alone, there are a myriad of possible points of view we can access, from the ant to the eagle and back again.

    3: "Sorcerers know that when an average person's inventory fails, the person either enlarges his inventory or his world of self-reflection collapses. The average person is willing to incorporate new items into his inventory if they don't contradict the inventory's underlying order. But if the items contradict that order, the person's mind collapses. The inventory is the mind. Sorcerers count on this when they attempt to break the mirror of self-reflection." Carlos Castaneda, *The Power of Silence.*

Further Reading

— — — — — — — — — — — — — — — — —

Taisha Abelar: *The Sorcerers' Crossing*
George C. Andrews: *Extraterrestrial Friends and Foes.*
William Blake: *The Marriage of Heaven and Hell*
Helena Blavatsky: *The Secret Doctrine.*
Paul Bowles: *The Sheltering Sky, Conversations with Paul Bowles.*
William Bramley: *The Gods of Eden.*
Albert Budden: *Psychic Close Encounters*
William Burroughs: *Nova Express, The Ticket That Exploded.*
Joseph Campbell: *Masks of God.*
Carlos Castaneda: *The Teachings of Don Juan, A Separate Reality, Journey to Ixtlan, Tales of Power, The Eagle's Gift,* etc
William Cooper: *Behold a Pale Horse*
Aleister Crowley: *Book 4, The Book of Thoth, Confessions,* etc.
Joan D'Arc (editor) *Paranoid Women Collect Their Thoughts*
Philip K. Dick: *Valis,* etc
Florinda Donner: *Being-In-Dreaming*
Fyodor Dostoyevsky: *The Brothers Karamazov*
Ramsey Dukes, *S.S.O.T.B.M.E, Words Made Flesh,* etc.
Mircea Eliade: *Shamanism, Archaic Techniques of Ecstasy*
David Fideler: *Jesus Christ, Sun of God.*
Charles Fort: *Complete Books*
Bob Frissel: *Nothing is this Book is True, But That's Exactly How Things Are.*
Robert C. Girard: *Futureman*
Joscelyn Godwin: *Arktos*
Kenneth Grant: *Aleister Crowley and the Hidden God, Hecate's Fountain,* etc.
Robert Graves: *King Jesus.*
Elizabeth Haich: *Initiation.*

Patrick Harpur: *Daemonic Reality*
Murray Hope: *Ancient Egypt: The Sirius Connection.*
Carl Gustav Jung: *Flying Saucers, Man and His Symbols.*
Franz Kafka: *Metamorphosis and Other Stories*
John Keats: *Letters.*
John Keel: *Our Haunted Planet, UFOs: Operation Trojan Horse, The Mothman Prophecies*
Jim Keith: *Casebook on Alternative Three, Black Helicopters Over America, Secret and Supressed* (editor only)
Eliphas Levi: *The Key to the Mysteries, Transcendental Magic,* etc.
Ira Levin: *Rosemary's Baby*
Gregory Little: *Grand Illusions*
William Lyne: *Space Aliens From the Pentagon*
John E. Mack: *Abductions, Passport to the Cosmos*
Kyriacos C. Markides: *The Magus of Strovolos, Homage to the Sun*
Terence McKenna: *True Hallucinations, The Archaic Revival,* etc.
Peter Moon and Preston B. Nichols: *The Pyramids of Montauk, Adventures in the Pleiades*
Frederich Nietzsche: *Thus Spoke Zarathustra, Beyond Good and Evil, The Anti-Christ.*
Adam Parfrey (editor): *Apocalypse Culture, Apocalypse Culture 2*
Louis Pauwels and Jacques Bergier: *The Morning of the Magicians, Impossible Possibilities.*
Leonard Peikoff: *The Ominous Parallels*
George Piccard: *Liquid Conspiracy: JFK, LSD, the CIA, Area 51, & UFOs*
Edgar Allan Poe: *Tales of Mystery and Imagination,* etc.
Paul Rydeen: *Jack Parsons and the Fall of Babylon*
Samuel Sagan: *Entities: Parasites of the Energy Body*
R.A. Schwaller de Lubicz: *Sacred Science.*
William Shakespeare: *Hamlet, Macbeth, Romeo and Juliet,* etc
Robert Shea & Robert Anton Wilson: *Illuminatus!*
Daragh Smyth: *A Guide to Irish Mythology.*
Whitley Strieber: *Communion, Transformation, Majestic, The Key.*
John Symmonds: *The Medusa's Head*
Robert G.K. Temple: *The Sirius Mystery*
Lao Tze: *Tao Teh Ching*
Valdamar Valerian: *Matrix II: The Abduction and Manipulation of Humans Using Advanced Technology.*
Jacques Vallee: *Passport to Magonia, Messengers of Deception, The Secret College*
Leslie Watkins: *Alternative 3*
Oscar Wilde: *De Profundis*
Robert Anton Wilson: *Cosmic Trigger, Masks of the Illuminati, The Earth Will Shake, The Widow's Son,* etc
William Butler Yeats: *The Second Coming*

CONSPIRACY & HISTORY

LIQUID CONSPIRACY
JFK, LSD, the CIA, Area 51 & UFOs
by George Piccard

Underground author George Piccard on the politics of LSD, mind control, and Kennedy's involvement with Area 51 and UFOs. Reveals JFK's LSD experiences with Mary Pinchot-Meyer. The plot thickens with an ever expanding web of CIA involvement, from underground bases with UFOs seen by JFK and Marilyn Monroe (among others) to a vaster conspiracy that affects every government agency from NASA to the Justice Department. This may have been the reason that Marilyn Monroe and actress-columnist Dorothy Kilgallen were both murdered. Focusing on the bizarre side of history, *Liquid Conspiracy* takes the reader on a psychedelic tour de force. This is your government on drugs!
264 PAGES. 6X9 PAPERBACK. ILLUSTRATED. $14.95. CODE: LIQC

INSIDE THE GEMSTONE FILE
Howard Hughes, Onassis & JFK
by Kenn Thomas & David Hatcher Childress

Steamshovel Press editor Thomas takes on the Gemstone File in this run-up and run-down of the most famous underground document ever circulated. Photocopied and distributed for over 20 years, the Gemstone File is the story of Bruce Roberts, the inventor of the synthetic ruby widely used in laser technology today, and his relationship with the Howard Hughes Company and ultimately with Aristotle Onassis, the Mafia, and the CIA. Hughes kidnapped and held a drugged-up prisoner for 10 years; Onassis and his role in the Kennedy Assassination; how the Mafia ran corporate America in the 1960s; the death of Onassis' son in the crash of a small private plane in Greece; Onassis as Ian Fleming's archvillain Ernst Stavro Blofeld; more.
320 PAGES. 6X9 PAPERBACK. ILLUSTRATED. $16.00. CODE: IGF

MASS CONTROL
Engineering Human Consciousness
by Jim Keith

Conspiracy expert Keith's final book on mind control, Project Monarch, and mass manipulation presents chilling evidence that we are indeed spinning a Matrix. Keith describes the New Man, where conception of reality is a dance of electronic images fired into his forebrain, a gossamer construction of his masters, designed so that he will not—under any circumstances—perceive the actual. His happiness is delivered to him through a tube or an electronic connection. His God lurks behind an electronic curtain; when the curtain is pulled away we find the CIA sorcerer, the media manipulatorÖ Chapters on the CIA, Tavistock, Jolly West and the Violence Center, Guerrilla Mindwar, Brice Taylor, other recent "victims," more.
256 PAGES. 6X9 PAPERBACK. ILLUSTRATED. INDEX. $16.95. CODE: MASC

THE ARCH CONSPIRATOR
Essays and Actions
by Len Bracken

Veteran conspiracy author Len Bracken's witty essays and articles lead us down the dark corridors of conspiracy, politics, murder and mayhem. In 12 chapters Bracken takes us through a maze of interwoven tales from the Russian Conspiracy to his interview with Costa Rican novelist Joaquin Gutierrez and his Psychogeographic Map into the Third Millennium. Other chapters in the book are A General Theory of Civil War; The New-Catiline Conspiracy for the Cancellation of Debt; Anti-Labor Day; 1997 with selected Aphorisms Against Work; Solar Economics; and more. Bracken's work has appeared in such pop-conspiracy publications as *Paranoia, Steamshovel Press* and the *Village Voice*. Len Bracken lives in Arlington, Virginia and haunts the back alleys of Washington D.C., keeping an eye on the predators who run our country.
256 PAGES. 6X9 PAPERBACK. ILLUSTRATED. BIBLIOGRAPHY. $14.95. CODE: ACON.

MIND CONTROL, WORLD CONTROL
by Jim Keith

Veteran author and investigator Jim Keith uncovers a surprising amount of information on the technology, experimentation and implementation of mind control. Various chapters in this shocking book are on early CIA experiments such as Project Artichoke and Project R.H.I.C.-EDOM, the methodology and technology of implants, mind control assassins and couriers, various famous Mind Control victims such as Sirhan Sirhan and Candy Jones. Also featured in this book are chapters on how mind control technology may be linked to some UFO activity and "UFO abductions."
256 PAGES. 6X9 PAPERBACK. ILLUSTRATED. FOOTNOTES. $14.95. CODE: MCWC

NASA, NAZIS & JFK:
The Torbitt Document & the JFK Assassination
introduction by Kenn Thomas

This book emphasizes the links between "Operation Paper Clip" Nazi scientists working for NASA, the assassination of JFK, and the secret Nevada air base Area 51. The Torbitt Document also talks about the roles played in the assassination by Division Five of the FBI, the Defense Industrial Security Command (DISC), the Las Vegas mob, and the shadow corporate entities Permindex and Centro-Mondiale Commerciale. The Torbitt Document claims that the same players planned the 1962 assassination attempt on Charles de Gaul, who ultimately pulled out of NATO because he traced the "Assassination Cabal" to Permindex in Switzerland and to NATO headquarters in Brussels. The Torbitt Document paints a dark picture of NASA, the military industrial complex, and the connections to Mercury, Nevada which headquarters the "secret space program."
258 PAGES. 5X8. PAPERBACK. ILLUSTRATED. $16.00. CODE: NNJ

MIND CONTROL, OSWALD & JFK:
Were We Controlled?
introduction by Kenn Thomas

Steamshovel Press editor Kenn Thomas examines the little-known book *Were We Controlled?*, first published in 1968. The book's author, the mysterious Lincoln Lawrence, maintained that Lee Harvey Oswald was a special agent who was a mind control subject, having received an implant in 1960 at a Russian hospital. Thomas examines the evidence for implant technology and the role it could have played in the Kennedy Assassination. Thomas also looks at the mind control aspects of the RFK assassination and details the history of implant technology. A growing number of people are interested in CIA experiments and its "Silent Weapons for Quiet Wars." Looks at the case that the reporter Damon Runyon, Jr. was murdered because of this book.
256 PAGES. 6X9 PAPERBACK. ILLUSTRATED. NOTES. $16.00. CODE: MCOJ

24 hour credit card orders—call: 815-253-6390 fax: 815-253-6300
email: auphq@frontiernet.net   www.adventuresunlimitedpress.com   www.wexclub.com

CONSPIRACY & HISTORY

SAUCERS OF THE ILLUMINATI
by Jim Keith, Foreword by Kenn Thomas
Seeking the truth behind stories of alien invasion, secret underground bases, and the secret plans of the New World Order, *Saucers of the Illuminati* offers ground breaking research, uncovering clues to the nature of UFOs and to forces even more sinister: the secret cabal behind planetary control! Includes mind control, saucer abductions, the MJ-12 documents, cattle mutilations, government anti-gravity testing, the Sirius Connection, science fiction author Philip K. Dick and his efforts to expose the Illuminati, plus more from veteran conspiracy and UFO author Keith. Conspiracy expert Keith's final book on UFOs and the highly secret group that manufactures them and uses them for their own purposes: the control and manipulation of the population of planet Earth.
148 PAGES. 6x9 PAPERBACK. ILLUSTRATED. $12.95. CODE: SOIL

TECHNOLOGY OF THE GODS
The Incredible Sciences of the Ancients
by David Hatcher Childress
Popular *Lost Cities* author David Hatcher Childress takes us into the amazing world of ancient technology, from computers in antiquity to the "flying machines of the gods." Childress looks at the technology that was allegedly used in Atlantis and the theory that the Great Pyramid of Egypt was originally a gigantic power station. He examines tales of ancient flight and the technology that it involved; how the ancients used electricity; megalithic building techniques; the use of crystal lenses and the fire from the gods; evidence of various high tech weapons in the past, including atomic weapons; ancient metallurgy and heavy machinery; the role of modern inventors such as Nikola Tesla in bringing ancient technology back into modern use; impossible artifacts; and more.
356 PAGES. 6x9 PAPERBACK. ILLUSTRATED. BIBLIOGRAPHY. $16.95. CODE: TGOD.

THE ORION PROPHECY
Egyptian & Mayan Prophecies on the Cataclysm of 2012
by Patrick Geryl and Gino Ratinckx
In the year 2012 the Earth awaits a super catastrophe: its magnetic field reverse in one go. Phenomenal earthquakes and tidal waves will completely destroy our civilization. Europe and North America will shift thousands of kilometers northwards into polar climes. Nearly everyone will perish in the apocalyptic happenings. These dire predictions stem from the Mayans and Egyptians—descendants of the legendary Atlantis. The Atlanteans had highly evolved astronomical knowledge and were able to exactly predict the previous world-wide flood in 9792 BC. Orion and several others stars will take the same 'code-positions' as in 9792 BC! For thousands of years historical sources have told of a forgotten time capsule of ancient wisdom located in a mythical labyrinth of secret chambers filled with artifacts and documents from the previous flood. We desperately need this information now—and this book gives one possible location.
324 PAGES. 6x9 PAPERBACK. ILLUSTRATED. BIBLIOGRAPHY. $16.95. CODE: ORP

THE HISTORY OF THE KNIGHTS TEMPLARS
by Charles G. Addison, introduction by David Hatcher Childress
Chapters on the origin of the Templars, their popularity in Europe and their rivalry with the Knights of St. John, later to be known as the Knights of Malta. Detailed information on the activities of the Templars in the Holy Land, and the 1312 AD suppression of the Templars in France and other countries, which culminated in the execution of Jacques de Molay and the continuation of the Knights Templars in England and Scotland; the formation of the society of Knights Templars in London; and the rebuilding of the Temple in 1816. Plus a lengthy intro about the lost Templar fleet and its connections to the ancient North American sea routes.
395 PAGES. 6x9 PAPERBACK. ILLUSTRATED. $16.95. CODE: HKT

DARK MOON
Apollo and the Whistleblowers
by Mary Bennett and David Percy
•Was Neil Armstrong really the first man on the Moon?
•Did you know that 'live' color TV from the Moon was not actually live at all?
•Did you know that the Lunar Surface Camera had no viewfinder?
•Do you know that lighting was used in the Apollo photographs—yet no lighting equipment was taken to the Moon?
All these questions, and more, are discussed in great detail by British researchers Bennett and Percy in *Dark Moon*, the definitive book (nearly 600 pages) on the possible faking of the Apollo Moon missions. Bennett and Percy delve into every possible aspect of this beguiling theory, one that rocks the very foundation of our beliefs concerning NASA and the space program. Tons of NASA photos analyzed for possible deceptions.
568 PAGES. 6x9 PAPERBACK. ILLUSTRATED. BIBLIOGRAPHY. INDEX. $25.00. CODE: DMO

WAKE UP DOWN THERE!
The Excluded Middle Anthology
by Greg Bishop
The great American tradition of dropout culture makes it over the millennium mark with a collection of the best from *The Excluded Middle*, the critically acclaimed underground zine of UFOs, the paranormal, conspiracies, psychedelia, and spirit. Contributions from Robert Anton Wilson, Ivan Stang, Martin Kottmeyer, John Shirley, Scott Corrales, Adam Gorightly and Robert Sterling; and interviews with James Moseley, Karla Turner, Bill Moore, Kenn Thomas, Richard Boylan, Dean Radin, Joe McMoneagle, and the mysterious Ira Einhorn (an *Excluded Middle* exclusive). Includes full versions of interviews and extra material not found in the newsstand versions.
420 PAGES. 8x11 PAPERBACK. ILLUSTRATED. $25.00. CODE: WUDT

ARKTOS
The Myth of the Pole in Science, Symbolism, and Nazi Survival
by Joscelyn Godwin
A scholarly treatment of catastrophes, ancient myths and the Nazi Occult beliefs. Explored are the many tales of an ancient race said to have lived in the Arctic regions, such as Thule and Hyperborea. Progressing onward, the book looks at modern polar legends including the survival of Hitler, German bases in Antarctica, UFOs, the hollow earth, Agartha and Shambala, more.
220 PAGES. 6x9 PAPERBACK. ILLUSTRATED. $16.95. CODE: ARK

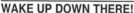

24 hour credit card orders—call: 815-253-6390 fax: 815-253-6300
email: auphq@frontiernet.net   www.adventuresunlimitedpress.com   www.wexclub.com

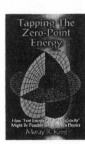

TESLA TECHNOLOGY

THE FANTASTIC INVENTIONS OF NIKOLA TESLA
Nikola Tesla with additional material by David Hatcher Childress

This book is a readable compendium of patents, diagrams, photos and explanations of the many incredible inventions of the originator of the modern era of electrification. In Tesla's own words are such topics as wireless transmission of power, death rays, and radio-controlled airships. In addition, rare material on German bases in Antarctica and South America, and a secret city built at a remote jungle site in South America are part of Tesla's students, Guglielmo Marconi. Marconi's secret group claims to have built flying saucers in the 1940s and to have gone to Mars in the early 1950s! Incredible photos of these Tesla craft are included. The Ancient Atlantean system of broadcasting energy through a grid system of obelisks and pyramids is discussed, and a fascinating concept comes out of one chapter: that Egyptian engineers had to wear protective metal head-shields while in these power plants, hence the Egyptian Pharoah's head covering as well as the Face on Mars!

•His plan to transmit free electricity into the atmosphere. •How electrical devices would work using only small antennas mounted on them.
•Why unlimited power could be utilized anywhere on earth. •How radio and radar technology can be used as death-ray weapons in Star Wars.
•Includes an appendix of Supreme Court documents on dismantling his free energy towers. •Tesla's Death Rays, Ozone generators, and more...
342 PAGES. 6x9 PAPERBACK. ILLUSTRATED. BIBLIOGRAPHY AND APPENDIX. $16.95. CODE: FINT

THE TESLA PAPERS
Nikola Tesla on Free Energy & Wireless Transmission of Power
by Nikola Tesla, edited by David Hatcher Childress

In the tradition of *The Fantastic Inventions of Nikola Tesla, The Anti-Gravity Handbook* and *The Free-Energy Device Handbook*, science and UFO author David Hatcher Childress takes us into the incredible world of Nikola Tesla and his amazing inventions. Tesla's rare article "The Problem of Increasing Human Energy with Special Reference to the Harnessing of the Sun's Energy" is included. This lengthy article was originally published in the June 1900 issue of *The Century Illustrated Monthly Magazine* and it was the outline for Tesla's master blueprint for the world. Tesla's fantastic vision of the future, including wireless power, anti-gravity, free energy and highly advanced solar power.
Also included are some of the papers, patents and material collected on Tesla at the Colorado Springs Tesla Symposiums, including papers on:
•The Secret History of Wireless Transmission •Tesla and the Magnifying Transmitter
•Design and Construction of a half-wave Tesla Coil •Electrostatics: A Key to Free Energy
•Progress in Zero-Point Energy Research •Electromagnetic Energy from Antennas to Atoms
•Tesla's Particle Beam Technology •Fundamental Excitatory Modes of the Earth-Ionosphere Cavity
325 PAGES. 8x10 PAPERBACK. ILLUSTRATED. $16.95. CODE: TTP

LOST SCIENCE
by Gerry Vassilatos

Secrets of Cold War Technology author Vassilatos on the remarkable lives, astounding discoveries, and incredible inventions of such famous people as Nikola Tesla, Dr. Royal Rife, T.T. Brown, and T. Henry Moray. Read about the aura research of Baron Karl von Reichenbach, the wireless technology of Antonio Meucci, the controlled fusion devices of Philo Farnsworth, the earth battery of Nathan Stubblefield, and more. What were the twisted intrigues which surrounded the often deliberate attempts to stop this technology? Vassilatos claims that we are living hundreds of years behind our intended level of technology and we must recapture this "lost science."
304 PAGES. 6x9 PAPERBACK. ILLUSTRATED. BIBLIOGRAPHY. $16.95. CODE: LOS

SECRETS OF COLD WAR TECHNOLOGY
Project HAARP and Beyond
by Gerry Vassilatos

Vassilatos reveals that "Death Ray" technology has been secretly researched and developed since the turn of the century. Included are chapters on such inventors and their devices as H.C. Vion, the developer of auroral energy receivers; Dr. Selim Lemstrom's pre-Tesla experiments; the early beam weapons of Grindell-Mathews, Ulivi, Turpain and others; John Hettenger and his early beam power systems. Learn about Project Argus, Project Teak and Project Orange; EMP experiments in the 60s; why the Air Force directed the construction of a huge Ionospheric "backscatter" telemetry system across the Pacific just after WWII; why Raytheon has collected every patent relevant to HAARP over the past few years; more.
250 PAGES. 6x9 PAPERBACK. ILLUSTRATED. $15.95. CODE: SCWT

HAARP
The Ultimate Weapon of the Conspiracy
by Jerry Smith

The HAARP project in Alaska is one of the most controversial projects ever undertaken by the U.S. Government. Jerry Smith gives us the history of the HAARP project and explains how works, in technically correct yet easy to understand language. At best, HAARP is science out-of-control; at worst, HAARP could be the most dangerous device ever created, a futuristic technology that is everything from super-beam weapon to world-wide mind control device. Topics include Over-the-Horizon Radar and HAARP, Mind Control, ELF and HAARP, The Telsa Connection, The Russian Woodpecker, GWEN, Earth Penetrating Tomography, Weather Modification, Secret Science of the Conspiracy, more. Includes the complete 1987 Eastlund patent for his pulsed super-weapon that he claims was stolen by the HAARP Project.
256 PAGES. 6x9 PAPERBACK. ILLUSTRATED. $14.95. CODE: HARP

HARNESSING THE WHEELWORK OF NATURE
Tesla's Science of Energy
by Thomas Valone, Ph.D., P.E.

Chapters include: Tesla: Scientific Superman who Launched the Westinghouse Industrial Firm by John Shatlan; Nikola Tesla—Electricity's Hidden Genius, excerpt from The Search for Free Energy; Tesla's History at Niagara Falls; Non-Hertzian Waves: True Meaning of the Wireless Transmission of Power by Toby Grotz; On the Transmission of Electricity Without Wires by Nikola Tesla; Tesla's Magnifying Transmitter by Andrija Puharich; Tesla's Self-Sustaining Electrical Generator and the Ether by Oliver Nichelson; Self-Sustaining Non-Hertzian Longitudinal Waves by Dr. Robert Bass; Modification of Maxwell's Equations in Free Space; Scalar Electromagnetic Waves; Disclosures Concerning Tesla's Operation of an ELF Oscillator; A Study of Tesla's Advanced Concepts & Glossary of Tesla Technology Terms; Electric Weather Forces: Tesla's Vision by Charles Yost; The New Art of Projecting Concentrated Non-Dispersive Energy Through Natural Media; The Homopolar Generator: Tesla's Contribution by Thomas Valone; Tesla's Ionizer and Ozonator: Implications for Indoor Air Pollution by Thomas Valone; How Cosmic Forces Shape Our Destiny by Nikola Tesla; Tesla's Death Ray plus Selected Tesla Patents; more.
288 PAGES. 6x9 PAPERBACK. ILLUSTRATED. $16.95. CODE: HWWN

24 hour credit card orders—call: 815-253-6390 fax: 815-253-6300
email: auphq@frontiernet.net   www.adventuresunlimitedpress.com   www.wexclub.com

ANTI-GRAVITY

THE A.T. FACTOR
A Scientists Encounter with UFOs: Piece For A Jigsaw Part 3
by Leonard Cramp
British aerospace engineer Cramp began much of the scientific anti-gravity and UFO propulsion analysis back in 1955 with his landmark book *Space, Gravity & the Flying Saucer* (out-of-print and rare). His next books (available from Adventures Unlimited) *UFOs & Anti-Gravity: Piece for a Jig-Saw* and *The Cosmic Matrix: Piece for a Jig-Saw Part 2* began Cramp's in depth look into gravity control, free-energy, and the interlocking web of energy that pervades the universe. In this final book, Cramp brings to a close his detailed and controversial study of UFOs and Anti-Gravity.
324 PAGES. 6X9 PAPERBACK. ILLUSTRATED. BIBLIOGRAPHY. INDEX. $16.95. CODE: ATF

COSMIC MATRIX
Piece for a Jig-Saw, Part Two
by Leonard G. Cramp
Cosmic Matrix is the long-awaited sequel to his 1966 book *UFOs & Anti-Gravity: Piece for a Jig-Saw.* Cramp has had a long history of examining UFO phenomena and has concluded that UFOs use the highest possible aeronautic science to move in the way they do. Cramp examines anti-gravity effects and theorizes that this super-science used by the craft—described in detail in the book—can lift mankind into a new level of technology, transportation and understanding of the universe. The book takes a close look at gravity control, time travel, and the interlocking web of energy between all planets in our solar system with Leonard's unique technical diagrams. A fantastic voyage into the present and future!
364 PAGES. 6X9 PAPERBACK. ILLUSTRATED. BIBLIOGRAPHY. $16.00. CODE: CMX

UFOS AND ANTI-GRAVITY
Piece For A Jig-Saw
by Leonard G. Cramp
Leonard G. Cramp's 1966 classic book on flying saucer propulsion and suppressed technology is a highly technical look at the UFO phenomena by a trained scientist. Cramp first introduces the idea of 'anti-gravity' and introduces us to the various theories of gravitation. He then examines the technology necessary to build a flying saucer and examines in great detail the technical aspects of such a craft. Cramp's book is a wealth of material and diagrams on flying saucers, anti-gravity, suppressed technology, G-fields and UFOs. Chapters include Crossroads of Aerodynamics, Aerodynamic Saucers, Limitations of Rocketry, Gravitation and the Ether, Gravitational Spaceships, G-Field Lift Effects, The Bi-Field Theory, VTOL and Hovercraft, Analysis of UFO photos, more.
388 PAGES. 6X9 PAPERBACK. ILLUSTRATED. $16.95. CODE: UAG

THE ENERGY GRID
Harmonic 695, The Pulse of the Universe
by Captain Bruce Cathie.
This is the breakthrough book that explores the incredible potential of the Energy Grid and the Earth's Unified Field all around us. Cathie's first book, *Harmonic 33*, was published in 1968 when he was a commercial pilot in New Zealand. Since then, Captain Bruce Cathie has been the premier investigator into the amazing potential of the infinite energy that surrounds our planet every microsecond. Cathie investigates the Harmonics of Light and how the Energy Grid is created. In this amazing book are chapters on UFO Propulsion, Nikola Tesla, Unified Equations, the Mysterious Aerials, Pythagoras & the Grid, Nuclear Detonation and the Grid, Maps of the Ancients, an Australian Stonehenge examined, more.
255 PAGES. 6X9 TRADEPAPER. ILLUSTRATED. $15.95. CODE: TEG

THE BRIDGE TO INFINITY
Harmonic 371244
by Captain Bruce Cathie
Cathie has popularized the concept that the earth is crisscrossed by an electromagnetic grid system that can be used for anti-gravity, free energy, levitation and more. The book includes a new analysis of the harmonic nature of reality, acoustic levitation, pyramid power, harmonic receiver towers and UFO propulsion. It concludes that today's scientists have at their command a fantastic store of knowledge with which to advance the welfare of the human race.
204 PAGES. 6X9 TRADEPAPER. ILLUSTRATED. $14.95. CODE: BTF

THE HARMONIC CONQUEST OF SPACE
by Captain Bruce Cathie
Chapters include: Mathematics of the World Grid; the Harmonics of Hiroshima and Nagasaki; Harmonic Transmission and Receiving; the Link Between Human Brain Waves; the Cavity Resonance between the Earth; the Ionosphere and Gravity; Edgar Cayce—the Harmonics of the Subconscious; Stonehenge; the Harmonics of the Moon; the Pyramids of Mars; Nikola Tesla's Electric Car; the Robert Adams Pulsed Electric Motor Generator; Harmonic Clues to the Unified Field; and more. Also included are tables showing the harmonic relations between the earth's magnetic field, the speed of light, and anti-gravity/gravity acceleration at different points on the earth's surface. New chapters in this edition on the giant stone spheres of Costa Rica, Atomic Tests and Volcanic Activity, and a chapter on Ayers Rock analysed with Stone Mountain, Georgia.
248 PAGES. 6X9. PAPERBACK. ILLUSTRATED. BIBLIOGRAPHY. $16.95. CODE: HCS

MAN-MADE UFOS 1944—1994
Fifty Years of Suppression
by Renato Vesco & David Hatcher Childress
A comprehensive look at the early "flying saucer" technology of Nazi Germany and the genesis of man-made UFOs. This book takes us from the work of captured German scientists to escaped battalions of Germans, secret communities in South America and Antarctica to todays state-of-the-art "Dreamland" flying machines. Heavily illustrated, this astonishing book blows the lid off the "government UFO conspiracy" and explains with technical diagrams the technology involved. Examined in detail are secret underground airfields and factories; German secret weapons; "suction" aircraft; the origin of NASA; gyroscopic stabilizers and engines; the secret Marconi aircraft factory in South America; and more. Introduction by W.A. Harbinson, author of the Dell novels *GENESIS* and *REVELATION*.
318 PAGES. 6X9 PAPERBACK. ILLUSTRATED. INDEX & FOOTNOTES. $18.95. CODE: MMU

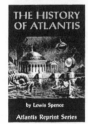

ANCIENT SCIENCE

THE LAND OF OSIRIS
An Introduction to Khemitology
by Stephen S. Mehler

Was there an advanced prehistoric civilization in ancient Egypt? Were they the people who built the great pyramids and carved the Great Sphinx? Did the pyramids serve as energy devices and not as tombs for kings? Independent Egyptologist Stephen S. Mehler has spent over 30 years researching the answers to these questions and believes the answers are yes! Mehler has uncovered an indigenous oral tradition that still exists in Egypt, and has been fortunate to have studied with a living master of this tradition, Abd'El Hakim Awyan. Mehler has also been given permission to present these teachings to the Western world, teachings that unfold a whole new understanding of ancient Egypt and have only been presented heretofore in fragments by other researchers. Chapters include: Egyptology and Its Paradigms; Khemitology—New Paradigms; Asgat Nefer—The Harmony of Water; Khemit and the Myth of Atlantis; The Extraterrestrial Question; 17 chapters in all.

272 PAGES. 6X9 PAPERBACK. ILLUSTRATED. COLOR SECTION. BIBLIOGRAPHY. $18.95. CODE: LOOS

A HITCHHIKER'S GUIDE TO ARMAGEDDON
by David Hatcher Childress

With wit and humor, popular Lost Cities author David Hatcher Childress takes us around the world and back in his trippy finalé to the Lost Cities series. He's off on an adventure in search of the apocalypse and end times. Childress hits the road from the fortress of Megiddo, the legendary citadel in northern Israel where Armageddon is prophesied to start. Hitchhiking around the world, Childress takes us from one adventure to another, to ancient cities in the deserts and the legends of worlds before our own. Childress muses on the rise and fall of civilizations, and the forces that have shaped mankind over the millennia, including wars, invasions and cataclysms. He discusses the ancient Armageddons of the past, and chronicles recent Middle East developments and their ominous undertones. In the meantime, he becomes a cargo cult god on a remote island off New Guinea, gets dragged into the Kennedy Assassination by one of the "conspirators," investigates a strange power operating out of the Altai Mountains of Mongolia, and discovers how the Knights Templar and their off-shoots have driven the world toward an epic battle centered around Jerusalem and the Middle East.

320 PAGES. 6X9 PAPERBACK. ILLUSTRATED. BIBLIOGRAPHY. INDEX. $16.95. CODE: HGA

CLOAK OF THE ILLUMINATI
Secrets, Transformations, Crossing the Star Gate
by William Henry

Thousands of years ago the stargate technology of the gods was lost. Mayan Prophecy says it will return by 2012, along with our alignment with the center of our galaxy. In this book: Find examples of stargates and wormholes in the ancient world; Examine myths and scripture with hidden references to a stargate cloak worn by the Illuminati, including Mari, Nimrod, Elijah, and Jesus; See rare images of gods and goddesses wearing the Cloak of the illuminati; Learn about Saddam Hussein and the secret missing library of Jesus; Uncover the secret Roman-era eugenics experiments at the Temple of Hathor in Denderah, Egypt; Explore the duplicate of the Stargate Pillar of the Gods in the Illuminists' secret garden in Nashville, TN; Discover the secrets of manna, the food of the angels; Share the lost Peace Prayer posture of Osiris, Jesus and the Illuminati; more. Chapters include: Seven Stars Under Three Stars; The Long Walk; Squaring the Circle; The Mill of the Host; The Miracle Garment; The Fig; Nimrod: The Mighty Man; Nebuchadnezzar's Gate; The New Mighty Man; more.

238 PAGES. 6X9 PAPERBACK. ILLUSTRATED. BIBLIOGRAPHY. INDEX. $16.95. CODE: COIL

LEY LINE & EARTH ENERGIES
An Extraordinary Journey into the Earth's Natural Energy System
by David Cowan & Anne Silk

The mysterious standing stones, burial grounds and stone circles that lace Europe, the British Isles and other areas have intrigued scientists, writers, artists and travellers through the centuries. They pose so many questions: Why do some places feel special? How do ley lines work? How did our ancestors use Earth energy to map their sacred sites and burial grounds? How do ghosts and poltergeists interact with Earth energy? How can Earth spirals and black spots affect our health? This exploration shows how natural forces affect our behavior, how they can be used to enhance our health and well being, and, ultimately, how they bring us closer to penetrating one of the deepest mysteries being explored. A fascinating and visual book about subtle Earth energies and how they affect us and the world around them.

368 PAGES. 6X9 PAPERBACK. ILLUSTRATED. BIBLIOGRAPHY. INDEX. $18.95. CODE: LLEE

THE ORION PROPHECY
Egyptian & Mayan Prophecies on the Cataclysm of 2012
by Patrick Geryl and Gino Ratinckx

In the year 2012 the Earth awaits a super catastrophe: its magnetic field reverse in one go. Phenomenal earthquakes and tidal waves will completely destroy our civilization. Europe and North America will shift thousands of kilometers northwards into polar climes. Nearly everyone will perish in the apocalyptic happenings. These dire predictions stem from the Mayans and Egyptians—descendants of the legendary Atlantis. The Atlanteans had highly evolved astronomical knowledge and were able to exactly predict the previous world-wide flood in 9792 BC. They built tens of thousands of boats and escaped to South America and Egypt. In the year 2012 Venus, Orion and several other stars will take the same 'code-positions' as in 9792 BC! For thousands of years historical sources have told of a forgotten time capsule of ancient wisdom located in a mythical labyrinth of secret chambers filled with artifacts and documents from the previous flood. We desperately need this information now—and this book gives one possible location.

324 PAGES. 6X9 PAPERBACK. ILLUSTRATED. BIBLIOGRAPHY. $16.95. CODE: ORP

ALTAI-HIMALAYA
A Travel Diary
by Nicholas Roerich

Nicholas Roerich's classic 1929 mystic travel book is back in print in this deluxe paperback edition. The famous Russian-American explorer's expedition through Sinkiang, Altai-Mongolia and Tibet from 1924 to 1928 is chronicled in 12 chapters and reproductions of Roerich's inspiring paintings. Roerich's "Travel Diary" style incorporates various mysteries and mystical arts of Central Asia including such arcane topics as the hidden city of Shambala, Agartha, more. Roerich is recognized as one of the great artists of this century and the book is richly illustrated with his original drawings.

407 PAGES. 6X9 PAPERBACK. ILLUSTRATED. $18.95. CODE: AHIM

24 hour credit card orders—call: 815-253-6390 fax: 815-253-6300
email: auphq@frontiernet.net   www.adventuresunlimitedpress.com   www.wexclub.com

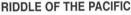

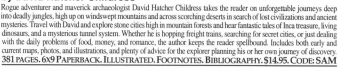

THE LUCID VIEW
Investigations in Occultism, Ufology & Paranoid Awareness
by Aeolus Kephas

An unorthodox analysis of conspiracy theory, ufology, extraterrestrialism and occultism. *The Lucid View* takes us on an impartial journey through secret history, including the Gnostics and Templars; Crowley and Hitler's occult alliance; the sorcery wars of Freemasonry and the Illuminati; "Alternative Three" covert space colonization; the JFK assassination; the Manson murders; Jonestown and 9/11. Also delves into UFOs and alien abductions, their relations to mind control technology and sorcery practices, with reference to inorganic beings and Kundalini energy. The book offers a balanced overview on religious, magical and paranoid beliefs pertaining to the 21st century, and their social, psychological, and spiritual implications for humanity, the leading game player in the grand mythic drama of Armageddon.
298 PAGES. 6x9 PAPERBACK. ILLUSTRATED. $16.95. CODE: LVEW

PIRATES & THE LOST TEMPLAR FLEET
The Secret Naval War Between the Templars & the Vatican
by David Hatcher Childress

Childress takes us into the fascinating world of maverick sea captains who were Knights Templar (and later Scottish Rite Free Masons) who battled the Vatican, and the Spanish and Italian ships that sailed for the Pope. The lost Templar fleet was originally based at La Rochelle in southern France, but fled to the deep fiords of Scotland upon the dissolution of the Order by King Phillip. This banned fleet of ships was later commanded by the St. Clair family of Rosslyn Chapel (birthplace of Free Masonry). St. Clair and his Templars made a voyage to Canada in the year 1298 AD, nearly 100 years before Columbus! Later, this fleet of ships and new ones to come, flew the Skull and Crossbones, the symbol of the Knights Templar. They preyed on the ships of the Vatican coming from the rich ports of the Americas and were ultimately known as the Pirates of the Caribbean. Chapters include: 10,000 Years of Seafaring; The Knights Templar & the Crusades; The Templars and the Assassins; The Lost Templar Fleet and the Jolly Roger; Maps of the Ancient Sea Kings; Pirates, Templars and the New World; Christopher Columbus—Secret Templar Pirate?; Later Day Pirates and the War with the Vatican; Pirate Utopias and the New Jerusalem; more.
320 PAGES. 6x9 PAPERBACK. ILLUSTRATED. BIBLIOGRAPHY. $16.95. CODE: PLTF

THE HISTORY OF THE KNIGHTS TEMPLARS
by Charles G. Addison, introduction by David Hatcher Childress

Chapters on the origin of the Templars, their popularity in Europe and their rivalry with the Knights of St. John, later to be known as the Knights of Malta. Detailed information on the activities of the Templars in the Holy Land, and the 1312 AD suppression of the Templars in France and other countries, which culminated in the execution of Jacques de Molay and the continuation of the Knights Templars in England and Scotland; the formation of the society of Knights Templars in London; and the rebuilding of the Temple in 1816. Plus a lengthy intro about the lost Templar fleet and its connections to the ancient North American sea routes.
395 PAGES. 6x9 PAPERBACK. ILLUSTRATED. $16.95. CODE: HKT

THE STONE PUZZLE OF ROSSLYN CHAPEL
by Philip Coppens

Rosslyn Chapel is revered by Freemasons as a vital part of their history, believed by some to hold evidence of pre-Columbian voyages to America, assumed by others to hold important relics, from the Holy Grail to the Head of Christ, the Scottish chapel is a place full of mystery. The history of the chapel, its relationship to freemasonry and the family behind the scenes, the Sinclairs, is brought to life, incorporating new, previously forgotten and heretofore unknown evidence. Significantly, the story is placed in the equally enigmatic landscape surrounding the chapel, which includes features from Templar commanderies to prehistoric markings, from an ancient kingly site to the South to Arthur's Seat directly north of the chapel. The true significance and meaning of the chapel is finally unveiled: it is a medieval stone book of esoteric knowledge "written" by the Sinclair family, one of the most powerful and wealthy families in Scotland, chosen patrons of Freemasonry.
124 PAGES. 6x9 PAPERBACK. ILLUSTRATED. $12.00. CODE: SPRC

TEMPLARS' LEGACY IN MONTREAL
The New Jerusalem
by Francine Bernier

Designed in the 17th century as the New Jerusalem of the Christian world, the people behind the scene in turning this dream into reality were the Société de Notre-Dame, half of whose members were in the elusive Compagnie du Saint-Sacrement. They took no formal vows and formed the interior elitist and invisible "heart of the church" following a "Johannite" doctrine of the Essene tradition, where men and women were considered equal apostles. The book reveals the links between Montreal and: John the Baptist as patron saint; Melchizedek, the first king-priest and a father figure to the Templars and the Essenes; Stella Maris, the Star of the Sea from Mount Carmel; the Phrygian goddess Cybele as the androgynous Mother of the Church; St. Blaise, the Armenian healer or "Therapeut"- the patron saint of the stonemasons and a major figure to the Benedictine Order and the Templars; the presence of two Black Virgins; an intriguing family coat of arms with twelve blue apples; and more.
352 PAGES. 6x9 PAPERBACK. ILLUSTRATED. BIBLIOGRAPHY. $21.95. CODE: TLIM

Co S3 016 cob

ADVENTURES UNLIMITED

One Adventure Place
P.O. Box 74
Kempton, Illinois 60946
United States of America
•Tel.: 1-800-718-4514 or 815-253-6390
•Fax: 815-253-6300
Email: auphq@frontiernet.net
http://www.adventuresunlimitedpress.com
or www.adventuresunlimited.nl

10% Discount when you order 3 or more items!

ORDERING INSTRUCTIONS

➤➤ Remit by USD$ Check, Money Order or Credit Card
➤➤ Visa, Master Card, Discover & AmEx Accepted
➤➤ Prices May Change Without Notice
➤➤ 10% Discount for 3 or more Items

SHIPPING CHARGES

United States

➤➤ Postal Book Rate { $3.00 First Item
50¢ Each Additional Item

➤➤ Priority Mail { $4.50 First Item
$2.00 Each Additional Item

➤➤ UPS { $5.00 First Item
$1.50 Each Additional Item

NOTE: UPS Delivery Available to Mainland USA Only

Canada

➤➤ Postal Book Rate { $6.00 First Item
$2.00 Each Additional Item

➤➤ Postal Air Mail { $8.00 First Item
$2.50 Each Additional Item

➤➤ Personal Checks or Bank Drafts MUST BE
USD$ and Drawn on a US Bank
➤➤ Canadian Postal Money Orders in US$ OK
➤➤ Payment MUST BE US$

All Other Countries

➤➤ Surface Delivery { $10.00 First Item
$4.00 Each Additional Item

➤➤ Postal Air Mail { $14.00 First Item
$5.00 Each Additional Item

➤➤ Checks and Money Orders MUST BE US $
and Drawn on a US Bank or branch.

➤➤ Payment by credit card preferred!

SPECIAL NOTES

➤➤ RETAILERS: Standard Discounts Available
➤➤ BACKORDERS: We Backorder all Out-of-
Stock Items Unless Otherwise Requested
➤➤ PRO FORMA INVOICES: Available on Request
➤➤ VIDEOS: NTSC Mode Only. Replacement only.
➤➤ For PAL mode videos contact our other offices:

European Office:
Adventures Unlimited, Pannewal 22,
Enkhuizen, 1602 KS, The Netherlands
http: www.adventuresunlimited.nl
Check Us Out Online at:
www.adventuresunlimitedpress.com

Please check: ☑

☐ This is my first order   ☐ I have ordered before   ☐ This is a new address

Name	
Address	
City	
State/Province	Postal Code
Country	
Phone day	Evening
Fax	Email

Item Code	Item Description	Price	Qty	Total

Please check: ☑

☐ Postal-Surface
☐ Postal-Air Mail (Priority in USA)
☐ UPS (Mainland USA only)

Subtotal ➡	
Less Discount-10% for 3 or more items ➡	
Balance ➡	
Illinois Residents 6.25% Sales Tax ➡	
Previous Credit ➡	
Shipping ➡	
Total (check/MO in USD$ only) ➡	

☐ Visa/MasterCard/Discover/Amex

Card Number

Expiration Date

10% Discount When You Order 3 or More Items!

Comments & Suggestions	Share Our Catalog with a Friend